# DATE DUE

|  |  |  |  |
|---|---|---|---|
|  |  |  |  |
|  |  |  |  |
|  |  |  |  |
|  |  |  |  |
|  |  |  |  |
|  |  |  |  |
|  |  |  |  |
|  |  |  |  |
|  |  |  |  |
|  |  |  |  |
|  |  |  |  |
|  |  |  |  |
|  |  |  |  |
|  |  |  |  |
|  |  |  |  |
|  |  |  |  |
|  |  |  |  |
|  |  |  |  |
|  |  |  |  |
|  |  |  |  |

HIGHSMITH #45115

# Domestic Slavery Considered as a Scriptural Institution

MERCER
UNIVERSITY PRESS

*Endowed by*
TOM WATSON BROWN
*and*
THE WATSON-BROWN FOUNDATION, INC.

# DOMESTIC SLAVERY CONSIDERED AS A SCRIPTURAL INSTITUTION

*Richard Fuller and Francis Wayland*

Edited by

Nathan A. Finn and Keith Harper

Mercer University Press
Macon, Georgia

MUP/H755

© 2008 Mercer University Press
1400 Coleman Avenue
Macon, Georgia 31207
First Mercer University Press Annotated Edition.

Original version of Fuller and Wayland Letters was published in 1847.

Books published by Mercer University Press are printed on acid free paper that
meets the requirements of American National Standard for Information
Sciences—Permanence of Paper for Printed Library Materials.

*Library of Congress Cataloging-in-Publication Data*

CIP data are available from the Library of Congress

ISBN    978-0-88146-107-7

# CONTENTS

Acknowledgments  vii

Introduction  ix

Introduction to the 1847 Edition  1

The Letter from Dr. Fuller to the Editor
 of the *Christian Reflector*  3


Dr. Wayland's Letters to Dr. Fuller  12

 Letter I—Errors on Both Sides  12

 Letter II—Definition of Slavery—Two Meanings
  of the Term Moral Evil—Slavery a Violation
  of Human Rights  18

 Letter III—The Holding of Slaves Does Not
  Necessarily Involve Guilt—Principles by
  Which the Innocence or Guilt Is to Be Determined  28

 Letter IV—Examination of the Argument in
  Favor of SLAVERY from the Old Testament  38

 Letter V—The Doctrine of Expediency  49

 Letter VI—The Argument in Favor of Slavery
  from the New Testament  58

 Letter VII—The Method of Prohibiting
  Slavery in the New Testament—Principles
  and Permission  71

 Letter VIII—The Duties Devolving on Christian
  Slaveholders  82


Dr. Fuller's Letters to Dr. Wayland  94

 Letter I—The Southern States Not Answerable
  for the Existence of Domestic Slavery  94

Letter II—Slavery Is Not to be Confounded with
the Abuses of Slavery                                                      102
Letter III—Slavery Proper, No Violation of Right—
Analogy with Civil Government—Despotism—
Comparison of the Condition of Slaves with
That of Laborers in Other Countries                          109
Letter IV—The Argument from the Old Testament          122
Letter V—The Argument form the New Testament—
Argument, Inference, Proof, Demonstration              136
Letter VI—The Mode of Teaching by Principle
in this Case at Variance with the Character
of God—The Practice of the Primitive Church        149

Dr Wayland's Closing Letter                                          166

Appendix I                                                                     187
Appendix II                                                                    198

# ACKNOWLEDGMENTS

They say, "Good help is hard to find." We do not know who "they" are but we have heard that *they* say it. We are happy to report that such was not the case with *us*. We received excellent assistance throughout this project and it is our great pleasure to recognize those who helped us in our work.

First, we want to thank Dr. Shawn Madden, librarian of Southeastern Baptist Theological Seminary. Shawn and his staff always provide expert, professional support to the seminary's administration, faculty, staff, and student body. We are especially happy to recognize our interlibrary loan department who tracked down numerous requests for obscure sources. They were very good help, indeed! Speaking of good help, we relied on Professor Fred Williams to translate the Latin phrases in this book that befuddled us. Thanks, Fred. Laura White did no translating, but she did an outstanding job of typing parts of the final manuscript. Last but by no means least, we would not think about sending a manuscript to the Press without first running it by Mike Travers for grammar and style issues. Thank you, all.

Beyond the gracious assistance we received at Southeastern, we are grateful for the help we received from other institutions. We tracked down an obscure French source at Duke University's archive and we found their staff both friendly and helpful. Jason Fowler, archivist at Southern Baptist Theological Seminary, was likewise helpful when it came to finding obscure sources.

Finally, we wish to acknowledge L. Russ Bush III, longtime academic vice president and dean of the faculty at Southeastern Baptist Theological Seminary, Wake Forest, North Carolina. Russ, stepped down from his administrative duties on June 1, 2006, to become academic vice president/dean of the faculty emeritus and the director of Southeastern's L. Russ Bush Center for Faith and Culture. Russ served Southeastern with distinction under three different presidents. He oversaw scores of curriculum revisions, endured innumerable meetings of various configurations, and survived the ordeal of accreditation reaffirmation –twice. And, he managed somehow to smile through it all. So, it seemed fitting that we dedicate this work to L. Russ Bush as a small token of our appreciation for his many contributions to Southeastern Baptist Theological Seminary. Sadly, Russ passed away on January 22, 2008, after a lengthy battle with cancer. We therefore dedicate this edition of *Domestic Slavery* to his memory.

    Nathan A. Finn
    Keith Harper

*Dedicated to the memory of L. Russ Bush III*

# INTRODUCTION

In late1844 and early 1845 the *Christian Reflector*, a Baptist newspaper in Boston, Massachusetts, ran a series of letters between Dr. Frances Wayland and Dr. Richard Fuller. Both were well known and well respected among their contemporaries. Wayland served as president of Brown University and had been a driving force in organized missionary work since the Triennial Convention's earliest days. Fuller hailed from South Carolina where he too supported missionary projects at home and abroad.[1] Their correspondence for the *Christian Reflector*, however, had nothing to do with missions. Rather, these men were offering two opposing understandings of slavery.

In all, these men exchanged sixteen letters that the *Reflector* carried in consecutive weeks. Rather than offering point/counterpoint understandings of slavery, the *Reflector* carried Wayland's letters and then published Fuller's letters. Once finished, Wayland, with Fuller's enthusiastic consent, wrote a closing letter and brief introduction for a bound copy of the correspondence. Their subsequent volume, *Domestic Slavery Considered as a Scriptural Institution*, or more commonly, *Domestic Slavery*, appeared in 1846 and quickly became required reading for anyone interested in slavery.

These letters continue to intrigue readers over a century and a half since they were first published. Both Fuller and Wayland were what may be best categorized as "moderates."[2] Wayland saw slavery as a "moral evil," but

---

[1 As important as each of these men was among their peers, Wayland may be the most under-appreciated Baptist leader of the nineteenth century and Fuller is scarcely known outside of Southern Baptist circles. For biographical informtion on these men see Thomas Halbrooks, "Francis Wayland: Contributor to Baptist Concepts of Church Order," (Ph.D. diss., Emory University, 1971). See also, *Historical Dictionary of the Baptists* (Lanham MD and London: Scarecrow Press, 1999) s.v. "Wayland, Francis," and *Dictionary of the Baptists in America* (Downers Grove IL: InterVarsity Press, 1994) s.v. "Wayland, Francis." For information on Fuller see the *Encyclopedia of Southern Baptists* (Nashville: Broadman Press, 1958) s.v. "Fuller, Richard."]

[2 For a discussion of Wayland's understandingof slavery see Deborah Bingham Van Broekhoven, "Suffering with Slaveholders: The Limits of Francis Wayland's Antislavery Witness," in John McKivigan and Mitchell Snay, eds., *Religion and the Antebellum Debate over Slavery* (Athens and London: University of Georgia Press, 1998) 196–220.]

he was not a staunch abolitionist. Fuller had no sympathy for cruelty and exploitation, but he saw no sin in an institution that he believed the United States Constitution and the Bible both sanctioned. One writer recently observed, "No one today would dispute the issue: Fuller was wrong and Wayland was right. What is significant in that book is the truly extraordinary degree to which these two friends on opposing sides of an explosive issue could relate to each other."[3] Indeed, these letters are remarkably measured in their content and kind in their tone.

For this edition of *Domestic Slavery* we have done nothing to the original text. However, Wayland and Fuller used abbreviated footnotes and we have edited these notes to be complete citations where possible. Our editorial additions are indicated by bracketed text in the footnotes. Also, we added a few information notes to help contemporary readers with obscure phrases and the like which are also designated by bracketed text. Moreover, we added the Wayland letter that Fuller referenced in his first letter (Appendix 1). We also added an editorial that the *Christian Reflector* ran in March 1845 (Appendix 2). The author anticipated a schism but exhorted his brethren to remain true to the cause of missions and to "adhere to their friends in New England." Other than these minor modifications, contemporary readers will read the same letters that stimulated mid-nineteenth century readers.

We hope this Mercer University Press edition of *Domestic Slavery* will stimulate renewed interest in an important era of American Baptist history. Wayland and Fuller seem to have sensed their task's importance. After all, few men exchange letters with footnotes. They were both well-read individuals who attempted to debate an emotionally charged issue apart from the rancor that such debate so often generated. If nothing else, these letters offer an enduring example of how interested individuals can publicly debate issues of national import without impugning the other's character.

---

[3 Thomas R. McKibbens, Jr., "Over Troubled Waters: Baptist Preachers Who Were Bridge Builders," *Baptist History & Heritage* 40/2 (Spring 2005): 62.]

# DOMESTIC SLAVERY

## *Introduction to the 1847 Edition*

In compliance with the wish of my friend and brother, the Rev. Dr. Fuller, the joint author with me of the following pages, I offer a few words by way of introduction.

The origin and progress of this correspondence may be thus briefly stated.

In the month of November last, at the request of the editor of the *Christian Reflector*, Dr. Fuller addressed a letter to that paper, presenting in brief his reasons for believing that Domestic Slavery is sanctioned by the Scriptures, and is therefore not always a sin. In this letter several allusions were made to the publications on this subject both of the late lamented Dr. Channing[1] and myself.[2] Had this eminent man been spared to us, the duty of defending what we both believed would have fallen into abler hands. It having pleased God to call him to his rest, this duty seemed to devolve upon me. I immediately communicated my intention to Dr. Fuller, and was gratified to learn that it met with his hearty concurrence.

I accordingly commenced a series of letters, in which I attempted to examine the various topics suggested in the letter above alluded to. These were immediately answered in a series of letters by Dr. Fuller. When at the request of several of our friends it was determined to publish the correspondence in a more permanent form, we preferred to print the whole in the same volume, in order that both of the views taken of this subject might lie presented together both at the North and the South. At the suggestion of Dr. Fuller, I have added the closing letter.

---

[1 William Ellery Channing (1780–1842) ranked among New England's leading Unitarian ministers. His widely-circulated pamphlet "Slavery" (Boston: James Monroe, 1835) offered a theological defense for abolition.]

[2Francis Wayland, "Domestic Slavery," *Christian Reflector* 12/18 and 19 (2 May 1844): 69–70 and 9 May 1844, 73. See Appendix 1 for the text of Wayland's letter.]

The design of this letter is not to prolong the correspondence by the addition of new matter, but rather to offer some explanations which seemed to be necessary, and also to present more clearly the bearing of the one argument upon the other, so that the points of agreement and difference might be rendered more manifest. I should have sent this letter to Dr. F. for his revisal, but the ink on the last page was not dry when the printer demanded the "copy."

Our different views are now laid before the public. I think that the letters of Dr. Fuller must in many cases modify the views, and in still more the feelings, of Christians at the North. Whether mine will have the same effect at the South, I am unable to determine. If, in any manner, the cause of truth shall be advanced; and, especially, if the disciples of Christ, by more clearly perceiving the sentiments of each other, shall find that the ground for the exercise of Christian charity is both wider and firmer than they had apprehended, some good at least will have arisen from this discussion.

In behalf of my brother and myself, I commend this correspondence to the disciples of Christ, both at the North and the South, in the humble hope that it may be the means of directing a calm yet earnest attention to this important subject.

F. W.

Providence, March 18, 1845.

# CORRESPONDENCE

*Letter from the Rev. Richard Fuller to the Editor of the* Christian Reflector[3]

Mr. Editor,

I comply at once, and in as few words as possible, with your request, and state why I, do deny that slavery is a moral evil; and let me request you, once for all, to bear in mind that this is the thing affirmed and denied. You say slavery is itself a sin; it is therefore always a sin; a sin amid any circumstances; a crime which must involve the criminal in perdition unless he repents, and should be abandoned at once, and without reference to consequences. This is the abolition doctrine; and at Philadelphia it was reiterated in every variety of phrase; and when even moderate men, and men seemingly very kind and calm in private, mounted the rostrum and felt the oratorical afflatus, we invariably heard, not arguments, but denunciations of this sort; we were sure to have eternal changes rung on the moral evil of slavery, the sin of slavery, the abominable guilt of slavery,—to be told that the ineffable horrors of slavery did not admit of discussion, and to be seriously asked what article of the decalogue slavery does not violate. And because the South listened to all this, unchafed and patiently, one or two papers at the north (and I believe the *Reflector* among them) forgot themselves, and, when the meetings were over, indulged in paeans and flourishes which showed they did not comprehend us. Now what I do entreat is, that you will cherish no delusion on this point. Even Dr. Channing censures this conduct of the abolitionists, and says, "They have done wrong, I believe; nor is their wrong to be winked at because; done fanatically, or with good intentions; for how much mischief may be wrought with good designs! *They have fallen into the common error of enthusiasts, that of exaggerating their object, of feeling as if no evil existed but that which they*

---

[3Richard Fuller, "Letter from the Rev. Richard Fuller, D.D., on the Subject of Slavery," *Christian Reflector* 12/45 (7 November 1844): 178.]

*opposed, and as if no guilt could be compared with that of countenancing and upholding it.* The tone of their newspapers, as far as I have seen them, has often been fierce, bitter, and abusive."[4] We are willing to weigh reasons, but assertion, and abuse, and blustering, will be heard in silence because this subject is not to be treated in that style. A correspondent in your last number holds up to me, as a model, the magnanimity of the Northern States in emancipating a few slaves who had become a burden to their owners. We understand this perfectly, and when in a similar situation will abolish, too. This writer is, however, utterly blind, if he supposes that the question with us now is about the value of so much slave property only. It regards all kinds of property, all civilization, and life itself; and in such a case to employ vituperation is at once a sin and a mistake. My chief hope for the Union is in the conservative power of religion, and the day is not far when that power will be required in all its stringency.

Look at the distracted condition of this land; reflect on the appalling character of a civil war; and if you love the country, or the slave, do not sever the bands which unite the Baptist churches. Compared with slavery, all other topics which now shake and inflame men's passions in these United States, are really trifling. They are only bonfires; but Ucalegon burns next, and in that quarter God forbid that Christians should throw the first torches.

If, however, slavery be a sin, surely it is the immediate duty of masters to abolish it, whatever be the result—this you urge, and this I grant; and this brings me to the single matter in hand, on which I submit to you the following observations.

1st. In affirming what you do, ought it not to give a pious mind pause, that you are brought into direct conflict with the Bible? The Old Testament did sanction slavery. God said,

> Both thy bondmen and thy bondmaids, which thou shalt
> have, shall be of the heathen that are round about you; of them

---

[[4]William Ellery Channing, "Slavery," in *The Works of William Ellery Channing* (Boston: American Unitarian Association, 1892) 732.]

shall ye buy bondmen and bondmaids. Moreover, of the children of the strangers that do sojourn among you, of them shall ye buy, and of their families that are with you, which they, begat in your land: and they shall be in your possession. And ye shall take them as an inheritance for your children after you, to inherit them for a possession; they shall b*e* your bondmen for ever [Levitivus 25:44–46a].

And in the Gospels and Epistles, the institution is, to say the least, tolerated. I do not now inquire as to the character of this slavery, nor is it important, for you pronounce slaveholding itself a sin; a sin, therefore, *semper et ubique*, always, and everywhere, and in all shapes. I, for my part, have no difficulty, and am in no sort of dilemma here, for I find my Bible condemning the abuses of slavery, but permitting the system itself, in cases where its abrogation would be a greater calamity than its existence. But you—how do you escape the charge of impiety?

2d. In the remark just made, I supposed, of course, that you admit some sort of slavery to have been allowed in the Old Testament, and suffered by Jesus and his apostles. A man who denies this will deny anything, and only proves how much stronger a passion is than the clearest truth. Both Dr. Channing and Dr. Wayland, with all respectable commentators, yield this point; but if this point be yielded, how can it be maintained that slaveholding is itself a crime? No one can regard the noble president of Brown University with more esteem and *affection* than I do; from his arguments, however, I am constrained to dissent. His position is this:[5] the moral precepts of the gospel condemn slavery; it is therefore criminal. Yet he admits that neither the Saviour nor his apostles commanded masters to emancipate their slaves; nay, they "go further," he adds, "and prescribe the duties suited to both parties in their present condition;" among which duties, be it remembered, there is not an intimation of manumission, but the whole code contemplates the

---

[5]I need hardly say that the argument is the same as Paley, chap. 3, book 3. [See William Paley, *Moral and Political Philosophy* (London: Printed for R. Faulder, 1785) 195–98.]

continuance of the relation. Here, then, we have the Author of the gospel, and the inspired propagators of the gospel, and the Holy Spirit inditing the gospel, all conniving at a practice which was a violation of the entire moral principle of the gospel! And the reason assigned by Dr. Wayland for this abstinence by God from censuring a wide-spread infraction of his law, is really nothing more nor less than expediency—the apprehension of consequences. The Lord Jesus and the apostles teaching expediency! They who proclaimed and prosecuted a war of extermination against all *the* most cherished passions of this guilty earth, and attacked with dauntless intrepidity all the multiform idolatry around them—they quailed, they shrank from breathing even a whisper against slavery, through fear of consequences!! And, through fear of consequences, the Holy Spirit has given us a canon of Scriptures, containing minute directions as *to* the duties of master and slave, without a word as to emancipation!!! Suppose our missionaries should be detected thus winking at idolatry, and tampering with crime in heathen lands.

Dr. Channing also says,—Paul satisfied himself with disseminating principles which would slowly subvert slavery.[6] "Satisfied himself!" but was he so easily satisfied in reference to any act which he regarded as a dereliction from duty? Hear how he speaks: "If any man that is called a brother be a fornicator, or covetous, or an idolater, railer, or a drunkard, or an extortioner, with such an one no not to eat [1 Corinthians 5:11]." "Be not deceived; neither fornicators, nor idolaters, nor adulterers, nor effeminate, nor abusers of themselves with mankind, nor thieves, nor covetous, nor drunkards, nor revilers nor extortioners, shall inherit the kingdom of God [1 Corinthians 6:9]." "Whoremongers and adulterers, God will judge [Hebrews 13:4]." "In the name of our Lord Jesus Christ, when ye are gathered together, and my spirit, with the power of our Lord Jesus Christ, to deliver such an one unto Satan for the destruction of the flesh, that the spirit may be saved in the day of the Lord Jesus [1 Corinthians 5:5]." Such was Paul's language; nothing but this

[6Channing, "Slavery," 723–25.]

unyielding, uncompromising. Condemnation of every sin could content him; yet, as to "the unutterable abomination of slavery," he is a temporizing palterer! As to slavery, which "violates every article in the decalogue," although the apostle saw it all around him, and members of the Church guilty of it, he declined uttering a word—he is cowed into a timeserver, a worker by concealed and tardy indirections! He "satisfies himself," while millions on all sides are sinking into hell through this crime—he "satisfies himself" with spreading principles which would slowly work a cure! Craven and faithless herald! And after this, with what face could he say, "I have kept back nothing"—"I have not shunned to declare the whole counsel of God [Acts 20:27]?" Arguments like these refute themselves; they are the signal failures of minds masterful for the truth, but impotent against it; and will convince every sincere inquirer that to denounce slaveholding as necessarily a sin, is to deal in loose assertion, and practically to range one's self with the infidel and scoffer.

3d. But will it not be laboring in the vocation of the infidel, to assert that the Bible does not condemn slavery, especially when we know that in the times of the Apostles, masters were allowed to torture their slaves, and starve them, and kill them as food for their fish? Is it not an insult to heaven, for one to defend such a system out of the Scriptures? This question is very plausible; but the answer is soon given, and it is the same which has been repeated over and over, viz., that the enormities often resulting from slavery, and which excite our abhorrence, are not inseparable from it—they are not elements in the system, but abuses of it. What, indeed, is slavery? *"I define slaver,"* says Paley, *"to be an obligation to labor for the benefit of the master, without the contract or consent of the slave."*[7] This is all that enters into the definition of slavery, and now what ingredient here is sinful? Suppose a master to "render unto his servant the things that are just and equal;" suppose the servant well clothed and religiously instructed, and to receive a fair reward for labor in modes of compensation best suited to his condition; might not the Bible permit the relation to continue, and might it not be best for the slave himself?

---

[7Paley, *Moral and Political Philosophy*, 195.]

Recollect that when you tell us of certain laws, and customs, and moral evils, and gross crimes, which are often incidents of slavery in this country, we agree with you, and are most anxious for their removal, and deprecate the incendiary movements of abolitionists as tending only to retard and even arrest our success. On these topics Christians throughout the land ought to communicate in the spirit of love, and combine their prayers and co-operations. The abolitionists, however, are not among those with whom we can thus associate. They occupy a position hostile alike to us, and to the word of God, and to every principle of charity. They do not attack the accidents of slavery, and attempt to show that they are essentials, but slavery itself they stigmatize, as an unutterable crime, and slaveholders as on a footing with thieves and pirates.

Is it to be expected that such libels will convince persons here, or that hard words will commend anybody as wiser and more courageous and better than the Saviour and his apostles? Examine all the anti-slavery publications, and what do they contain? Denude them of bold assertion and unmeasured invective against the accessories of slavery, and what is left? The simple question is, *whether it is necessarily, and amidst all circumstances, a crime to hold men in a condition where they labor for another without their consent or contract?* And in settling this matter all impertinences must be retrenched. But, if impertinences be removed, what remains in the abolition treatises? For example, slavery in these States may or may not be different from that mentioned in the Bible, and this may be a very important inquiry; but it is not the inquiry before us. So, with regard to the cruelty too often practiced by unprincipled men: here is guilt, guilt punishable by our laws, and which should exclude such persons from Christian fellowship; the crime, however, is not slaveholding, but cruelty. The popular argument, that a human being should not be treated as a chattel, is in the same category of impertinences. The proposition is self-evident, but wholly irrelevant, since it is by no means an attribute of slavery that a master may treat his slave as a chattel; the Bible forbids this, and every feeling of our nature rises up and must forever and effectually prevent it. Slavery is bondage, and nothing more. The slave has his rights, many of which are protected by our laws, and all by the Bible. The power of the master to transfer his authority, surely does not alter the character of that authority; and to confound this with his right in things which he may destroy at pleasure, is to overlook the plainest distinctions. It seems monstrous to you that a man should be the property of another man; but why is it so monstrous? Simply because you suppose that the word *"property"* involves a degradation to the state of a chattel. This, however, is plainly fallacious. Property in my furniture is one thing; property in my horse is a very different thing; and property in a slave entirely distinct still. To treat the brute as I might a chair, would be barbarous; and to use the slave as I might the brute, would justly make me infamous in any society, and draw down the vengeance of laws, human and divine. Property in a slave is only a *right to his service without his consent or contract*; and if this be necessarily criminal, then the authority of a father over his child, and of a government over its citizens, must be criminal too.

I might easily protract these remarks, but it is unnecessary. Let it be recollected that the only proposition is this abstract assertion: *slavery is itself a sin—always and by necessity a sin*; and it appears to me you must either abandon the Bible, or make it teach an expediency and "keeping back" of truth, which it abhors, or modify your views. The matter stands thus: the Bible did authorize some sort of slavery; if now the abuses admitted and deplored by me be essentials of all slavery, then the Bible did allow those abuses; if it be impossible that revelation should permit such evils, then you must either reject the Scriptures, as some abolitionists are doing, or concede that these sins are only accidents of slavery, which may; and perhaps, in cases of many Christians, do exist without them. Before I dismiss this subject, I would glance at two arguments which are sometimes urged, and require a passing notice.

The first is thus summed up by Dr. Wayland: "The manner in which the duty of servants or slaves is inculcated, therefore, affords no ground for the assertion, that the gospel authorizes one man to hold another in bondage, any more than the command to honor the king, when that king was Nero, authorized the tyranny of the emperor, or that the command to turn the other cheek when one is smitten, justifies the infliction of violence by an injurious man."[8] To this the reply is easy. The gospel does not recognize either Nero or the injurious man as a Christian brother, but it does so recognize those who hold slaves.

The second argument is thus put by Dr. Channing. "Polygamy was allowed to the Israelites, was the practice of the holiest men, and was common and licensed in the age of the apostles. But the apostles nowhere condemn it, nor was the renunciation of it made an essential condition of admission into the Christian Church."[9] And of this the sophistry is hardly specious. What if all that is affirmed be granted? It would only prove that polygamy is not sinful, and how is this connected with the matter at issue? But the gospel does forbid, and did at once abolish polygamy.

That those who hold slaves are unfit members for a Christian church, is a novel doctrine, a new light, which would have been scouted from our churches fifty years ago. But no polygamist has ever been admitted or tolerated as a Christian since the establishment of Christianity. The Saviour expressly gave a new law as to divorce; and the very letter of that precept, and every word in the epistles as to marriage, recognize and require only one wife. Jesus says, "*Whosoever putteth away his wife and marrieth another, committeth adultery* [Luke 16:18]." Now what constitutes the adultery? Not "*putting away his wife*," but "*marrying another:*" therefore he who marrieth another without putting away is guilty. Paul says, "For the woman which hath a husband, is bound by the law to her husband so long as he liveth; but if the husband be dead, she is loosed from the law of her husband; so then if while her husband liveth she be married to another man, she shall be called an adulteress [Romans 7:3]." "To avoid fornication, let every man have his own wife, and let every woman have her own husband [1 Corinthians 7:2]." Is not this express enough? Besides, it is a mistake in Dr. Channing and others to suppose that polygamy was common in the days of the Saviour and his

---

[8Francis Wayland, *The Elements of Moral Science*, abridged ed. (Boston: Gould and Lincoln, 1852) 213–14.]

[9Channing, "Slavery," 723.]

apostles. The Roman and Grecian laws did not permit it; and such are the inconveniences and evils of the custom, that it had nearly ceased in Judea: hence, in the whole New Testament not a single instance is even alluded to. No further notice was therefore required than the language of Christ and the directions in the Epistles. But slavery was everywhere a part the social organization of the earth; and slaves and their masters were members together of the churches; and minute instructions are given to each as to their duties, without even an insinuation that it was the duty of masters to emancipate. Now I ask, could this possibly be so, if slavery were "a heinous sin?" No! Every candid man will answer, no! What, then, are we to think, of those who revile us as pirates and thieves, and fulminate anathemas and excommunications against every Christian at the South, no matter what his conduct or character, simply because he will not submit to the arrogant behests of mortals who at best are, like himself, loaded with imperfections; and because he esteems the Bible a safer directory than the dogmas of men, most of whom are every day proving themselves destitute of the sound mind and charity of the gospel—of people who are essentially monomaniacs—who cannot live without running into some insanity—who, if slavery were abolished, would be just as mad upon amalgamation, or masonry, or Millerism,[10] or some other matter—and with whom, in, fine, whatever your course may be as to us, neither you, nor anybody at North who loves Christ and the gospel better than self, and strife, and fanatical intolerance, will lo be able to harmonize?

In the charity of the gospel, and with all respect,

I am, &c.,

R. Fuller, Beaufort, S.C.

---

[[10]Millerism refers to the teachings of of William Miller (1782–1849) a millenarian preacher in upstate New York who predicted the second coming of Christ would occur on 21 March 1843. When that date passed without incident, Miller revised his prediction to 22 October 1844.]

# DR. WAYLAND'S LETTERS

*Letter I*[11]

*To the Rev. Richard Fuller, D.D.*

My Dear Brother,

I have read with great interest your letter on Domestic Slavery in the *Christian Reflector* of the present week. Although it is addressed to the editor, yet as you have specially referred to sentiments which I have elsewhere advocated, I presume you will not consider it obtrusive, if I ask the privilege of offering a few remarks in illustration of the doctrines from which you dissent. I fully believe that you, equally with myself, desire to arrive at the truth on this question. If by the kind and fraternal exhibition of our views we can throw any light upon this difficult subject, we shall, I am sure, perform an acceptable service, both to the Church of Christ, and to our beloved country.

With many of the sentiments in your letter I heartily coincide. I unite with you and the late lamented Dr. Channing, in the opinion that the tone of the abolitionists at the north has been frequently, I fear I must say generally, "fierce, bitter, and abusive." The abolition press has, I believe, from the beginning, too commonly indulged in exaggerated statement, in violent denunciation, and in coarse and lacerating invective. At our late Missionary Convention in Philadelphia, I heard many things from men who claim to be the exclusive friends of the slave, which pained me more than I can express. It seemed to me that the spirit which many of them manifested was very different from the spirit of Christ. I also cheerfully bear testimony to, the general courtesy, the Christian urbanity, and the calmness under provocation, which, in a remarkable degree, characterized the conduct of the members from the South.

---

[11*Christian Reflector* 12/46 (14 November 1844): 182.]

While, however, I say this, justice requires me to add that I seem to have perceived grave errors, in the manner in which this subject has been treated in the slaveholding States. If, at the north, right of free discussion has been abused, I think that frequently, at the south, this right has been denied to American citizens. I have seen legislative messages which have, in substance, asserted that the people of this country have no right to discuss the subject of slavery at all. I am sure that you will agree with me in condemning every assumption of this kind. There is no subject whatever which I have not a perfect right to discuss, in the freest and fullest manner, in public or in private, provided I act with an honest intention to set before men what I consider to be important truth, and address myself to their understanding and conscience. I claim this right as a citizen of the United States; or rather, I claim it by a far higher title, as an intelligent creature of God. I can only surrender it with my life. I must always treat the threat of abridging it as an insult to the nature which has been given me by my Creator. If I abuse this right, I may be justly punished, and I grant that the punishment, both civil and social, should be exemplary. The right, however, as I have stated it, still remains interwoven with the essential elements of my intellectual and moral nature.

I rejoice that the question is assuming a new aspect. I rejoice that a brother from the south has invited this discussion, and that there is now an opportunity afforded for freely exchanging our sentiments with each other. Should I abuse this right, should I utter a word that would tend needlessly to wound the feelings of my Southern brethren, there is not one of them that will be as deeply pained as myself. I have never yet visited the Southern States. There may be cases in which, from ignorance of the modes of thinking and forms of expression which prevail among my Southern fellow-citizens, I may, inadvertently, seem not sufficiently to regard their feelings. I do not anticipate that such a case will occur. But should it occur, I have only to ask that I may be considered as an honest and kind man, desiring to hold forth what he believes to be truth; and that if I may seem in this respect to err, it may be imputed, not to an intention to give pain, but merely to my ignorance of the modes of thought peculiar to a state of society with which I am not familiar.

I would, in passing, offer another suggestion. The ground which is at present taken by the South, in regard to the whole question of slavery, seems to me to be of recent origin. At the time of the adoption of the Constitution, I suppose it to have been very generally acknowledged throughout this country, that slavery was an evil, and a wrong, and that it was, tacitly at least, understood to be the duty of those States in which it existed, to remove it as soon as practicable. Pennsylvania had already commenced this work, and she moved on steadily by successive acts to its completion. New York very soon followed her example. There was at that time much less distinction than at present between slaveholding and non-slaveholding States. It was, I think, considered as an evil and a wrong, in which the whole country was in different degrees involved, and which the whole country was under a solemn moral obligation to remove. The subject was everywhere freely discussed. I have before me, at this moment, a speech delivered in the Convention held at Danville, Kentucky, by the Rev. David Rice, proving that "slavery is inconsistent with justice and good policy," printed in Philadelphia, 1792.[12] It is as thorough, manly, and able discussion of this whole subject, as within the same compass I have ever seen. This was delivered in the Convention for forming a constitution for that State, and I have no reason to suppose that it gave any offence. This same freedom of discussion was enjoyed in Kentucky until quite lately. Some ten or fifteen years since, a motion was entertained in the Legislature of that State to call a convention for the express purpose of abolishing slavery, and it failed of success only by the casting vote of the speaker. Nay, even as late as the year 1830, in the Convention for forming the present Constitution for Virginia, the whole subject of slavery was publicly discussed, with a freedom and an eloquence which even in that State, so fertile in orators, has never been excelled.

---

[12David Rice was a leading Presbyterian pastor in early Kentucky. In 1792, he argued unsuccessfully that Kentucky's first state constitution should not allow slavery.]

The presentation of memorials to Congress, on the subject of slavery, has of late been esteemed an intolerable grievance. Formerly it was not so considered. On the 8th day of December, 1791, memorials from Societies for the abolition of slavery, from the States of Rhode Island, Connecticut, New York, Pennsylvania, Maryland, and Virginia, were *presented and read* in the House of Representatives, and *were referred to a select Committee.* In the memorial from Connecticut it is stated, "that the whole system of African slavery is unjust in its nature, impolitic in its principles, and in its consequences ruinous to the industry and enterprise of the citizens of these States." The memorialists from Pennsylvania say, "we wish not to trespass on your time by referring to the different declarations made by Congress, *on the unalienable right of all men to equal liberty*; neither would we attempt in this place to point out the inconsistency of extending freedom *to a part only* of *the human race.*" The memorialists from Baltimore declare that the *objects* of their association are founded in justice and humanity; "that in addition to *an avowed enmity to slavery in every form,* your memorialists in their exertions contemplate amelioration of the condition of that part of the human race who are doomed to fill the degraded rank of slaves in our country," &c. The strongest expression of opinion, however, on this subject, occurs in the memorial from Virginia. It commences as follows: "Your memorialists, fully believing that 'righteousness exalteth a nation,' and that slavery is not only an odious degradation but an outrageous violation of one of the most essential rights of human nature, and utterly repugnant to the precepts of the gospel, which breathes peace on earth and good-will to men, they lament that a practice so inconsistent with true policy, and the *unalienable rights of men,* should subsist in an enlightened age and among a people professing that all mankind are by nature equally entitled to freedom." These noble sentiments, I repeat it, originated from Virginia, and were read and referred to a select Committee of the House of Representatives.

Much has also been said on the interference of Associations, and other ecclesiastical bodies, on this subject. I do not here enter upon the question whether or not such assemblies should, in their corporate capacity, take action on the matter of slavery. I will merely state that such action can claim very ancient precedents. At the meeting of the Philadelphia Baptist Association, held Aug. 7th, 1789, the following declaration was made: "Agreeably to a letter from the church at *Baltimore*, this Association declare their high approbation of the several societies formed in the United States, and Europe, for the gradual abolition of slavery of Africans, and for the guarding against their being detained or sent off as slaves after having obtained their liberty, and do hereby recommend to *the churches we represent to form similar societies*, to become members thereof, and to exert themselves to obtain this important object."[13] To this action I know not that any exception was ever taken.

These facts seem to me conclusively to show that during the period of our history immediately succeeding the Revolution, the right or wrong of slavery was considered throughout the Union as a perfectly open question, on which any one, without offence to any class of persons, might freely express his opinions; on which any citizens might memorialize Congress, and in these memorials, express their opinions, assured that such opinions would meet with respectful attention; and also that in at least three of the slaveholding States themselves any citizen might, appealing to the understanding and conscience of his fellow-men, utter his sentiments as freely on this as on any other subject.

I deeply deplore the change in this respect that has come over the South. It seems to me unwise and unreasonable. The institution of slavery, whether it be considered in the light of political economy, of philanthropy, or of Christianity, is surely important enough to demand a full and impartial discussion. If it can be defended on either of these grounds, "a decent respect for the opinions of mankind" would certainly require that its defence should be attempted. If it cannot be so defended, but on the contrary can be shown to be at variance both with virtue and self-interest, the sooner we are convinced of this the better. But I

---

[13]A. D. Gillette, ed., *Minutes of the Philadelphia Baptist Association 1707 to 1807: Being the First One Hundred Years of Its Existence*, tricentennial edition (Springfield MO: Particular Baptist Press, 2002) 247.]

especially deplore the intolerance on this subject, which I believe now to exist in the slaveholding States themselves. I know that there are at this moment many of our Southern citizens, some of them slaveholders, who are convinced both of the moral evil of slavery, and of its ruinous influence on national prosperity. They long for an opportunity to express their sentiments to their fellow-citizens. But in the present state of public opinion they dare not do it. They are deprived of the opportunity of giving utterance to their honest convictions. Under such circumstances, how can we ever hope to arrive at the truth?

To this it may be replied, that the violence and fanaticism of abolitionists has been the cause of this universal irritability of our Southern fellow citizens. I have no doubt that this, to a considerable degree, has been the fact. I admit the existence of the cause, and presume that it has in part at least produced this effect. But the question still remains, *ought* it to have produced this effect? Suppose that a man addresses me unkindly and abusively on a question of duty; this *may* be a reason why I should not hear *him*, but it is surely no sufficient reason why I should not hear another man who addresses me on the same subject kindly and respectfully; much less is it a reason why I should determine never to hear the subject discussed by any person in any manner whatever, If abolitionists have treated this subject offensively, this is a no sufficient reason why any citizen of a *Southern State* should not be allowed, without offence, to declare his views of it in any suitable manner that he pleases. It is conceded that the institution of slavery is a matter peculiarly and exclusively belonging to the States in which it exits. For this reason, were there no other, the discussion of it should in those States be specially free, thorough, and universal. I cannot but believe that the public feeling, on this subject, was much more healthy with our fathers than with us. I cannot be persuaded that irritability and menace are either manly or dignified, or that the employment of physical force to arrest the discussion of an important subject, a either useful or wise. I wish most sincerely, that the temper and conduct of the Southern members of the late Convention at Philadelphia might be imitated by all their brethren. But I am protracting this letter to an unreasonable length, and will conclude by subscribing myself with the highest personal esteem and Christian affection,

## THE AUTHOR OF THE MORAL SCIENCE.

*Letter II*[14]

*To the Rev. Richard Fuller, D.D.*

My Dear Brother,

In my last letter I took notice of some incidental topics alluded to in your letter on domestic slavery. My object was to show that while the North had erred in its manner of treating this subject, this error had been by no means peculiar to the North; and also that the sensitiveness in regard to it, which has of late become so universal at the South, had no existence in the early periods of the history of this country. It seems to me desirable that the position of both parties should be changed; that the North should treat this subject by calm yet earnest appeal to the understanding and conscience of their fellow-citizens at the South, and that the South should invite the freest possible discussion of it, from what quarter soever it may proceed, so long as it confine itself within these limits. In your letter it is stated that "the thing affirmed and denied is, that slavery is a moral evil," "that slavery is, in itself, a sin; a sin amid any circumstances." You also, with great truth and frankness, add, if slavery be a sin, "it is the immediate duty of masters to abolish it, whatever be the result;" this you, urge and this I grant. I believe that in these latter expressions you give utterance to the real sentiments of your heart. I believe that you have submitted yourself without reserve to the whole will of God in so far as He shall reveal it to you. I well know the flattering prospects which you abandoned in order to become a preacher of the gospel of Christ. I believe that the same principles would govern

---

[[14]*Christian Reflector* 12/47 (21 November 1844): 186.]

you in this case; and that as soon as you shall be convinced that the rule of Christian duty requires of you any other course of conduct than that which you now adopt, you will, at any sacrifice whatever, act in accordance with your convictions. It is in this confidence that I address you on this subject with peculiar pleasure. I hope that if I am convinced of error, I shall be enabled to act from the same principles.

It may perhaps be proper to state that I have never expressed my views of slavery in the form to which you have alluded. The assertion is ambiguous in its meaning, and may admit of several very different answers. I could not pretend either to affirm or deny it, in this indefinite and indeterminate shape. It will be necessary therefore to fix its different meanings, and then offer my views upon each of them.

You remark, it is affirmed that "slavery is a moral evil." This you deny; and you assert, as I suppose, on the contrary, that slavery is not, in itself a moral evil. You define slavery to be "an obligation to labor for the benefit of the master, without the contract or consent of the slave." I understand you, then, to assert, that the master has a right to oblige the *slave* to labor for his (the master's) benefit, without the contract or consent of the slave. Now if the master enjoy this right, he enjoys also the right to use all the means necessary both to enforce and to render it permanent. He has a right to protect himself against every thing that would interfere with the exercise of this right. If the intellectual or moral cultivation of the slave would interfere with the master's power to enforce this right, he has the right to arrest this cultivation at any point he chooses, or to abolish it altogether. If this right exist, therefore, I do not perceive that any exception can be taken to the sternest laws which have ever been enacted in any of the Southern States, even though they prohibit, under the severest penalties, the education of negroes, and forbid them to assemble for the worship of God, except under the strictest surveillance.

I do not really see how these two rights can be separated. Either the right of the master to oblige the slave to labor without his consent, confers the right over his intellectual and moral nature, or it does not. If it does, then it may be rightfully exercised. It is a right given me by God, over another, and I may use it innocently, at my own discretion; that is, I may, control his intellectual and moral nature just in so far as is necessary in order to secure to myself the exercise of the original right which God has given me. If, on the other hand, it does not exist, then the slave in these respects stands to me in precisely the same relation as any other man. I have no more right to interfere with his intellectual or moral improvement than with that of any other man. He is in these respects as free as I am myself; and to interfere with him is both cruel and unjust. Nay more, I am bound to use all the means in my power to elevate and improve him, just as I am bound to do good to all other men, as I have opportunity. Or to state the matter in another form. The right of the master over the slave, and the right of the slave freely to enjoy the blessings of moral and intellectual cultivation, and the privileges of domestic society, are manifestly conflicting rights. One or the other must overrule. If the right of the master be the predominant right, it innocently controls the other. If the right of the_slave be the predominant right, it abolishes the right of the master wherever this right interferes with it.

Were I, therefore, to define the right of slavery, I should go somewhat further than you have gone. I suppose it to be the right to oblige another to labor, for me, without his contract or consent, with the additional right to use all the means necessary to insure the exercise of the original right.

But it is asserted that "slavery is not a moral evil." Here I think a most important distinction is to be taken. The terms *moral evil* may be used to designate two ideas widely dissimilar from each other, and depending upon entirely different principles. In the one sense it means wrong, the violation of the relations which exist between the parties, the transgression of a moral law of God. In the other sense it signifies the *personal guilt* which attaches to the being who does the wrong, violates the obligation, or transgresses the law. In the first sense, moral evil depends upon the immutable relations which God has established between his moral creatures. In the second sense, meaning personal guilt, it depends upon light, knowledge of duty, means of obtaining information on the subject, and may be different in different persons and at different times. It is manifest that we can take no proper view of the question before us, without considering these two meanings separately.

It has seemed to me that much of the misunderstanding which has existed on this subject has arisen from the want of attention to this obvious distinction. We, at the North have considered too exclusively the first, and you, at the South as exclusively the second, of these meanings of the terms moral evil. The one party has shown that slavery is always a violation of right, and has inferred that therefore it always involves equal guilt. The other party has urged the circumstances in which they and their slaves are placed, and has aimed to show that in their present condition they are not necessarily chargeable with guilt, and hence have inferred that slavery is not a wrong, or the violation of any moral law.

Let us endeavor calmly to consider both of these meanings of the phrase "moral *evil.*" In the first sense, when we affirm that slavery is not a moral evil, we affirm that to hold a man in slavery as it has been above explained is right, that it violates no law of God, and is at variance with no moral relation existing between man and man. Now I believe directly the reverse of this. I believe it to be wrong, utterly and absolutely at variance with the relations which God has established between his moral and intelligent creatures. My reasons for holding this opinion are briefly as follows:

I suppose that "God, of one blood, made all men that dwell upon the earth,"—that we are all partakers of the same nature, as we are all the children of one common parent. I suppose that this *common nature* is not affected, in any respect, by the color of the skin, the difference of the hair, or by any other variety of physical formation. I believe also that this common nature remains the same under every degree of intellectual development. A man may be wiser or less wise, he may be more or less richly endowed with mental capacity, he may be more or less ignorant than myself, but these differences affect not our *common nature*. He is in every respect, notwithstanding all this, as perfectly a human being as myself; and he stands with me in precisely the same relations to the Creator and Father of us all.

I believe that every human being is endowed with an immortal soul, and that he is placed in the present state of probation, a candidate for everlasting happiness or everlasting woe. He has an intellect capable of endless progression in knowledge, and is animated with a desire to improve that intellect to the utmost; and God has given one a right to improve it, to whatever extent he pleases. He is endowed with a conscience which renders him susceptible of moral obligations both to God and to man. In virtue of this endowment, it is his imperative duty to seek by all the means in his power to know the will of God, and it is his inalienable right to serve God in the manner which he believes will be most pleasing to the Creator. He has powers of external action, and by means of his intellect he may use these powers for the improvement of his own condition, and, provided he use them not in violation of the equal rights of his brethren, he may employ them as he will, and the result of this employment is strictly and exclusively his own.

But more than this. Every human being is a fallen creature. He is a sinner against God, and is exposed, for his transgressions, to the condemnation of everlasting death. God so loved him "that he gave his only-begotten Son, that whosoever believeth in him should not perish, but have everlasting life [John 3:16]." To every one possessing this nature, Jesus Christ has made, in the gospel, the offer of eternal salvation. The New Testament constitutes this message, and it is addressed to every child of Adam. Upon our understanding and obeying it, the eternal destiny of every one of us depends. Every human being has a perfect right to know every word that God has addressed to him, and as perfect a right to the use of all the means by which this knowledge may be obtained. These rights and obligations seem to me to arise specially and exclusively from the relations established by God, between the creature and himself; and therefore with them no other creature of God, not even the angels of heaven, have a right to interfere. They were ordained from the beginning, ere ever

"The hills were formed, the fountains opened,
Or the sea with all its roaring multitude of waves;"
and no ordinance of man can in any manner vary or annul them. [15]

I may go farther, and observe, that by the will of the Creator certain subordinate and temporary relations are established among human beings. Among these are the relations of husband and wife, and parent and child. From these relations certain obligations arise, and for the fulfilment of these obligations, God holds the parties individually responsible to him. With these obligations no other human being has a right to interfere. The laws which God has given respecting them in his word, transcend and overrule and abrogate all counteracting laws of man. Every man is bound to obey these laws which God himself has enacted, nor can any man rightfully present any obstacle to this obedience. I might pursue this subject further, but I have said enough to illustrate the nature of my belief.

That all these ideas are involved in the conception of *a human nature*, I think no one can deny. And if this be not denied, I do not perceive how the subject in this view admits of any argument. It is a matter of immediate moral consciousness. I know and feel that by virtue of my creation, I possess such a nature. I feel that the rights which I have described were conferred on me by the immediate endowment of God. I feel that with the exercise of these my rights, no created being can interfere, without doing me an aggravated wrong, and violating the law to which we are both subjected by our Creator. I am sure, my brother, that you feel all this as keenly as any man alive. You feel it, not by virtue of any constitution of government, or any enactment of civil law, but simply and truly because you are a man. And is not every other man, for precisely the same reason, endowed with the same rights, and is not the violation of these rights as great a wrong in his case as in either yours or my own?

[15 The editors were unable to locate the source for this quotation.]

To present this subject in a simple light. Let us suppose that your family and mine were neighbors. We, our wives and children, are all human beings in the sense that I have described, and, in consequence of that common nature, and by the will of our common Creator, are subject to the law, *Thou shalt love thy neighbor as thyself* [Matthew 19:19]. Suppose that I should set fire to your house, shoot you as you came out of it, and seizing upon your wife and children, "oblige them to labor for my benefit, without their contract or consent." Suppose, moreover, aware that I could not thus oblige them, unless they were inferior in intellect to myself, I should forbid them to read, and thus consign them to intellectual and moral imbecility. Suppose I should measure out to them the knowledge of God on the same principle. Suppose I should exercise this dominion over them and their children as long as I lived, and then do all in my power to render it certain that my children should exercise it after me. The question before us I suppose to be simply this, would I, in so doing, act at variance with the relations existing between us as creatures God? Would I, in other words, violate the supreme law of my Creator, Thou shalt love thy neighbor as thyself, or that other, Whatsoever ye would that men should do unto you, do ye even so unto them [Matthew 7:12]? I do not see how any intelligent creature can give more than one answer to this question. Then I think that every intelligent creature must affirm that to do this is wrong, or, in the other form of expression, that it is a great moral evil. Can we conceive of any greater?

Again, suppose my neighbor offers me money, and I, for the sake of this money, transfer some of these children to him, and he proceeds, as I did before him, to oblige them "to labor for his benefit, without their contract or consent;" and takes all the means, as before stated, which shall enable him to exercise this power. Does this transfer of money from him to me in any respect modify the relations which exist between him and them, as creatures of God, or abolish that law by which God has ordained that all our actions towards each other shall be governed? They are the same human beings, possessing the same human nature, and they stand in the same relations to God and to each other as before. The transfer of silver from him to me neither makes one party more nor the other party less than human beings; hence their actions are to be judged of by precisely the same rule as if no such transfer had been made. Hence I cannot resist the conclusion that the act in question is, as before, wrong; and that slavery, with this modification, is again, as before, a "moral evil."

I will offer but one more supposition. Suppose that any number, for instance, one half of the families in our neighborhood, should agree to treat the other half in the manner that I have described. Suppose we should by law enact that the weaker half should be slaves, that we would exercise over them the authority of masters, prohibit by law their instruction, and concert among ourselves the means for holding them permanently in their present situation. In what manner would this alter the moral aspect of the case?

A law, in this instance, is merely *a determination* of the stronger party to hold the weaker party in bondage; and *a contract* with each other, by which their whole power is pledged to each individual, so far as it shall be necessary, in order to enable him to hold in bondage his portion of the weaker party.

Now I cannot see that this in any respect changes the *nature* of the parties. They remain, as before, human beings, possessing the same intellectual and moral nature, holding the same relations to each other and to God, and still under the same unchangeable law, Thou shalt love thy neighbor as thyself. By the act of holding a man in bondage, this law is violated. Wrong is done, moral evil is committed. In the former case it was done by the individual; now it is done by the individual and the society. Before the formation of this compact, the individual was responsible only for his own wrong; now he is responsible both for his own, and also, since he is a member of the society, for all the wrong which the society binds itself to uphold and render perpetual.

The Scriptures frequently allude to the fact, that wrong done by law, that is, by society, is amenable to the same retribution *as* wrong done by the individual. Thus, Psalm 94:20–23: "Shall the *throne* of iniquity have fellowship with Thee, which *frame mischief by a law*, and gather themselves together against the soul of the righteous, and condemn the innocent blood? But the Lord is my defense; and my God is the rock of my refuge. And he shall bring upon them their own iniquity, and shall cut them off in their own wickedness; yea, the Lord our God shall cut them off." So also Isaiah 10:1–4:

> Woe unto them that *decree* unrighteous decrees, and that write grievousness which they have *prescribed;* to turn aside the needy from judgment, and to take away the right from the poor of my people, that widows may be their prey, and that they may rob the fatherless! And what will ye do in the day of visitation, and in the desolation which shall come from far? To whom will ye flee for help? And where will ye leave your glory? Without me they shall bow down under the prisoners, and they shall fall under the slain. For all this his anger is not turned away, but his hand is stretched out still.

Besides, persecution for the sake of religious opinion is always perpetrated by law; but this in no manner affects its moral character.

There is, however, one point of difference, which arises from the fact that this wrong has been established by law. It becomes a social wrong. The individual, or those who preceded him, may have surrendered their individual right over it to the society. In this case it may happen that the individual cannot act as he might have acted if the law had not been made. In this case the evil can only be eradicated by changing the opinions of the society, and thus persuading them to abolish the law. It will however be apparent that this, as I said before, does not change the relation of the parties either to each other or to God. There wrong exists as before. The individual act is wrong. The law which protects it is wrong. The whole society, in putting the law into execution, is doing wrong. Before, only the individual, now, the whole society becomes the wrong-doer, and for that wrong both the individual and the society are held responsible in the sight of God.

I have thus endeavored as clearly as possible to illustrate my views upon the question—is slavery a moral evil? Understanding by these terms, wrong, or violation of moral law. The consideration of the second meaning of the phrase I must reserve for another occasion. It may, perhaps, be proper for me here to state, once for all, that in these remarks and those that may follow, I speak as the organ of no party and of no sect. I belong to none. I am not and I never have been connected with any abolition society, and I believe that I have read as much on one side of this question as on the other. I write what seem to me the simple dictates of my individual understanding and conscience, enlightened I hope by the teachings of the Holy Scriptures. Nay, I may claim that the doctrines which I have advanced are by necessity involved in the character which I hold as an American citizen. I do not know that I have uttered a single sentiment which is not comprehended in the notable words which, form the introduction to our Declaration of Independence: " We hold these truths to be *self-evident*," (that is, so evident that they are, from the principles of the human mind, admitted as soon as they are stated,) "that all men are *created equal*," (that is, equal in right to use the endowments of the Creator as they choose, though not equal in endowments,) "that they are endowed by their Creator with certain *inalienable* rights," (that is, rights from which they cannot be rightfully alienated,) "and that among these are life, liberty, and, the pursuit of happiness." I do not know how else in so few words I could express my opinions on this subject.

I am, my dear brother, yours with every sentiment of regard,

The Author of the Moral Science.

*Letter III*[16]

*To the Rev. Richard fuller, D.D.*

My Dear Brother,

In my last letter, I endeavored to show that the right of slavery, if it exists, is not only the right "to oblige another to labor for our benefit, without his contract or consent," but also the right to use all the means necessary for the establishment and perpetuity of this right. Wherever slavery is established by law, I believe this power is conferred by society upon the master, and therefore it would be absurd to suppose that it is not generally exercised. I also attempted to show that when we assert or deny that slavery is a moral evil, the terms "moral evil," are susceptible of two very dissimilar meanings. They may mean either wrong, violation of right, transgression of moral law; or they may mean the guilt that attaches to the person doing the wrong. I endeavored also to show that, taken in the first of these senses, slavery is, from the very nature of the case, essentially a moral evil—that it is a violation of the rights of man, and a transgression of that law under which all human beings are created, "Thou shalt love thy neighbor as thyself [Matthew 19:19];" and that the moral character of the relation is the same, whether the master be the captor or the purchaser of the slave; whether his power be upheld by his own individual prowess, or by the combined authority of society.

I proceed now to consider the second meaning of the assertion—slavery is or is not a moral evil. We now mean by this assertion, that whoever holds a fellow-man in bondage is guilty of sin. To this assertion let us now direct our attention.

Supposing a moral law to exist, our guilt in violating it, as well as our virtue in obeying it, depends in the first place upon our knowledge of its existence. If we have never known that such a law has been enacted, we may be free from guilt though we violate it. If, on the other hand, we

---

[16]*Christian Reflector* 12/48 (28 November 1844): 190.]

know of its existence, and, with adequate knowledge of our duty, violate it, we incur, without mitigation, the guilt of our transgression.

Again, the guilt of violating a moral law must depend not only upon our knowledge, but upon our opportunities for the acquisition of knowledge. Two men may both violate a law in ignorance, but the one may have had every opportunity for acquiring a complete knowledge of his duty; the other may have been deprived of all such opportunities whatever. Their guilt will, in these cases, be very dissimilar. He who refuses to be informed concerning his duty, is voluntarily ignorant. His ignorance is his own fault, and he is justly responsible for all the consequences of his own act. The maxim in law clearly applies to this case: "No man may take advantage of his own wrong;" in other words, no man may plead ignorance as an excuse, when ignorance rather than knowledge is his own deliberate choice.

I am prepared to go further than this. Knowledge of my duty may be offered to me, but offered so commingled with error, and in a manner so repulsive to all my feelings of self-respect, that I instinctively reject it. In this case the guilt of rejecting knowledge of my duty is obviously less than it would have been if the same truth, unmixed with error, and clothed in the charity of the gospel, had been presented to my understanding. For instance, I am an instructor. In the discharge of my duties I may unwittingly adopt unsound principles. Suppose a stranger wishes to correct my errors, and introduces himself by stating as facts what I know to be exaggerations, and by loading me with gross and offensive personal abuse. I know that I ought to bear it calmly, and, carefully discriminating between the good and the bad, to use both as a means of self-improvement. I fear, however, that I should be, at the best, prejudiced against such instructions, and that some time would elapse before this discrimination could take place. I grant that I should do wrong in allowing my judgment to be biased by this abuse. But it is certainly as true that he did wrong in abusing me. It is his abuse that has rendered me unwilling to be convinced, when I might have been convinced on the instant, if he had treated me with Christian courtesy. My ignorance is therefore the combined result of his unchristian want of kindness and my unchristian want of meekness. The responsibility clearly attaches to both of us. Which of us will bear the larger portion of it, can only be known when the secrets of all hearts shall be revealed.

I see not why these principles do not apply to the present case. And hence, among those who, as I believe, in violation of right, hold human beings in bondage, there may be found every possible gradation of guiltiness. There may be many persons in our Southern states who have been reared in the midst of slavery, who have uniformly treated their slaves humanely; and who, having always seen the subject discussed in such a manner that they have been instinctively repelled from it, have never yet deliberately investigated it as a question of duty. Slaves have been held by those whom the slaveholders most venerate among the dead, and by those whom they most respect among the living. It is surprising to observe how long even a good man, under such circumstances, may continue in the practice of wrong, without ever suspecting its moral character. Of this fact the temperance reformation has furnished a thousand remarkable instances. It is only a few years since many of our most estimable citizens were acquiring their wealth by the manufacture and sale of spirituous liquors; that is, by means of the wholesale destruction, both temporal and eternal, of their fellow-men. Yet, strange as it may now seem, it never occurred to them that they were doing wrong. I remember very well that when this subject was first agitated in New England, I made it the theme of two fast-day discourses. In the course of the following week, a member of my church, one of the most conscientious men I have ever known, a wholesale grocer, said to me, "If your doctrine be true, I do not see how I can continue to deal in spirituous liquors." I believe that the thought had never crossed his mind before. He examined the subject carefully, became fully convinced of his duty, and abandoned the traffic. Yet he had attained to more than middle life, and had been from youth a man of exemplary piety, without having been aware that he was doing wrong. The *wrong* was ever the same. *Guilt* commenced as soon as he was convinced of the wrong, and continued in the practice of it.

Now all this absence of consideration may exist among many persons at the South, on the subject of slavery. It has, under almost as peculiar circumstances, existed at the North. I have been told that the Rev. Dr. Stiles,[17] afterwards President of Yale College, during his residence in Newport, R. I., being in want of a domestic, sent by the captain of a slave-ship a barrel of rum to the coast of Africa, to be exchanged for a slave. The venture was successful, and in due time a negro boy was brought back. It chanced that some time afterwards, in passing through his kitchen, he observed the boy in tears. He asked him the reason of his sorrow, and the poor fellow answered that he was thinking of his parents, and brothers and sisters, whom he should never see again. In an instant, the whole truth flashed upon the master's mind, and he saw the evil he had done. He could not return the boy to Africa, but he made every reparation in his power. He provided for him every means of improvement, was the means of his conversion, and treated him ever afterwards not as a servant, but as a brother beloved. *Newport*, for that was his name, survived Dr. Stiles several years, and was, to the end of his life, supported by a legacy which his former master had left him.

Such cases as these may exist now in the Southern states. On the other hand, it is no violation of charity to suppose that there are others who, utterly regardless of justice, knowing what they do to be wrong, and intentionally steeled against every monition of conscience, deliberately sacrifice every right of their slaves to their own pecuniary advantage, or the gratification of their love of power; who decide the question in how many years they shall work their fellow-men to death, by a calculation of profit and loss, and who exult in the power of subjecting to their uncontrolled will—a will avaricious, lustful, tyrannical and cruel—as many human beings as by purchase they can appropriate to themselves.

Let us now take these two extremes. These men are both slaveholders. They both do a wrong act in holding a fellow-man in

---

[17]Ezra Stiles served as president of Yale College from 1778 until his death in 1795.]

bondage. But would any one confound the moral character of the one with that of the other? The one may be a brother beloved, desirous from his heart of doing the will of God, so far as it shall be revealed to him. The other is a monster in iniquity—since the slave-trade exists I will not say without a *parallel*—*but* surely without many superiors in wickedness. And who does not see that the interval between these extremes may be filled up with every gradation of guiltiness? And hence it is that I perceive, in reflecting on this subject, wide ground for the exercise of Christian charity. With a deep conviction of the universal wrong of the act, I have very dissimilar views of the guilt of the actors. Some of them, with pain, I believe to be unjust, tyrannical, and cruel in the face of knowledge, acting in utter disregard of the dearest rights of their fellow-men. Others, I rejoice to believe, uphold this institution, in the belief that it is innocent, and exercise the power which they suppose themselves rightfully to possess with exemplary kindness, with paternal tenderness, and with a religious care for the souls that are, as they believe, committed to their charge. I cannot include these two classes in the same sweeping sentence of condemnation. In the one, though I see and lament their errors, I perceive the lineaments of the Christian character, in many cases strongly and beautifully expressed. Such men, while I testify against what seem to me their errors, I must receive as brethren, and I delight to co-operate with them in every good work, provided I so do it as not to imply any participation with what I believe to be wrong. Towards the others, I entertain the same sentiments which I entertain towards any other wicked and injurious men. I believe them to be not only doing wrong, but to be also exceedingly guilty—excluded by their guilt from all hope of salvation, unless they repent of this sin.

Hence I can never approve of those appeals which treat all men at the South as though they were, in respect to slavery, under the same condemnation; and which apply to all indiscriminately epithets which certainly belong to no more than a part. Hence I consider much of the action of churches and associations at the North, to be false in principle and unchristian in practice. It affirms *guilt* of the action, instead of affirming it of the mind of the actor; hence it makes the act, at all times and under all circumstances, of the same guiltiness; and it uniformly attaches to an action the worst motives, instead of ascribing to it as good motives as the circumstances attending upon it will allow.

I should also add, that the degree of guilt attendant upon a wrong action, must be continually changing with the progress of light and knowledge. Every one sees that Dr. Stiles, in the case above alluded to, could not, at the present time, send a barrel of rum to Africa in exchange for a human being, without being a very wicked man. Sixty or seventy years since he did it, and he was a very good man. It is much more difficult for a man at the present time to hold his fellow-men in bondage, and be guiltless, through ignorance, than it was twenty years since. The whole civilized world has been agitated upon this question. Great Britain, from a conviction of moral obligation, has liberated her slaves at an expenditure of a hundred millions of dollars. The subject is producing fearful excitement throughout our whole country, and threatens us with evils which I dare scarcely contemplate, and to which, in your letter, you have so eloquently alluded. Under these circumstances, it surely becomes every man who holds men in bondage, to inquire whether he can be innocent in the sight of "the Judge of the whole earth." If Jefferson "trembled for his country when he remembered that God is just," and declared that "in case of insurrection the Almighty has no attribute that can take part with us in such a contest,"[18] surely it becomes *a disciple of Jesus Christ to* pause and reflect. And besides, although this subject has been pressed offensively, and has naturally produced irritation, it should be borne in mind that anger in the bosom of a wise man is always short-lived. It is time for us to abstract the truth from the circumstances that surround it, and endeavor to ascertain our duty, each one for himself.

I will refer to one other condition, by which the personal guilt of holding men in bondage may be modified; it is the law of the community in which we live. I have already shown that such laws can never affect the *right* or *wrong* of an action. They may, however, affect the *guilt* or *innocence* of the actor. For instance, the law of the state may forbid me to

[[18]Thomas Jefferson, *Notes on the State of Virginia* (reprint; New York: Harper and Row, 1964) 156.]

manumit a slave without giving to the public, securities for his maintenance through life, and I may be unable to give such securities. It may forbid me to manumit my slaves without removing them out of the State, and they may themselves be unwilling to be removed, and may be unable, young and old together, to support themselves by labor in another climate. Or, the laws may be of such a nature that I can only manumit them under circumstances which would render their return to relentless bondage almost inevitable. I do not pretend to specify all the cases that may arise of this nature. In such circumstances as these, I can easily conceive of a course of action which might be innocent, even though the relation of master and slave existed. The master might become convinced of the wrong of slavery, and feel that he had no right over these human beings. The law, however, will not allow him to liberate them on any conditions with which it is in his power to comply. What then can he do? I answer, he may, from the moment that he is thus convinced, hold them not for *his* benefit but for *theirs*. If they, in their present condition, are unable to support themselves in other States, he may change that condition by teaching them habits of self-reliance and profitable industry. He may cultivate their intellects and improve their morals; and having done this, he may emancipate them just as rapidly as divine Providence shall present the opportunity. He who acts thus, or in any other way, in the fear of God, acts upon the principle that he holds this relation for the good of the slave, honestly and earnestly laboring, at any personal sacrifice, to terminate it as soon as he is able, seems to me innocent of the guilt of slavery.

Now I doubt not that there are many just such men among our brethren at the South. I have known Christian slaveholders who have devoted themselves through life to the welfare, temporal and spiritual, of their slaves, with the spirit of the most self-denying missionaries; and who, I confidently believe, if they could do it with a reasonable prospect of improving the condition of their slaves, would gladly manumit them and support themselves by daily labor at the North. Such men and women do honor to human nature. They are the true friends of their race. I am pained at the circumstances in which they are placed; but being so placed, I know not how they could act more worthily.

This is one extreme. Here, as in the previous case, there is another extreme. No one will deny that there are slaveholders of a very different character from these to whom I have now alluded. There are men who love the very law which gives them the power over their fellow-men; who daily strive to render that law more stringent; who, without regard either to the rights of man or the law of God, use the power which the law has given them over the slave, to the uttermost; and who resist by menace and, outcry every modification of the law by which those who think differently from them shall be enabled to act towards their slaves as their consciences shall dictate.

Here then we have men who are slaveholders equally in form, but of the most dissimilar moral character. The one class may be honestly and prayerfully laboring, to the best of their ability, to obey the Christian precept, "As ye would that men should do unto you, do ye even so unto them [Matthew 7:12a]." The other class allow no law, human or divine, to interfere with the exercise of their oppressive and tyrannical will. And between these extremes, as I said before, how many gradations of guiltiness may intervene!

Here then, again, is there room for the exercise of charity. I am not so simple as to believe, because there are some slaveholders of the first class, that all slaveholders are such; nor do I hold that the existence of slavery under some circumstances without moral guilt, proves that slavery under other circumstances is innocent; or that by the innocency of the one, the guilt of the other is in the smallest degree diminished. I do, however, believe, that we should look at the facts as they are, and instead of dealing in wholesale denunciation, until we can find a better rule, treat that man as a Christian in whom we can recognize the spirit of Christ.

While, however, I thus state the grounds of Christian charity, I hope that no one will suppose for a moment that I mean to extenuate the moral wrong of slavery. Should a man enslave me or my family, I should consider it the greatest wrong that he could inflict upon us. It is just as great a wrong to enslave any other family as to enslave mine. Nor would the wrong rendered be less, but in fact greater, were he so to stupify and debase us, that we were willing to submit our whole nature, physical, intellectual, and moral, to the will of a master. Still, were this done to me, I can conceive that the guilt of the oppressor might be and would be materially affected by his knowledge, his means of information, and the laws of the society to which he was obliged for the present to submit.

I remark again, that these modifications of the guilt of slavery can avail only where they exist. A man who knowingly, or with the power of knowing, voluntarily does wrong, is guilty for the full amount of that wrong; and, at the bar of God, he must answer for it. The only plea in abatement of guilt is, that a man has not the means of knowing better; or, that it is physically out of his power to obey the precept. But, while this abatement may be pleaded when it actually exists, it furnishes ground for no plea of abatement beyond the precise limits of its existence. If therefore a man allow that slavery is a violation of right—a violation of the law, "Thou shalt love thy neighbor as thyself"—before he can plead that he is guiltless, he must show that he has done, and is doing, every thing in his power to discontinue and make reparation for the wrong.

Once more. In what I have said above, I have alluded to the course which a slaveholder might be supposed to pursue, and be innocent of the guilt of slavery. I have, however, in these remarks, referred only to his conduct as an *individual*. There remains yet to be considered his duty as a member of society. If the laws are wrong, he, as a member of society, is bound to exert his full constitutional power to effect their abolition. If the moral sentiment of the State is wicked, he is bound to labor with his whole power to correct it. If his fellow-citizens oppress him, he is called upon by every sentiment of manliness, constitutionally to resist this oppression. If they oppress his fellow-men, he is bound by every sentiment of philanthropy to defend the oppressed and raise up the down-trodden. Unless he do this, he cannot, as a member of the society, be free from the guilt of the wrong which the society perpetrates. There is, however, no opportunity in this letter to discuss this part of the subject. It may present itself again, at a later period of our inquiry.

In the above remarks I have endeavored to illustrate the principles by which the personal guilt of holding a man in bondage may be modified. In what degree they apply to the case of every separate individual, can be known only to the Searcher of hearts. You and I, however, my brother, believe in the moral corruption of the human soul. We have been taught by the Bible that men are by nature influenced by direful passions and unholy lusts; by an insane love of wealth and a reckless desire for power. We know, too, how universally these corrupt affections darken the understanding and stupify the conscience. Taking these truths into view, we may form some estimate of the proportion of cases in which, on the above principles, the holding of slaves does or does not involve guiltiness; in how far insensibility to duty results from a want of knowledge, and in how far it results from a selfish and sinful indisposition to know the truth. You, who are well acquainted with slavery in all its phases, can form, I presume, a more correct judgment in this matter than myself. Of one thing, however, there can be no doubt. So far as slavery is a wrong perpetrated by society, no modification of guilt can arise from the *want of power* to remedy it. The power resides in the society. Its members have placed themselves in their present position in regard to slavery. They can, whenever they please, change that position. And for not changing it, every member of the society who has not exerted his full constitutional power to remove it, must at the bar of God be held guilty.

I am, my dear brother, yours with every sentiment of Christian affection—

The Author of the Moral Science.

*Letter IV[19]*

*To the Rev. Richard Fuller, D.D.*

My Dear Brother,

In my last two letters I have attempted to show what I mean when I assert that slavery is a moral evil. I have wished to make it clear that slavery, or the holding of men in bondage, and "obliging them to labor for our benefit, without their contract or consent," is always and everywhere, or, as you well express it, *simper et ubique*, a moral wrong, a violation of the obligations under which we are created to our fellow-men, and a transgression of the law of our Creator, *Thou shalt love thy neighbor as thyself;* that, however, while this is true, it is also true that the guilt of any individual doing this wrong may be modified by his means of obtaining a knowledge of his duty, and also by the laws of the community of which he may chance to be a member.

The objection to this view of the subject is founded on the precept and example of the Old and New Testaments. With pleasure I proceed to consider the argument on this part of the question. Believing as we both do that the Bible is a perfect rule of duty, if we can ascertain what it teaches, we may reasonably hope that our opinions may yet coincide. In this letter I propose to examine the argument derived from the Old Testament alone.

Your view, I think, may be briefly expressed as follows: Slavery was sanctioned in the Old Testament; and, since the Old Testament is a revelation from God, and since He would not sanction any thing morally evil, therefore slavery is not a moral evil.

Before, however, I proceed to consider this argument, permit me to remark, that I do not perceive in the views which I have expressed any thing at variance with the teachings of the Old Testament. I will briefly explain my opinions on the subject:

I grant, at once, that the Hebrews held slaves from the time of the conquest of Canaan, and that Abraham and the patriarchs had held them

---

[[19]*Christian Reflector* 12/49 (5 December 1844): 194.]

many centuries before. I grant also that Moses enacted laws with special reference to that relation. Of the nature of these laws it may be convenient to speak shortly. I wonder that any one should have had the hardihood to deny so plain a matter of record. I should almost as soon deny the delivery of the ten commandments to Moses.

Granting all this, I do not see that it contradicts aught that I have said. I believe slavery then, as now, to have been wrong, a violation of our obligations to man, and at variance with the moral laws of God. But I believe that God did not see fit to reveal his will on this subject, nor indeed on many others, to the ancient Hebrews. He made known to them just as much of his moral law as he chose, and the law on this subject belonged to the part which he did not choose to make known. Hence, although they did what was in itself *wrong*, yet, God not having made known to them his will, they were not *guilty*.

But more than this. God saw fit to institute peculiar relations between the Hebrews and the inhabitants of Canaan, relations such as he has never instituted between any other portions of the human family. When the iniquity of the Canaanites was full, God gave them and their lands and possessions, by *special revelation*, to the Hebrews. The Hebrews were authorized *by a divine commission* to invade their territory, to take possession of their houses and fields, and slay without mercy the inhabitants. The limitation and extent of this grant were definitely marked out. They were, however, directed to pause before the work of destruction was fully completed, lest the land, being deserted of its inhabitants, should be overrun by beasts of prey. Still, the people within these limits remained under the primitive curse. The Hebrews were authorized to destroy them, and seize upon their land whenever they needed it. The authority to take them as slaves seems to me to be a part of this original, peculiar, and I may perhaps say anomalous grant.

But this grant was made to one people, and to one people only, *the Hebrews*. It *had respect to one people only*, the Canaanites. It can be of force at no other time and to no other people. If the Jews were now to return to Palestine, the Old Testament would furnish no warrant by which they would be authorized, were it in their power, to devote to destruction or to enslave the Druses or Maronites of Mount Lebanon, the Arabs of Damascus, or the Turks of Acre. Much less would it authorize American citizens, residing in Palestine, to destroy or to enslave them; and much less does it authorize American citizens here at home to destroy, or to enslave, or to hold in slavery, the people of another continent. To the Jews it would have been unlawful, except by the special direction of Jehovah. To us and to all men it is unlawful to do the same thing, unless we can show the same special direction. These seem to me to be the general principles which we always apply when reasoning concerning the revelation made by the Most High to the Hebrew commonwealth. They comprehend the case of slavery; and by them is the bearing upon us of the permission in question to be determined.

The view which you take of the case, however, differs materially from this. I will now proceed to examine it. It may be stated briefly thus: Slavery was sanctioned by revelation among the Hebrews; it is therefore sanctioned to us.

Let us reduce this argument to a syllogism, and it will be expressed thus:

1. Whatever God sanctioned among the Hebrews, he sanctions for all men and at all times.
2. God sanctioned slavery among the Hebrews.
Therefore,
3. God sanctions slavery for all men and at all times.

I believe that in these words I express the argument correctly. If I do not, it is solely because I do not know how to state it more exactly.

Let us, then, in the first place, examine the major premise. *"Whatever God sanctioned among the Hebrews, he sanctions for all men and at all times."* Now this proposition surely is not self-evident. If it be true, it must be provable either by reason, or by revelation. Can it be proved by reason? The only argument by which it could be supported is, I think, the following:

1. Whatever God sanctions to any men at any time he sanctions to all men at all times.
2. The Hebrews are men.

Therefore,

3. Whatever he sanctioned to the Hebrews at any time he sanctioned to all men at all times.

Now I think that the major premise of this syllogism is wholly untenable. It appears to me to be diametrically at variance with the whole theory of the divine dispensation. Every one, I think, knows that God has seen fit to enlighten our race progressively; and that he has enlightened different portions in different degrees. He has first given us the light of nature. Millions at the present day have no other light. We know from revelation that by the truth alone which this light reveals, will they be judged. They will therefore be held guilty for the transgression of no other laws than those which this light has discovered to them. The rest of their transgressions of moral law will not be laid to their account. Thus in this sense of the word, these transgressions are *sanctioned* to them; that is, they are not forbidden, and they are not reckoned against them as sin. But I ask, are they sanctioned to us? Could we who have the light of the gospel go back to the morality of Socrates, Plato, Aristotle, or Confucius, for the reason that what the light of nature allowed to them is allowable in us? Yet I see not but this proposition would lead us to precisely this conclusion.

The same principle applies to the other gradual revelations of moral light which God has at different periods made to mankind. He increased the light of the patriarchs by the direct communication of a small part of his will. A large part of that will, however, he saw fit still to withhold. The violations of this latter part he did not forbid, but on the contrary he allowed them to remain unchecked, that is, in this sense he sanctioned them. But could any of us, in the fear of God, go back to the patriarchal dispensation, and take for our moral rule the revelation, and only the revelation, made to the patriarchs?

So of the Mosaic dispensation. By this revelation the light was more fully discovered, but still much of it was withheld. We cannot plead in this case, more than in the other, that what was permitted without rebuke in a darker age is permitted to us to whom greater light has been given. I suppose, therefore, that directly the reverse of the proposition in question is true; that God reveals his will in different degrees, at different times, and to different people at the same time; that he holds men accountable for precisely as much light as he has given them; that he allows without rebuke those actions on the moral character of which that light has not shined, and, in this sense, he sanctions them; but that this allowance can never be pleaded in behalf of those who enjoy a more perfect revelation, that is, on whom a better light has shined.

But suppose we take the strongest meaning of the word *sanction*,—*that* of *approve* or *command*—the proposition will not be, I think, more tenable, as I have before said. God commanded the Hebrews to destroy the Canaanites. He commanded Saul to destroy the Amalekites. But were these commands given to all men and at all times? It is therefore, I think, manifest, that this proposition, on which the argument from reason must rest, is, in every sense of the word *sanction*, without foundation.

I hope, my dear brother, you will excuse this use of formal syllogisms in a familiar letter. It is not done for the sake of formality, or with the design of appearing precise and logical. I have adopted this mode of discussion simply because I have thought that thus I could present the points at issue with greater distinctness than seemed possible in any other. But can the proposition, "whatever was sanctioned to the Hebrews is sanctioned to all men at all times," be proved from revelation? It seems to me that precisely the reverse is the fact. To arrive at the truth in this case it is only necessary to inquire whether there were any acts sanctioned to the Hebrews by Moses which are not sanctioned to all men.

Take for instance the whole Mosaic code of civil law, its severe enactments, its very frequent capital punishments, its cities of refuge, its tenure of real estate. Could any legislator at the present day enact similar laws, and justly plead as a sufficient reason that God had sanctioned, nay enacted, such laws for the Jews? Would this be a sufficient reason for abolishing the trial by jury in a case of accidental homicide, (as for instance when the head of an axe slipped from the helve and wounded a man to death,) and enacting that the next akin might slay an innocent person if he overtook him before he arrived at a city of refuge? I think every one must immediately perceive that this law was a humane limitation to the spirit of Oriental vindictiveness, but that it would be very wrong to put it in practice at the present day.

But we are not left to our own reasonings on this subject. We know full well that polygamy and divorce are wrong, that they violate the obligations established by God between the sexes, and are transgressions of his positive law. On this subject I presume we can have no difference of opinion. Yet these sins were not forbidden by Moses. Nay more, laws were enacted by the Hebrew legislator in respect to both of these practices. When a man was already united to one wife, and chose to take another, the manner in which the first wife was to be put away was prescribed. The right of the first-born was also in such a case defined. When, again, a Hebrew wished to divorce a wife, the manner in which this should be done was a matter of positive enactment. The discussion of our Saviour with the Jews on this subject is given us in Matthew 19:3–9. I will quote the whole passage.

"The Pharisees also came unto him, tempting him, and saying unto him, Is it lawful for a man to put away his wife for every cause? And he answered and said unto them, Have ye not read that at the beginning, when the Creator made man, he formed a male and a female, and said, For this cause a man shall leave father and mother and adhere to his wife, and they two shall be one flesh. Wherefore they are no longer two, but one flesh. What therefore God hath conjoined, let not man separate. They replied, Why then did Moses command to give her a writing of divorcement and dismiss her? He answered, Moses indeed, because of your *untractable disposition, permitted* you to divorce your wives, but it was not so from the beginning. Therefore I say unto you, whosoever divorceth his wife except for whoredom, and marrieth another, committeth adultery."

You perceive I have used the translation of Dr. Campbell,[20] who seems to have understood the scope of the argument better than the authors of our version.

Now concerning this decision of our Lord, several things are to be remarked:

1. Our Lord authoritatively lays down the law of marriage, defining it to be an exclusive engagement between two parties for life.

2. He not only does this, but he declares that this doctrine was taught from the creation, quoting Genesis 2:24, in confirmation of his assertion.

3. Notwithstanding this, Moses had sanctioned divorce; that is, he had not forbidden it, and had enacted laws for the regulation of it.

4, And moreover, the reason of this is given; it was because of the hardness of their hearts, or their untractable disposition.

Here then is an institution sanctioned; that permitted and made a subject of legislation, which is wrong in itself, and therefore forbidden by our Saviour to them and to all men. Nay, it had been thus sanctioned, although a prior revelation had discountenanced it. It is therefore clear, that a practice may have been sanctioned to the Hebrews, which is not sanctioned to all men at all times; nay, which before and after a particular period was not sanctioned even to the Hebrews themselves. I think, therefore, that the teaching of the Scriptures is diametrically at variance with the proposition on which the whole argument from the Old Testament is founded.

I will, in passing, add a single remark respecting the manner in which the inspired legislator of the Hebrews has dealt with this subject. Polygamy and divorce at this time were universally practised among the Jews, and indeed among all other Oriental nations. Moses did not at

---

[20George Campbell was a British clergyman who published a translation of the gospels in 1789.]

once directly forbid these wrongs. He only permitted them and modified some of their worst features. He, however, did not leave the subject here. He inculcated such principles as would, by appealing to their reason and conscience, gradually abolish these abuses. And the result took place as he had intended. Hence we observe that the prophets rebuked their countrymen for the practice of these very wrongs,—wrongs *permitted*, or (in the manner which we have explained) *sanctioned* by Moses, and they denounced the wrath of God in consequence of them. A most touching expostulation on this subject is found in Malachi 2:13–16.

"And this have ye done again, covering the altar of the Lord with tears, with weeping, and with crying out, insomuch that he regardeth not the offering any more, or receiveth it with good-will at your hand. Yet ye say, Wherefore? Because the Lord hath been witness between thee and the wife of thy youth, against whom thou hast dealt treacherously: yet is she thy companion, and the wife of thy covenant. And did not he make one? Yet had he the residue of the Spirit. And wherefore one? That he might seek a godly seed. Therefore take heed to your spirit, and let none deal treacherously against the wife of his youth. For the Lord, the God of Israel, saith, that *he hateth putting away*: for one covereth violence with his garment, saith the Lord of hosts: therefore take heed to your spirit, that ye deal not treacherously."

It was in consequence of these very fundamental truths inculcated by Moses, truths diametrically opposed to polygamy and divorce, that these evils had to a great degree ceased, as you have remarked, at the time of the coming of Christ.

But to return. Suppose this proposition, that whatever was sanctioned to the Hebrews is sanctioned to all men at all times, be granted, I do not see in what manner it could justify slavery in the United States. It is, I presume, conceded, that a permission of this kind is to be understood according to the utmost strictness of application. If slavery be justified by the law of Moses, it is, of course, only justified *in the manner* and *with the restrictions* under which it was placed by that law. Let us look at some of the provisions respecting it, which Moses established.

1. A distinction was made between their brethren and the Canaanites. The former could be held in slavery only for six years, but strangers might be held for life.

2. The slaves of the stranger were circumcised and admitted to the ordinary privileges of the Hebrew church and commonwealth.

3. If a master in any manner maimed such a servant, even to the breaking of a tooth, he was obliged to manumit him.

4. The Hebrews were not only positively forbidden to deliver up a slave who had escaped from his master, but were commanded to allow him to dwell in the place which he chose, in any of the gates where it hiked him best [Deuteronomy 23:15–16]. It is not necessary that I attempt to contrast these laws with the laws of the Southern States, respecting slavery. Every one must, I think, perceive the unreasonableness of pleading the Jewish laws as authority for an institution so entirely dissimilar, and so forgetful of the limitations by which that practice was originally guarded. If it be said that the Jewish commonwealth was so peculiar that it is impossible for us to conform ourselves to its laws in this respect, this I think establishes the very point in dispute; namely, that the Jewish law was made exclusively for that people, and can be pleaded in justification by no other people whatever.

And again, this last precept, I think, clearly shows that Moses intended to abolish slavery. How could slavery long continue in a country where every one was forbidden to deliver up a fugitive slave? How different would be the condition of slaves, and how soon would slavery itself cease, were this the law of compulsory bondage among us!

I have already been so long detained upon the first proposition of the argument derived from the Old Testament, that I have room for but few words to devote to the second. The remarks above will, however, render extended discussion unnecessary. The second proposition is as follows: "God sanctioned slavery among the Hebrews."

If by the word *sanctioned* it is meant that God in any manner testified his *approbation* of slavery, I am obliged to say, that the evidence of such sanction nowhere exists, to my knowledge, in the Old Testament. Precisely as in the case of divorce the institution was permitted and regulated; absolutely nothing more. In the mean time principles were inculcated, and laws were enacted, which must naturally, in the end, undermine and overthrow it. Slavery, so far as I can perceive, is no more sanctioned in the Old Testament than polygamy and divorce, and these institutions were, in precisely the same manner as slavery, tolerated and regulated, while they were, both before and afterwards, declared to be totally at variance with the whole will of God. From the fact of toleration and regulation of these practices, therefore, we can no more infer the approbation of God in the one case than in the other.

The passage from Leviticus 25:44–46, is not, that I can see, at all at variance with the view which I have taken on this subject. "Both thy bond-men, and thy bond-maids, which thou shall have, shall be of the heathen that are round about you; of them shall ye buy bond-men and bondmaids. Moreover, of the children of the strangers that do sojourn among you, of them shall ye buy, and of their families that are with you, which they begat in your land: and they shall be your possession. And ye shall take them as an inheritance for your children after you, to inherit them for a possession; they shall be your bond-men for ever: but over your brethren the children of Israel, ye shall not rule one over another with rigor." If any one will take the trouble to turn to the chapter and read from the beginning, he will perceive that its general intention is to inculcate the duty of kindness to their Jewish brethren as distinguished from the heathen. The verses above quoted are a particular exemplification of a general law. They really say no more than that the Hebrews might hold slaves for life of the Canaanites, but not of the Hebrews. I know that the word "shalt" is used when speaking of this subject, but it is clearly used as prophetic and not as mandatory; it tells what *would* or what *might* be, and not what *should* or *must* be. No one can for a moment confound this use of it with that in the ten commandments; nor can any one suppose it to impose any obligation on the Hebrews to hold slaves, either of their own brethren or of strangers. As this is the strongest passage in the Old Testament in favor of the view which we are examining, I do not know that it is necessary to extend this part of the discussion any farther.

Let us now review the ground which we have passed over. I have supposed that the argument by which slavery is justified from the Old Testament is properly expressed by the following syllogism.

1. Whatever God sanctioned among the Hebrews he sanctioned for all men and at all times.
2. God sanctioned slavery among the Hebrews.
Therefore,
3. God sanctioned slavery among all men and at all times.

I suppose myself to have shown that the first of these propositions is at variance with reason and the Scriptures, whether the word *sanction* mean *tolerate* or *enact*; that the second proposition is untrue, if the word sanction mean any thing more than tolerate; and as with this meaning it can at the present day afford no justification of slavery, therefore the conclusion that God in the Old Testament sanctions slavery to all men, that is, to us, is without foundation.

I merely use this technical formality, as I have said before, because I wish to expose my views in the clearest light, so that if I err, I may the more easily be corrected. There is no one, my dear brother, who is more capable of detecting my error, if it exist, than yourself; and there is no man living before whom I would more willingly stand corrected.

I am, my dear brother, yours with every sentiment of Christian affection,

The Author of the Moral Science.

*Letter V[21]*

*To the Rev. Richard Fuller, D.D.*

My Dear Brother,

In my last letter I attempted an examination of the argument derived from the Old Testament in favor of slavery. It becomes me next to consider the manner in which this institution is treated in the New Testament. Before, however, I do this, it will be proper to offer a few suggestions on the subject of *expediency*. This topic, as I am aware, is introduced only incidentally into the discussion. Nevertheless, as it is liable to embarrass our judgments, in the further prosecution of this inquiry, I propose briefly to consider it in this place.

It gives me great pleasure to declare that I cheerfully and heartily coincide with you in the spirit and intention of your remarks on this subject. I admire the indignation with which you repel the suspicion that the Saviour or his apostles would, for the sake of escaping persecution, shun to declare the whole counsel of God. I sympathize in the scorn with which you contemplate that craven spirit, which, while it "speaks great swelling words," yet has "men's persons in admiration because of advantage." I know of nothing more utterly contemptible. Disgraceful, however, as it is everywhere, it is specially so in the Christian church, and more than all in the Christian ministry. We have all seen the evils of this sort of expediency. It has too frequently brought the ministry of the gospel into contempt in the eyes of all honorable and high-minded men. Holding these views, I should be thoroughly ashamed if any thing that I have ever said or written, has justly led any one to suppose that I consider our Lord or his apostles capable of so unmanly a wickedness. I am, therefore, gratified with your allusion to the subject, as it will enable me to explain my views more explicitly. I hope that I may be able so to illustrate them, that on this point at least there may be no difference of opinion between us.

---

[21*Christian Reflector* 12/50 (12 December 1844): 198.]

The word *"expedient"* means, "fitness or suitableness to effect some end, or purpose intended." In this sense it is morally neutral, being in itself neither good nor bad, but deriving its moral quality from some circumstance extraneous to itself. I have said that it is morally neutral. This, however, expresses not the whole truth. Expediency, that is, the use of means suitable or fitted to accomplish an end, is the simple and universal dictate of intelligence. A man would scarcely be deemed of sound mind unless he obeyed the dictates of such an expediency. Nay, if he failed to avail himself of such means, he might be morally delinquent. For instance, if a man were charged with the accomplishment of some good design, and neglected to use the means suited to effect it, or still more if he used means of a directly opposite tendency, we should all declare him culpable. His conduct would show that his interest in the good work was not sufficient to prompt him to the use of the proper means to insure his success.

We see then, clearly, that simple expediency, that is, the use of the means suitable to accomplish an end, is in itself innocent, that it may be commendable, and that the want of it may justly expose us to censure. On the other hand, it is equally evident that expediency may be mean, contemptible, cowardly, and wicked. In what manner, then, may these two cases be distinguished from each other.

The end which we desire to accomplish may be either bad or good. As, however, no means which we use to accomplish a bad end can be innocent, we may at once dismiss this class of cases from our consideration. The question then will be reduced to the following: "Under what circumstances is expediency in the accomplishment of a good end wicked, and under what circumstances is it innocent?"

We have seen that expediency, in itself, is not only innocent, but that it may be even commendable. When it is wicked, the wickedness must arise, therefore, from some cause aside from the fact that the act seems to be expedient. In other words, then, expediency is wicked either when the act which we deem expedient is in itself wicked; or when the act itself is performed from a wicked motive. When neither of these is the case, when the act violates no moral law, either in act or in motive, it is as innocent an act as any other. And moreover, we see that these two qualities of the act are entirely distinct from each other. Let an act seem ever so expedient, this does not affect its moral character. If it be wicked, it is just as wicked as if it did not seem expedient; if it be virtuous, it is just as virtuous whether it seen to be expedient or otherwise.

Let us now illustrate this distinction by a reference to some of the cases in which expediency clearly partakes of one or the other of these characters.

I may for instance desire to promulgate the knowledge of the gospel among the heathen; and, in order to convince them of its truth, may make use of pious frauds, and work before them false miracles. I may suppose that by so doing I shall convert men's souls. But I have done wickedly. I have lied; and more than this, I have lied in the name of the Most High God. Again, suppose I wish to increase the interest of the public at home in the cause of missions, or any other scheme of benevolence, and I utter exaggerated statements, I tell stories which I know to be false, or which I have no reason to believe to be true, and do this for the sake of "*advancing the cause*;" this also is wicked. It is a sheer lie just as much when uttered to support a good cause, as a bad one. The cause makes it no better, and my hypocrisy makes it worse.

Again, suppose that I understand the Scriptures to reveal a particular system of truth to the human race, and I profess to be moved by the Holy Ghost to enforce this truth upon my fellow-men. I however think that I can make it more acceptable *to them* by totally withholding a part of it, or by adding to it, or by modifying the whole or any part of it. In so doing I am guilty of a great wickedness. God has authorized me to preach the preaching that he bids me, and no other; to preach the truth, the whole truth, and nothing but the truth. I am guilty of telling a lie in his name, of usurping the prerogative of the Most High, and for the consequences of my sin I am responsible in his sight.

Or again, suppose that I understand the revelation which he has given, but I fear that to deliver it just as he has revealed it, will expose me to, persecution, or will endanger my property, my influence, my reputation, or my life; and I, from fear of consequences *to myself*, abridge, or alter, or modify the message which God has given me: in this case again I do wickedly. I violate the commandment of my Maker, and I prefer my temporal happiness to the will of God, and the eternal salvation of the souls of my fellow-men. I deny Christ before men, and he will deny me before the angels of God.

Or again, suppose that while I myself hold firmly to the doctrines of the gospel, I, from the fear of popular clamor, adopt means for advancing what I believe to be truth, of which my conscience and reason disapprove. In this case also I do wickedly. I obey men rather than God. I ruin men's souls rather than incur their displeasure. I do, as if by the command of God, what I do not believe that he has commanded, and do this because my fellow-men desire it. I am guilty, and to God I must answer it.

In these instances, and in all such as these, it is in vain to plead that I desire to do good, that I wish to advance the cause of truth, or that I wish to preserve my influence for the sake of using it on some other occasion. God does not choose to be served by abandoning *his* service, and serving *man* in his place. He has not commanded us to serve him by doing wickedness. Our influence is not more valuable than truth and righteousness. When we can only preserve it by doing wrong, it is clear that God does not intend us to hold it any longer; and we cannot hold it longer, except on the peril of our souls.

Again, expediency may become wicked, not only by doing an act in itself wrong, but by doing an act in itself innocent from an impure motive. We have a striking illustration of this in the case of the apostles Peter and Paul. In the commencement of the gospel dispensation, when Judaism was fading, but had not yet entirely vanished away, there was a considerable mingling of the Jewish rites with Christianity. Many of the sincere believers in Jesus, from the force of old association, adhered to the rites of Judaism; looking upon them as by no means obligatory, but yet pleasant and perhaps profitable. And yet more, as the Jews would much more readily hear the truth from one who respected their law than from a Gentile, a concession to their prejudices, for their own good, was in many cases innocent. The innocency, however, depended wholly on the motive. Peter, *from the fear of man*, was led into sin. He conformed to the Mosaic ritual, to avoid the offence of the cross; and so acted as to lead men to believe that he considered its rites and ceremonies as of yet binding obligation. For this cause Paul "rebuked him to the face, in the presence of them all, because he was to be blamed [Galatians 2:11]." Yet Paul himself circumcised Timothy, kept the feast of Pentecost, and in many other cases yielded obedience to the law. What then was the difference in the moral character of these actions? Simply this; Paul yielded this obedience for *the good of others*, everywhere, and at all times, stating the grounds on which he acted, and in the face of all opposition, and in despite of the bitterest persecution, contending, that Christ having fulfilled the law, it was no longer of binding efficacy upon the Jews, or upon any other men. Peter, on the contrary for *the sake of avoiding persecution*, kept the law, and urged the Gentiles to keep it, as though it were still an ordinance of God, and as if our salvation depended on the keeping of it. No man ever understood this distinction better than the apostle Paul, and no man ever acted upon it with more promptness or precision. He circumcised Timothy, in order to render him more acceptable as a preacher of the gospel to the Jews. But, when the performance of this rite upon Titus was pressed upon the apostle as a matter of *moral obligation*, he utterly refused to perform it, and that because of false brethren, who desired to bring the disciples into bondage; "to whom," says he indignantly, "we gave place by subjection, no not for an hour, that the truth of the gospel might continue with you [Galatians 2:5]."

Such are some of the cases in which the acting from expediency involves moral guilt, and frequently guilt of no ordinary turpitude. Let us now examine some of the cases in which expediency may be employed innocently. I suppose they may all be comprehended under the following rule. We may innocently employ any means for the accomplishing of our purposes, which are innocent in themselves, and which we employ with a virtuous intention.

Let us examine a few cases which come under this rule.

Suppose that I am communicating to another a system of truth or of duty, and think that he will be most likely to be influenced by my teaching, if I unfold my views gradually, allowing one portion to work its part of the change which I hope to effect, before I introduce another. In this is there the violation of any moral law? Am I obliged to present the truth in such a manner as will be most likely to ensure its entire rejection? Am I not bound, in such a case, to consult the dictates of my own reason, and the best good of him whom it is my duty to benefit? The Bible is filled with cases of just such expediency as this. The gradual development of the truths of revelation under the several dispensations, illustrate it on the widest possible scale, and show that the Deity frequently allows ages to intervene between the discovery of one truth and the discovery of the next which is intimately associated with it. Our Saviour disclosed his doctrines to his disciples, as their minds by becoming expanded were able to receive them. Even at the close of his ministry he affirmed, "I have yet many things to say unto you, but *ye cannot bear them now*." John 16:12. To precisely the same effect is the saying of the apostle Paul to the Corinthians, 1 Corinthians 3:1–2: "And I, brethren, could not speak to you as unto spiritual but as unto carnal, even as unto babes in Christ. I have fed you with *milk* and not with *meat*; for hitherto, *ye were not able to bear it*, nor *now are ye able*." Here the apostle distinctly recognises the principle that he delivered divine truth to the Corinthians, not in its totality, but in such portions, and in such manner, as the weakened understandings and benighted consciences of his hearers would enable them to receive it. This, then, is, undoubtedly, a proper and innocent use of expediency.

But again, there may be a choice not only in respect to the succession of the several parts, but also in respect to the manner in which the whole or any part of the truth shall be presented. Thus, for instance, suppose that in the discussion of the subject of slavery there were no wrong in applying opprobrious epithets to fellow-citizens, and to Christian brethren; inasmuch as the use of these epithets would disincline men to receive what we believe to be the truth, would not both wisdom as well as Christian charity suggest the expediency of laying them aside?

Again, it is frequently the case that we wish to inculcate a duty upon another, to which he is particularly adverse, and of which the obligation depends upon principles with which he is not familiar. In such a case, while he will not hearken for a moment to the *precept*, he may be willing attentively to consider the *principles* on which it is founded. Here I see no reason why I may not inculcate the *principle*, and leave it to work out its result, instead of directly inculcating the *precept*. For instance, I find a man violently enraged, and burning with vindictiveness towards another who has injured him. It is his duty to forgive the offender. But the suggestion of this duty might only enrage him the more. May I not, then, instead of inculcating the duty directly, unfold to him our relations to God, how much we have sinned against him, how much we all need his forgiveness, and how much and how often we have all offended our brethren and needed their forgiveness? I well know, that if these sentiments once gain possession of his mind, his wrath will be quelled, and he will not dare to ask forgiveness of God until he has exercised forgiveness to his brother. This is almost precisely what our Lord himself has done, when he taught charity to the Pharisee with whom he was dining, Luke 7:39–49. So when he was called upon to interfere in the case of the brother who was defrauded of his inheritance, Luke 12:13–20. Thus also he inculcates the duty of forgiveness, Matthew 28:23–35. Here he gives a very general precept, but explains the principle at length. A beautiful instance of this kind of expediency is also seen in 2 Corinthians 8. St. Paul is desirous of inculcating upon the Corinthians the duty of liberality. He does not, however, as he had a right to do, make use of his apostolical authority; he does not demand this or that portion of their income; but he merely tells them what other churches had done, and adds, "Ye know the grace of our Lord Jesus Christ, who, though he was rich, yet for your sakes became poor, that ye through his poverty might become rich [2 Corinthians 8:9]." Indeed, if we were disposed to generalize this idea, we might easily show that the gospel of Christ is rather a system of principles than of precepts. It is a treasure-house of elementary and all-controlling moral truth. This truth it presents to the understanding, and presses upon the conscience, leaving it to every individual to carry it into practice according to the peculiarities of his individual situation, provided only he do it *honestly*, *earnestly*, with pure love to God and ardent charity to man.

This form of expediency—the inculcating of a fundamental truth, rather than of the duty which springs immediately out of it, seems to me *innocent*. I go further: in some cases it may be really *demanded*. Thus, suppose a particular wrong to have become a social evil, to have become interwoven with the whole framework of society, and to be established by positive enactment and immemorial usage; suppose that all departments of society have become adjusted to it, and that much instruction is necessary before any party can avail itself of the advantages of a righteous change; suppose also the whole community to be ignorant of the moral principles by which both the wrong is condemned and the right established. In such a case, the wrong could only be abolished by changing the sentiments and enlightening the consciences of the whole community. Here it seems to me that it would be not only allowable, but a matter of imperative duty, to inculcate the principles on which the duty rested, rather than the duty itself. The one being fixed in the mind, would necessarily produce the other; and thus the end would be in the most certain manner accomplished.

It is in this manner that the New Testament has generally dealt with the various forms of social evil. Take for instance civil government. At the time of Christ and his apostles, the only form of government known in the civilized world, was a most abominable and oppressive tyranny. Yet the New Testament utters no precepts in regard to forms of government, or the special duties of rulers. It goes further. It commands men everywhere to obey the powers that be, so far as this could be done with a good conscience towards God. But it at the same time inculcates those truths concerning the character, rights, responsibilities, and obligations of man, which have been ever since working out the freedom of the human race; and which have received, as I believe, their fullest development in the principles of the American Declaration of

Independence. Indeed, in no other manner could the New Testament have become a system of religion for the whole human race, adapted to meet the varying aspects of human depravity. If it had merely taught precepts, whatever was not forbidden must have been taken as permitted. Hence, unchecked wickedness would soon have abounded, and the revelation of God must have become a nullity. But by teaching principles of universal application, it is prepared to meet every rising form of moral deviation, and its authority is now as all-pervading as at the moment when it was first delivered. Our Saviour, as it appears to me, carries out this principle to the utmost, when, setting aside as it were all other precepts, he declares that our whole duty is summed up in these two commandments, "Thou shalt love the Lord thy God with all thy heart, and thy neighbor as thyself; for this is the law and the prophets [Matthew 22:39]." That is, I suppose him to mean that cherishing these principles in our hearts and carrying them out into all our actions, we shall do the whole will of God without any other precept.

I have thus, my dear brother, endeavored, in as distinct a manner as I am able, to develop my views on the subject of expediency. I have done it with great diffidence, because I know it is one from a misconception of which great misunderstanding is likely to arise. It seemed, however, to be required by the nature of our discussion; and I hope that what I have suggested may throw some little light upon the subject. I know of but few points in casuistry which at the present moment require a more thorough examination. It is from a misconception here that Jesuitism has arisen on the one hand, and fanaticism on the other. The Jesuit, whether Protestant or Catholic, believes himself at liberty to use any devices whatever, to accomplish a good design; or, in other words, he declares that the end sanctifies the means. The fanatic, provided his end be good, considers himself at liberty to deride the dictates of reason, and use the means which have the least possible tendency to accomplish the end which he has in view. He declares that he has no regard for *consequences.* He seems, however, to forget that the end which he has in view is *a consequence,* and that it must be a consequent, that is, an *effect* of certain *causes*, which, in the providence of God, are ordained to produce it. If, therefore, he has no regard to consequences, and sets in action causes without regard their effects, he is as likely to produce any other end as that which he intends. I think, besides, it may sometimes be observed that while men are so entirely reckless of the consequences of their conduct upon the *cause* which they espouse, they are not at all unmindful of the consequences to *themselves*, and not unfrequently pursue the same courses which shrewd, selfish, and intriguing men adopt, to advance, by means of a cause, their own personal interests.

But I am wandering from the subject immediately before us, and will therefore close by assuring you that I am, with the greatest personal esteem and Christian affection, yours very truly,

The Author of the Moral Science.


*Letter VI*[22]

*To the Rev. Richard Fuller, D.D.*

My Dear Brother,

You will at least give me credit for being an indefatigable correspondent. I hope, however, that you are not wearied either with the number, or the length, of my replies. Although I have commenced my sixth letter, I believe that I have alluded to no topic on which both you and our brethren at the South have not placed reliance, in the construction of their argument in favor of slavery. I rejoice that my labor is drawing to a close. But one more subject remains to be considered; it is the argument derived from the New Testament. With this I shall close my remarks, after having asked your attention to some incidental reflections which could not so well have been interwoven with the main body of the discussion.

In my letter on the Old Testament argument in favor of slavery, I suppose myself to have shown, that the Mosaic law contains nothing more than the permission of slavery; that this permission was granted

---

[22*Christian Reflector* 12/51 (19 December 1944): 202.]

specially and exclusively to the Jews and that we could not assume it as a law for ourselves, without claiming every other permission that was granted to them, and subjecting ourselves to every precept that was enacted for them. I cannot but believe that you, as a preacher of the New Testament, will agree with me in this view of the subject. I am confident that you would hardly reason with a man who should endeavor to enforce any other Mosaic usage, or plead any other Mosaic license, on the same grounds that are used to sustain the institution of American slavery. Indeed, I can hardly suppose that any of our Southern brethren place any great reliance on this part of the argument. I feel assured that they will not, if they reflect on the consequences which it necessarily involves.

I think, then, that the Scriptural argument in defence of slavery is narrowed down to the limits of the New Testament. Let us, then, endeavor carefully to inquire whether this institution is supported by the instructions of the Saviour and his apostles. You say that "slavery was at least tolerated by Christ and his apostles," and hence you argue that it is no wrong; and, therefore, I presume, consider that this toleration is universal; and, if so, that slavery is right and proper everywhere, or, as you well remark, *simper et ubtque*. You do not, I know, thus generalize the doctrine; but I do not see how such generalization is to be avoided. The New Testament was not given, like the Mosaic law, to one people, but to the whole race; not for one period, but for all time. If, therefore, it tolerates slavery really and truly—if this is the doctrine of our Saviour, it justifies this institution to all men; and Pagans, Christians, and Mohammedans who have united in abolishing it, have greatly erred in supposing it to be at variance with the clearest principles either of natural justice or of Christian duty.

It is then important to us as disciples of Christ, to ascertain in how far the New Testament really upholds what the natural conscience of man, from at least as far back as the time of Aristotle, has declared to be a violation of the plainest dictates of natural justice. I will not detain you by inquiring into the meaning of the word *tolerate*. It may perhaps convey a stronger sense than the facts will warrant. I will at once come to the passages in the New Testament in which this subject is mentioned. By calmly considering these, we may, I think, ascertain what foundation is furnished for the superstructure which has so frequently been erected upon them.

1. Slaves are frequently alluded to by our Saviour in the Gospels. Several parables are founded upon this relation. But as the object of these parables is to enforce some duty which had no respect to slavery, no one will for a moment pretend that this sort of allusion has any bearing upon the question. Our Lord illustrates the wisdom of men in temporal, contrasted with their folly in spiritual concerns, by the parable of the steward who had wasted his lord's goods. But this is never pleaded in justification of dishonesty in a confidential agent. The same principle applies equally to one case as to the other.

2. In the Epistles the relation between masters and slaves is several times averted to. I will quote, so far as I remember, all the passages which are considered to be of importance in the settlement of this question.

1. Of the duties of slaves.

Ephesians 6:5–8: "Servants, be obedient to them that are your masters according to the flesh, with fear and trembling, in singleness of your heart, *as unto Christ*. Not with eye-service, as men-pleasers; but *as the servants of Christ*, doing the will of God from the heart; with good will doing service, *as to the Lord*, and not to men; knowing that whatsoever good thing any man doeth, the same shall he receive of the Lord, whether he be bond or free."

Colossians 3:22–25: "Servants, obey in all things your masters according to the flesh; not with eye-service, as men-pleasers; but in singleness of heart, fearing God: and whatsoever ye do, do it heartily, *as to the Lord*, and not unto men; knowing that of the Lord ye shall receive the reward of the inheritance: *for ye serve the Lord Christ*. But he that doeth wrong, shall receive for the wrong which he hath done: and there is no respect of persons."

1 Timothy 6:1–5: "Let as many servants as are under the yoke count their own masters worthy of all honor, *that the name of God and his*

*doctrine be not blasphemed.* And they that have believing masters, let them not despise them, because they are brethren; but rather do them service, because they are faithful and beloved, partakers of the benefit. These things teach and exhort. If any man teach otherwise, and consent not to wholesome words, even the words of our Lord Jesus Christ, and to the doctrine which is according to godliness, he is proud, knowing nothing, but doting about questions and strifes of words, whereof cometh envy, strife, railings, evil surmisings, perverse disputings of men of corrupt minds, and destitute of the truth, supposing that gain is godliness: from such withdraw thyself."

Titus 2:9–10: "Exhort servants to be obedient unto their own masters, and to please them well in all things; not answering again; not purloining, but showing all good fidelity; that they *may adorn the doctrine of God our Saviour in all things.*"

1 Peter 2:18–23: "Servants, be subject to your masters with all fear; not only to the good and gentle, but also to the froward. For this is thankworthy, if a man for conscience toward God endure grief, suffering wrongfully. For what glory is it, if, when ye be buffeted for your faults, ye shall take it patiently? But if, when ye do well, and suffer for it, ye take it patiently, *this is acceptable with God.* For even hereunto were ye called: because Christ also suffered for us, leaving us an example, that ye should follow his steps: who did no sin, neither was guile found in his mouth: who when he was reviled, reviled not again; when he suffered, he threatened not; but committed himself to him that judgeth righteously."

Now I do not see that the scope of these passages can be misunderstood. They teach patience, meekness, fidelity, and charity—duties which are obligatory on Christians towards all men, and of course towards masters. These duties are obligatory on us towards enemies, because an enemy, like every other man, is a moral creature of God. They are demanded of Christians, because by acting otherwise they would bring reproach upon the cause of Christ. And it is to be observed, that the apostles are in every case careful not to utter a syllable by which they concede the right of the master, but they always add as a reason for these precepts, the relation in which the slave stands to

Christ. The fact seems to be simply this. There are certain vices to which ignorant, and ill-instructed persons, when laboring for others, are specially liable; such, for instance, are disobedience, lying, purloining, eye-service, and the like. These practices are inconsistent with the Christian character, and the apostles forbid them, referring always to the principles of love and piety which the gospel inculcates. These instructions, then, would have been appropriate (as indeed they are everywhere appropriate at this moment, and just as appropriate to free laborers as slaves had there been no such institution as slavery in existence. They were therefore appropriate to slaves, who stood in the relation *of persons doing service.* These precepts seem to me to emanate directly from the principles of Christianity, and hence, in 1 Timothy 6:3–5, the apostle sternly rebukes those that teach any other doctrine. But in this very rebuke he makes no allusion to the right of the master over the slave; and boldly exposes the motives of those who would excite insubordination for the sake of their own personal gain. To present this subject in the clearest light, I ask, do our obligations to practice fidelity, honesty, charity, to avoid purloining, lying, eye-service, depend on the justice of the authority which the master claims, over the slave? If not, the inculcation of these duties in no manner involves a concession of the claim of the master to that authority. Supposing slavery to be wrong, will this wrong justify a Christian in lying, stealing, deception, or even in rebellion against the authority by which he is unjustly held in bondage?

If this be so, the only foundation for the argument in favor of slavery from the New Testament must be found in the precepts which it addresses to *masters.* These are as follows:

Ephesians 6:8: "And ye masters, do the same things unto them, forbearing threatening, knowing that your Master also is in heaven; neither is there respect of persons with him." This passage immediately follows that above quoted from Ephesians 6:5–8, and merely inculcates reciprocity of duties between master and servant.

Colossians 4:1: "Masters, render to your servants that which is just and equal; knowing that ye also have a Master in heaven."

These precepts simply inculcate on masters the duty of treating the slave as he himself would wish to be treated; and of allowing to him suitable means of subsistence. And this is all.

Let us now see the use that is made of these two passages. They are supposed to sanction the whole system of domestic slavery; and to grant a universal permission to establish and maintain it everywhere and at all times; for, as I have said, if it be a permission of *the New Testament*, it is of course without limitation. Let us see what this permission involves. It is the right to compel another man, a fellow-creature of God, in every respect made like to myself, in his social, intellectual, and moral nature, and held at the bar of God to precisely the same responsibility as myself, to labor for me without his contract and consent. This right also, as I have shown, involves the right to use all the means necessary to its establishment and perpetuity; and of course the right to crush his intellectual and social nature, and to stupify his conscience, in so far as may be necessary to enable me to enjoy this right with the least possible peril. Nay, more, I do not see that it does not sanction the whole system of the slave-trade. If I have a right to a thing after I have gotten it, I have a natural right to the means necessary for getting it. If this be so, I should be as much justified in sending a vessel to Africa, murdering a part of the inhabitants of a village, and making slaves of the rest, as I should be in hunting a herd of wild animals, and either slaying them or subjecting them to the yoke. If I err in making these inferences, I err innocently; for they seem to me to be of necessity involved in the principles which would be established by the argument in question.

Now I ask, was there ever such a moral superstructure raised from such a foundation? The doctrine of purgatory, from a verse in Maccabees, the doctrine of the papacy, from the saying of Christ to Peter, the establishment of the inquisition, from the obligation to extend the knowledge of religious truth, all of these seem to me as nothing to it. I say it with entire kindness, for on such a subject I am incapable of any other feeling, if the religion of Christ allows us to take such a license from such precepts as these, the New Testament would be the greatest curse that ever was inflicted on our race.

I need not say, my dear brother, that I know you would abhor such an inference as much as any man on earth. I know well your kindness of heart, and what is still better, your entire will, fully to subject yourself to the whole doctrine of Christ. But, I ask, do not the principles which our Southern brethren adopt, lead to precisely these results? Let us test the case by an example. Suppose that a foreign foe should land an over whelming force on your shores, for the sake of reducing the State of South Carolina to bondage; would not the language of every man, because he is a man, be, "Give me liberty or give me death!" And do you suppose that the apostolic precept respecting masters and slaves was intended to stifle this first and strongest aspiration of a human soul? Suppose that such an enemy should establish this authority, and reduce you to servitude, it would be your duty as men, and especially as Christians, to be kind, charitable, and forbearing; to avoid lying, purloining, and deceit. But would it not be, a most cruel mockery to plead the apostolic precepts on this subject in justification of the tyranny and oppression under which you were crushed? Now, strong as this case may seem, I think it is put fairly. For we are always to remember that a New Testament rule is a universal rule. It was not made for the Northern or the Southern States, for white men or for black men, but for all men. And hence the precept which would justify slavery in one case, would justify it equally in all similar cases.

But it may be said, that although these precepts, taken *by themselves*, will not authorize slavery, yet that it is really authorized by the inference which may be drawn from *a consideration of the circumstances* under which the precepts were delivered. At the time of our Saviour and his apostles, slavery was universal, and was of a very oppressive character. These precepts were given for the sake of correcting its abuses. But inasmuch as the abuses were thus corrected, and nothing was said respecting the institution itself, it is inferred that the gospel considers slavery in itself as innocent, and only reproves those incidental wrongs which are by no means essential to it. If this be so, it will, I think, be true, that we are to learn our duty, the universal duty of man respecting slavery, from a consideration of Roman slavery in connection with the precepts of the

New Testament. Roman slavery is the basis on which we are to rest. This, in its principles, was right, and agreeable to the will of God, and became at variance with the gospel only by abuse. The New Testament undertook to correct these abuses, and what is not thus corrected is therefore according to the will of God.

Let us, then inquire what were some of the features of slavery among the Romans at the time of Christ.

1. Slavery[23] was universal throughout the empire, and the number of slaves almost exceeds belief. Some rich individuals possessed 10,000, and others even 20,000 of their fellow-creatures.

In Italy it is computed that there were three slaves to one freeman, and that their number in this part of the empire alone, was, at this time, more than twenty millions.

2. Persons. became slaves by being made *captives in war, by purchase* from slave dealers, by *birth*, and by the *operation of law*; as for instance in consequence of debt or as a punishment for crime. Ceesar is said to have taken 400,000 captives in his Gallic wars alone. The islands of the Mediterranean were almost universally slave markets. In Delos alone, 10,000 slaves were sometimes bought and sold in a single day.

3. On the condition of slaves, it may be remarked that—

1. The master had the power of life and death over the slave.

2. Slaves were not permitted to marry.

3. They were permitted to hold no property as their own; whatever they acquired being the property of their masters.

4. They were exposed to the most unrelenting barbarity, being perfectly unprotected by law, and left entirely in the power of their owners. They were liable to every kind of torture; and cruel masters sometimes kept on their estates tormentors by profession, for the purpose of punishing their slaves. Burning alive was sometimes resorted

---

[23]For these statements respecting slavery among the Romans, I am indebted to an article by the Rev. Prof. B. B. Edwards, of the Theological Seminary, Andover. [See B. B. Edwards, "Roman Slavery in the Early Centuries of the Christian Era," in *The Writings of Prof. B. B. Edwards, with a Memoir*, 2 vols., ed. Edwards Amasa Park (Boston: John P. Jewett and Co., 1853) 2:79–112.]

to, and crucifixion was frequently made the fate of a slave for trifling misconduct, or from mere caprice. In fine, a slave was considered in no other light than as a representative of so much value. Hence it is not wonderful that they should be slain in order to make food for fishes, or, that the question should arise, whether, in a storm, a man should sacrifice a valuable horse or a less valuable slave.

I need not pursue this subject more at large. It is too revolting to humanity. I only present a few of the more prominent points for consideration. Enough, however, has been adduced to answer the purpose of the argument.

If, then, the view which we are considering be correct, the New Testament, with all these facts in sight, did really justify Roman slavery in the main; and set itself to correct its abuses. This correction is contained in the few lines which I have quoted above. All the rest is, therefore, permitted to us and to all men, on the sanction of inspiration. The selling of prisoners of war, the slave-trade itself, (for, as I have said, the Mediterranean then was full of slavers,) the power of life and death over the slave, the prohibition of marriage, and the infliction of death at the master's will, all these are sanctioned by the word of God himself. The master has only to forbear threatening, to give his slave suitable physical comforts, as the reward for his toil, and the master's right, and the authority to exercise this right, remains as it was under the Roman empire, in the time of Christ. If this be so, there is no reason why Christians at the South should be grieved with the severity of the laws respecting slaves. These are as yet very far within the power confided to the master by the New Testament itself. The gospel of Christ, on the subject of human rights, falls infinitely below the Declaration of American Independence.

It is said, however, that the gospel allows of slavery, but forbids the abuse of it. The distinction between the proper use and the abuse of it, however, most evidently is not to be found in the precepts which we have quoted. Where then is it to be found? Where shall we find the direction in the Scriptures by which we shall be guided? Let us take a few instances. Under what circumstances may a man be made a slave? By war, by purchase, by birth, or by all of them? If unlawfully enslaved at first, how is the right over him afterwards to be lawfully acquired? Has he a right to marry; and is the relation of marriage protected by the rules of Christ on this subject? The Roman law allowed slaves to read, and many of them were learned men; can this permission be abrogated? Can a slave be rightfully forbidden to read the sacred Scriptures? I will not, however, multiply such questions. If it be said that the New Testament intends to discriminate between the use and the abuse of slavery, it must certainly present us with precepts bearing on these questions, for they are all eminently practical, and they are of daily occurrence. But where in the New Testament shall we find any precept by which such questions can be decided? Who would ever think of going to the New Testament for such a decision? Where have we ever known the New Testament to be called upon to decide the question, what constitutes the proper use, and what the abuse of the institution of slavery? Would it not be utterly impossible to find the elements for such a decision in any part of the word of God?

If this be so, I think it must be evident that the precepts of the New Testament furnish no justification of slavery, whether they be considered either absolutely, or in relation to the usage of the Roman empire at the time of Christ. All that can justly be said seems to me to be this, the New Testament contains no *precept* prohibitory of slavery. This must, I think, be granted; but this is all.

But if the New Testament has left no precept justifying, and no prohibition forbidding slavery, are we to conclude that it is wholly indifferent on the subject? I answer, by no means. It has, in my opinion, prohibited it in a manner far more emphatic than could have been done by any precept whatever.

The universal existence of slavery at the time of Christ, took its origin from the moral darkness of the age. The immortality of the soul was unknown. Out of the Hebrew nation, not a man on earth had any true conception either of the character of the Deity or of our relations and obligations to Him. The law of universal love to man had never been heard of. Every nation considered every other nation a fit object for plunder. A stranger and an enemy were equivalent terms. It was, moreover, an age of great intellectual refinement, and of unbounded wealth, and hence an age of thorough and universal sensuality. Combine these elements together, and slavery must naturally result from them, and must continue as long as they existed.

In what manner, then, did the Saviour and his apostles deal with this universal sin? I answer, by promulgating such truths concerning the nature and destiny of man, his relations and obligations both to man and to his Maker, as should render the slavery of a human being a manifest moral absurdity; that is, a notion diametrically opposed to our elementary moral suggestions. I have, in my second letter, alluded to those ideas of human nature, which the Scriptures have revealed. Let us observe how strangely they are in contrast with all that was then known of the *character* and *value* of a man.

To men who had scarcely an idea of the character, or even the existence, of a Supreme Intelligence, and whose objects of adoration were images of "gold and silver and stone, graven with art and man's device [Acts 17:29]," and whose worship consisted in the orgies of Venus and Bacchus, the gospel revealed the existence of one only living and true Jehovah, all-wise, all-just, all-holy, everywhere present beholding the evil and the good, knowing the thoughts and intents of the heart, who will bring every secret thing into judgment, whether it be good or whether it be evil, and who has placed us all under one and the same law, that law which declares, "Thou shalt love the Lord thy God with all thy heart, and thy neighbor as thyself [Luke 10:27]."

To men who had scarcely an idea of existence after death, whose notions of futurity were the fables of Charon's boat, the Styx, and Tartarus fables which were already held up as objects of inextinguishable laughter—the gospel revealed the doctrine of man's immortality; it taught that every human being was a never-dying soul; that the world to come was a state either of endless acid inconceivable happiness or of woe; that for this infinitely important state, the present brief existence was the probation and the only probation that God had allotted to us;

and that, during this probation, every one of our race must by his own moral character determine his destiny for himself.

To men who had scarcely formed an idea of their moral relations, the gospel revealed the fact that our race were universally sinners, and were, without exception, under the condemnation of that law which denounces eternal death as the desert of every transgression; that God placed such an estimate upon, a human soul, nay, that he so loved the world that he gave his only-begotten Son, that whosoever believeth on him should not perish, but have everlasting life; and that, in consequence of this atonement, eternal salvation is freely offered to every human being, who, repenting of his rebellion, will return to the love and service of God.

To men steeped in the most debasing and universal sensuality, whose motto was, "Let us eat and drink, for to-morrow we die [1 Corinthians 15:32]," the gospel revealed the truth, that while this salvation was thus freely offered to all, yet still every individual of our race was placed on earth to work out his salvation: with fear and trembling; that he was still, in the strictest possible sense, in a state of probation; and that in a world lying in wickedness, surrounded by every temptation to sin, exposed to all the allurements of vice, and assailed by all the arts of the adversary of souls, he must come off conqueror over every moral enemy, or else he will after all perish under a most aggravated condemnation.

And lastly, to men who esteemed the people of another nation as by nature foes whom they had a right to subdue, murder, or enslave, whenever and in what manner soever they were able, the gospel revealed the fact that all men are, by the act of their creation, *brethren*; that all are equally beloved by the same Father of all; that Christ died equally for all; that all are equally exposed to the same perdition; that to all is equally offered a mansion in the same Father's house, and that the title to that inheritance, the same to all, can be secured in no other way, than by obedience to the universal law of love, a law enforced by the solemn sanction, "Inasmuch as ye did it not *to one of the least of these*, ye did it not *unto me* [Matthew 25:40]."

Such, then, were some of the effulgent truths which the gospel poured upon the moral darkness of the heathen world. Such was the entire revolution (the word, you perceive, is feebleness itself when applied to such a case) which the gospel effected in all the notions which were then entertained respecting the character, the destiny, the responsibilities, and the *inestimable value* of a man. We feel at once that the highest seraph around the throne would not dare to violate the meanest right of the meanest creature who stood in such a relation to God; infinitely less would he dare, for the sake of his own temporary convenience, to interfere with any of the means to which such a creature was entitled, for ascertaining and doing the will of God, and thus escaping eternal death, and laying hold on everlasting life. "Are *they* not all ministering spirits, sent forth to minister to those that are heirs of salvation [Hebrews 1:14]?" What shall we say then, if a creature of yesterday, himself subject to the same law, exposed to the same condemnation, and going to the same judgment-seat, abolishes, at his own pleasure, and on the authority of physical force, the social, intellectual, and moral rights of his brother; and for the sake of pecuniary gain interferes with the most solemn relations which can exist between the God and Father of us all, and his child here on earth—a child redeemed with the precious blood of his only begotten Son.

It is obvious that such principles as these, instilled into the public mind, must of necessity abolish slavery, and every other form of wrong. Just in so far as slavery is, either in its principles or its practice, at variance with these elementary truths of revealed religion, it is forbidden. Whether it be thus at variance, let every man judge.

Suppose, then, that slavery were permitted in the New Testament, and that, at the same time, these truths at variance with it were inculcated, it would be evident that the *permission* must yield to the *principle*. Divorce was *permitted*, but the Hebrews were censured for availing themselves of the permission. You may give your child, if he were approaching to years of discretion, permission to do an act, while you inculcate upon him principles which forbid it, for the sake of teaching him to be governed by principles rather than by any direct enactment. In such a case you would expect him to obey the principle, and not avail himself of the permission. So in the present instance, were the permission proved, we, as moral creatures of God, would be bound by the principles which controlled it.

But if no such permission was ever given, if, on the question of right, the New Testament has never uttered an approving syllable, then we are left entirely to the direction of the principle; and what this principle is I have endeavored to show.

But why was this mode of teaching adopted? This question must be reserved for the next letter.

I am, my dear brother, yours with every sentiment of affection,

The Author of the Moral Science.


*Letter VII*[24]

*To the Rev. Richard Fuller, D.D.*

My Dear Brother,

In my last letter I endeavored to illustrate the manner in which I suppose the New Testament to have prohibited the existence of domestic slavery. It is not by any precept forbidding it, but by the inculcation of such truths respecting the character, the value, and the responsibility of man, and his relation to his fellow-man and to his Maker, as are utterly inconsistent with the institution. The next question which naturally occurs is this, why was this mode of expressing the divine will adopted? This inquiry I propose to consider, in the present letter. I fear that this correspondence is becoming wearisome by its length, and shall, therefore, in the remarks that follow, study the utmost brevity.

You will perceive at once, that I am by no means obliged to reply to this inquiry. If such is proved to have been the method chosen by

---

[24*Christian Reflector* 12/52 (26 December 1844): 206. The *Reflector* erroneously denotes this as Wayland's sixth letter; it is in fact his seventh.]

Omniscient Wisdom, we all concede that it must have been chosen for the best possible reason. The fact is all that we need be anxious to discover. Nevertheless, if we are able to show probable reasons for the course adopted by inspiration, it may anticipate various objections that might otherwise suggest themselves. I remark then in the first place; this mode of teaching is, in all respects, conformable to that universally adopted by the Saviour and his apostles. In the words of Archbishop Whately,

> "It was no part of the scheme of the gospel revelation to lay down any thing approaching to a complete system of *moral precepts*—to enumerate every thing that *is enjoined nor forbidden* by our religion, nor again to give a *detailed* general description of *Christian* duty—or to *delineate*, after the manner of systematic ethical writers, *each separate habit of virtue or vice*. New and higher *motives* were implanted, a more exalted and perfect example was proposed for imitation, a loftier standard of morality was established, rewards more glorious and punishments more appalling were held out, and supernatural aid was bestowed, and the Christian, with these incentives and advantages, is left to apply for himself in each case, the principles of the gospel. He is left to act at his own discretion, according to the dictates of his conscience; to cultivate Christian dispositions, and thus become a law unto himself." [25]

Nay, still farther, care was taken in the revelation of the New Testament, to guard the disciple of Christ against *expecting* a system of precise moral *enactments*. For this reason, the precepts which are given

---

[25] Whately's Essays, vol. 2, p. 263: London, 1833. See this whole subject treated in a masterly manner in the essay on "the mode of conveying moral precepts in the New Testament." Like everything else from the pen of this great and good man, this essay is full of the "seeds of things." [Richard Whately, *Essays on Some of the Difficulties in the Writings of St. Paul and in Other Parts of the New Testament*, 2 vols. (London: B. Fellowes, 1833) 2:263.]

are sometimes contradictory, as when we are commanded to "let our light shine before men [Matthew 5:16]," and also, "not to let our left hand know what our right hand doeth [Matthew 6:3]." Sometimes the literal precept was extravagant and irrational, as when we are commanded "to pluck out a right eye [Matthew 5:29]," or "cut off a right hand [Matthew 5:30]." Sometimes the precept was in itself insignificant, as when we are told "to wash each other's feet [John 13:14]." In all these and similar cases, it is plain that we are taught to disregard the *precept itself*; and looking beyond it, to adopt as the rule of our universal conduct, the *principle* which it is evidently intended to inculcate. If any one has any doubts on the mode of New Testament instruction in this respect, I beg him to read the essay to which I have referred.

I think it must appear obvious to every reflecting mind, that this is the only method in which a universal revelation, which should possess any moral stringency, could have been given, for all coming time. A simple precept, or prohibition, is of all things the easiest to be evaded. Lord Eldon[26] used to say, that "no man in England could construct an act of Parliament through which he could not drive a coach and four." We find this to have been illustrated by the case of the Jews in the time of our Saviour. The Pharisees, who prided themselves on their strict obedience to the *letter*, violated the *spirit* of every precept of the Mosaic code. Besides, suppose the New Testament had been intended to give us a system of precepts, there were but two courses which could have been adopted. The first would have been to forbid merely every wrong practice of *that particular time*, the second to go forward into futurity and forbid every wrong practice *that could ever afterwards arise*. If the first mode had been adopted, every wrong practice that might in after ages arise would have been unprovided for, and of course unforbidden. If the second had been adopted, the New Testament would have formed a library in itself more voluminous than the laws of the realm of Great Britain. Both of these courses would have been manifestly absurd. The only remaining scheme that could be devised is, to present the great

---

[26]John Scott, who served as Lord Chancellor of England from 1801 to 1827.]

principles of moral duty, to reveal the great moral facts on which all duty must rest, the unchangeable relations in which moral creatures stand to each other, and to God, and without any precepts in each particular case, to leave the course of conduct to be determined by the conscience of every individual acting in the presence of the all-seeing Deity. To illustrate the practical difference of these modes of teaching, I ask, is there any danger that either you or I, acting in the spirit of the principle which teaches us, thou shalt love thy neighbor as thyself, would violate any law of the United States? We have lived many years without even knowing what these laws are, and yet have never violated one of them. But yet the precepts which are intended to guard against such a violation are the study of a lifetime; and the number of them is annually increasing, and must increase, in order to render our rights in any manner secure.

Now such being the mode in which it was necessary to make known to men the moral laws of the New Testament, it is plain that to this mode, the instruction in respect to slavery must be subjected. If this form of wrong had been singled out from all the others, and had alone been treated preceptively, the whole system would have been vitiated. We should have been authorized to inquire why were not similar precepts in other cases delivered; and if they were not delivered, we should have been at liberty to conclude that they were intentionally omitted, and that the acts which they would have forbidden are innocent. I cannot but consider this as a sufficient reason why no precept should be given on the subject of slavery, and why, like almost every other, certainly like *every other social* wrong, it should be left to the results of the inculcation of a moral principle.

There seem to me other reasons also why this mode of instruction should be adopted in this particular instance.

1. The reason of the duty to abolish slavery is found in the moral relations and responsibilities of a human being. But these moral relations and responsibilities were at this time wholly unknown. This I have attempted to illustrate in my last letter. It was certainly reasonable to postpone the inculcation of the *duty* until the *truths* were promulgated

on which this duty *was founded.* The fundamental truths of the Declaration of Independence had, during the previous struggles of our colonial history, become fully known and universally acknowledged. On the ground of these, our Fathers declared our connection with the mother country severed. But of what use would have been such a declaration if these principles had never been either promulgated or understood. Every one sees that such an act would have been inoperative and absurd.

2. Again, slavery, at the time of our Saviour and his Apostles, was a social evil. It was established by law. The whole community enforced the law on every individual. The master could only manumit such a portion of his slaves as the law permitted. He could go to no other country and there set them free, for the whole civilized world was under the same dominion. If he set them free contrary to law, they were liable to be reduced again to a worse bondage than that from which he had delivered them. Hence it was manifest that the system could only be abolished by a change in the public mind, by inculcating those principles which would show the whole community that it was wrong, and induce them, from a general conviction of its moral evil, to abandon it.

I can also perceive other practical benefits of great importance which would necessarily attend this method of abolishing slavery. To have inculcated the right of the slave to freedom, and the duty of the master to liberate him, absolutely and immediately, while both were ignorant of the principles on which the precept was founded, and wholly uninfluenced by these principles, must have led to a universal social war. The masters would not have obeyed the precept, the slaves would have risen in rebellion. This attempt had been frequently made before, and had been put down by horrible bloodshed. There is no reason to suppose that the same result would not have taken place again. Myriads of unarmed and ignorant slaves could never have stood the shock of the Roman legions, commanded by able generals and supported by the wealth of the empire. Hence, to have adopted the method of abolishing slavery by precept, would have defeated the great object in view, and rendered the condition of the slave worse than before. Such, in all cases except in insular situations, has been the result of servile insurrections.

The result of the abolition of slavery by the inculcation of the principles of the Gospel would be the reverse of all this. By teaching the master his own accountability, by instilling into his mind the mild and humanizing truths of Christianity; by showing him the folly of sensuality and luxury, and the happiness derived from industry, frugality, and benevolence, it would prepare him of his own accord to liberate his slave, and to use all his influence towards the abolition of those laws by which slavery was sustained. By teaching the slave his value and his responsibility as a man, and subjecting his passions and appetites to the laws of Christianity, and thus raising him to his true rank as an intellectual and moral being, it would prepare him for the freedom to which he was entitled, and render the liberty which it conferred a blessing to him as well as to the State of which he now, for the first time, formed a part.

Such was, in fact, the result of the promulgation of Christianity upon the Roman Empire. As the gospel spread from city to city, and began to exert an influence upon the public mind, the laws respecting slavery were gradually relaxed, and every change in legislation was, in this respect, a change for the better. This tendency continued and increased until, throughout the whole empire, slavery was at last abolished. And, by the admission of all, this abolition was purely the result of the teachings of the gospel. And still more, it was first commenced, and its progress was accelerated by the noble example of the *Christian Church*. To liberate their fellow-men from servitude was, very early in the history of Christianity, deemed to be one of the most urgent duties of the disciples of Christ. Clemens, in his Epistle to the Corinthians, remarks: "We have known many among ourselves who have delivered themselves into bonds and slavery that they might restore others to their liberty. Paulinus, Bishop of Nola, expended his whole estate, and then sold himself, in order to accomplish the same object. Cyprian sent to the Bishop of Numidia 2,500 crowns, in order to redeem some captives. Socrates, the historian, says that after the Romans had taken 7,000 Persian captives, Acacius, Bishop of Amida, melted down the gold and silver plate of his church with which he redeemed the captives. Ambrose, of Milan, did the same in respect to the furniture of his church. It was the only case in which the imperial constitutions allowed plate to be sold." These facts sufficiently illustrate the manner in which the early church interpreted the teaching of the gospel respecting slavery, and also the effect which this teaching had upon their practice.[27]

And thus we see that *the very reason* why this mode of teaching was adopted, was to *accomplish the universal abolition of slavery.* A precept could not have done this, for, in the changing condition of human society, the means would have easily been devised for eluding it. But by teaching truths, the very truths in which Christianity consisted, utterly and absolutely opposed to slavery, truths founded in the essential moral relations of creatures to their Creator, it was rendered certain that wherever Christianity was understood and obeyed, this institution must cease to exist. Thus the principles of the gospel have once abolished slavery from the face of the earth. They have almost done it for the second time. May we not hope that the work will be speedily accomplished, and accomplished forever.

And here I think that the New Testament, having adopted this as the correct and only universal mode of accomplishing this object, is perfectly consistent with itself, in giving no precept to *Christian masters.* The gospel is a universal rule. It prescribes no moral duty for one man, and excuses from that duty another, when both are under the same circumstances. If it prescribed the duty of manumitting their slaves to *Christian* masters, it must have prescribed it to *all masters*; that is, it must have adopted that other mode of teaching, by *precept,* instead of teaching *by principle.* It therefore left the whole matter to the operation of principle, and the manner in which that principle was acted upon by Christians, I have already illustrated. In all this I see nothing but the benevolence and long-mindedness of the Deity. God treats his intelligent creatures according to the nature which he has given them.

[27]Biblical Repository, before cited, October 1835. Art. *Roman Slavery.* [See Edwards, "Roman Slavery."]

He reveals his will. He promulgates truth of universal efficacy, but frequently allows long time to elapse before the effect of it appears, in order that that effect may be the more radical and comprehensive. These seem to me to be sufficient reasons for the mode of teaching which the New Testament has adopted in respect to slavery. On this subject I do not see that there can be any question between us. I have always remarked that our Southern brethren are specially opposed to *immediate* abolition. They consider it absurd, ruinous, inhuman, and destructive to society itself. They also declare that if abolition is ever to be accomplished, it must be accomplished by means of the inculcation of principles which naturally lead to it; and not by force of arms, or by the passage of arbitrary acts. It would, therefore, seem peculiarly unreasonable for them to assert that there is only one method in which the abolition of slavery could, with benevolence to all parties, be accomplished, and then to assert that the gospel could not certainly mean to abolish it, because it had adopted this very method. Before leaving this part of the subject, it may be well to consider very briefly in what manner the principles which we have been discussing, bear upon the question of slavery in our Southern States.

In the first place, if slavery be inconsistent with the principles of the Gospel, it is wrong, and God requires us to abandon it. And besides, God does not require us to abandon it simply because we are Christians, but because we are men, his creatures, and because it is at variance with the moral law under which we are created. If it be asked, when? I ask again, when is it our duty to obey God? Is it not our duty always and everywhere, *semper et ubique*, as soon as we hear his commandments? A reason that would be sufficient for delaying to obey God for a moment, would be a sufficient reason for disobeying him forever. If the physical act to which his commandment tends, be in any respect out of our power, we are to act honestly and in his fear, from the principle of obedience, and remove, as far as possible, every obstacle that exists to perfect obedience to the commandment.

2. What are we to learn from the *manner* which the gospel adopted to accomplish the abolition of slavery? I answer, we are at liberty to use

the same manner, in just so far as our circumstances and those of the early Christians correspond.

The reason for the gradual abolition of slavery under the gospel, was that all parties were ignorant of the principles on which the rights, and duties, and responsibilities of men were founded. The world then knew of nothing better than polytheism, and all the absurdities of heathen mythology. It was necessary that this darkness should be dispelled, before the moral light could shine upon slavery, or upon almost any other wrong. Slavery was then universal, and there existed small opportunity to know its moral evil in the sight of God. The case with us is different. We have from our earliest youth been instructed in the gospel of our salvation. The fundamental principles on which our duty rests, are as familiar to us as household words; we have only to apply them to our particular case, and the will of God in respect to us cannot be mistaken. Nay, we, in our Declaration of Independence, have already acknowledged the very principles now in question. We have seen slavery abolished all around us. There is, therefore, no need for delay for *the purpose of inculcating on us the principles on which our duty rests.*

Again, slavery was then, and it is now, a social evil. It is established and maintained by the power of society, and it can be universally abolished only by legislation. The case was the same in the early ages of Christianity. There is, however, this one remarkable difference. Then, the laws were nothing but the published will of a despot. The subject had no power to make or unmake them. It is by no means the same with us. *We make our own laws.* Every citizen who exercises the right of suffrage, is himself responsible for every law that is made, unless he has put forth his full constitutional power to prevent it. Hence, a grave responsibility rests upon every Christian citizen in respect to the laws by which he is governed. If he favor, or if he do not constitutionally resist, laws at variance with the gospel which he professes, he is responsible to God for all the wrong which these laws create.

In a word, I believe that slavery is forbidden in the Scriptures just as almost every other sin is forbidden; that is, by the inculcation of moral principles which are utterly at variance with it. Is not this the almost universal method of the teaching of the New Testament? Do you not, my brother, so interpret it? When you attempt to teach men that they are sinners against God, do you enumerate the precepts which they have broken, or do you set before them the character of God, and their universal relations to him? If their conduct has been at variance with all these relations, does not their own conscience pronounce them guilty? The case is, as I esteem it, similar here. God has thus taught us that slavery wrong, a violation of his most holy law. And if so, it is our duty at once to abandon it.

The manner in which this is to be done, may, I apprehend, vary with our circumstances. Such, I think, we may believe to be the teaching by example of the New Testament. A man, I suppose delivers himself from the guilt of slavery at the very moment when he, in the sight of God, renounces all right in his fellow-man, and acts in sincerity of heart, in the presence of his Judge, in conformity with that renunciation. The manner of his acting out this renunciation may, however, vary with the circumstances of the case. All that the gospel requires is, that, unbiased by interest, unawed by persecution, he carry out the principles of the gospel, wheresoever they may lead him. He is to do this as an individual, with respect to those whom he now believes that he has unjustly held in bondage. He is to do it in respect to the community whom, by his former precept and example, he has either led into or confirmed in error. He is to bear his testimony to the truth, whatever sacrifice it may cost him. So soon as the Church of Christ acts upon these principles, our land will be freed from the sin of slavery. Until she do this, the stain of blood-guiltiness (and if it be a sin at all, it is a sin of appalling magnitude) is found on her garments.

I think I can illustrate my view of this subject by a familiar example. I am obliged to take a case which we all know to be sinful, for the sake of the illustration. I do not intend to do it offensively. Suppose a man to have been guilty of great dishonesty. He holds in his hands the property of several of his fellow-men, of which he as obtained possession unjustly. He repents of his sin, and wishes to obey the gospel of Jesus Christ. I tell him that he has offended God and injured his neighbor—that he has not a right to hold a farthing or a fraction of all this part of his possession. The moment he repents of this sin, and in the sight of God renounces all right to this property, and holds it only for the good of the rightful owner, he ceases to be guilty of the sin of dishonesty. But to carry out this principle may be a work of time and labor. One whom he has defrauded may be his next door neighbor. To him he will make restitution immediately. Another may live a thousand miles off. To him he will restore his own in such a manner as will most directly and safely accomplish the object. The property of another may have been inherited by heirs; to these he will restore their portion according to the principles of law and justice. He may thus be obliged to hold this possession in his own hands for some time after he has renounced all right to hold it *as his own*. He holds it, however, not for *his own benefit*, but merely for the sake of being the better enabled to do justice. He is innocent of dishonesty in just so far as he thus holds it. If he allow any unnecessary delay to intervene—if because the rightful owner does not know of his loss—if, because he cannot restore it to-day, he resolve that he will not restore it at all—or if, because he finds some difficulty in carrying out the principle of right, he quietly relapse into his former state, and uses as his own, and for his own benefit, what on the eternal principles of justice belongs to another—in the sight of God and man he is guilty of dishonesty.

Such, my dear brother, seem to me some of the reasons why the Scriptures selected this mode of teaching us our duty on this subject, and of the bearing which this mode of teaching should have upon our present practice.

I am, my dear brother, yours, with every sentiment of Christian affection,

The Author of the Moral Science.

*Letter VIII*[28]

## To the Rev. Richard Fuller, D.D.

My Dear Brother,

In my last letter I attempted to exhibit the reasons why the inspired writers of the New Testament preferred to teach the will of God on the subject of slavery by principle rather than by precept; and to show that, such being the revealed will of God, a most solemn and imperative duty is imposed upon the disciples of Christ in the slaveholding States. I shall ask your attention to a few additional remarks on the latter of these topics, and with these shall close my part of this correspondence, already, I fear, too much protracted.

I remarked in the preceding letter, that if the views which I have taken of this subject be correct, it is the immediate duty of every slaveholder at once to free himself from the guilt of slavery, and, also, by the use of his whole constitutional power, to free his country from this guilt.

In pursuing this subject somewhat farther, I would suggest that this, as it seems to me, would be the duty of every man, especially of every disciple of Christ, were slavery nothing more than you have represented it to be—the "obliging another to labor for our benefit without his contract or consent." By our very constitution as men, we are under solemn and unchangeable obligations to respect the rights of the meanest thing that lives. Every other man is created with the same rights as ourselves; and, most of all, he is created with the inalienable "right to life, liberty, and the pursuit of happiness." To deprive him of these as a punishment for crime, while yet he continues under the protection of law, is one of the severest infliction that the criminal code of any human government can recognise, even when the punishment is confined to his own person. But what crime can be conceived of so atrocious as to justify the consigning of a human being to servitude for life, and the extension of this punishment to his posterity down to the remotest generations?

---

[28*Christian Reflector* 13/1 (2 January 1845): 2.]

Were this the penalty even for murder, every man in the civilized world would rise up in indignation at its enormous injustice. How great, then, must be the injustice when such a doom is inflicted, not upon criminals convicted of atrocious wickedness, but upon men, women, and children, who have never been accused of any crime, and against whom there is not even the suspicion of guilt! Can any moral creature of God be innocent that inflicts such punishment upon his fellow-creatures, who have never done any thing to deserve it? I ask, what have those poor, defenseless, and undefended black men done, that they and their children forever should thus be consigned to hopeless servitude? If they have done nothing, how can we be innocent if we inflict such punishment upon them? But yet more. The spirit of Christianity, if I understand it aright, teaches us not merely the principles of pure and elevated justice, but those of the most tender and all-embracing charity. The Captain of our salvation was anointed "to preach the gospel to the poor; he was sent to heal the broken-hearted, to preach deliverance to the captives, and recovering of sight to the blind; to set at liberty them that are bruised [Luke 4:18]." "He is the comforter of them that are cast down [2 Corinthians 7:6]." Can the disciple of such a Saviour, then, inflict the *least*, how much less the *greatest*, of punishments upon a human being who, has never been guilty of a crime that should deserve it?

All this, as it seems to me, must then be the duty of every man, especially of every disciple of Christ, even were slavery such as you have defined it; that is, if the slave were merely held to compulsory labor, but fed and clothed with considerate care—if he were as perfectly as ourselves under the protection of law—if the laws affecting him were made with the greatest respect for his condition and helplessness—if no other inconvenience were imposed upon him except merely what might be necessary to ensure his faithful labor—and if, in the division of the profits of his labor, a cautious love of right awarded to him his just portion of the joint proceeds of labor and capital.

But if, under such circumstances as these, it would be our duty to free ourselves from the responsibility which attaches to such an act of injustice, how much more imperative must be this duty, if all these modifying circumstances are totally reversed!

What if these human beings, thus punished without crime, or the suspicion of it, are placed wholly *without the protection of law*, and are surrendered up by society to the will of their masters, absolutely, without the power of resistance or the hope of redress, to be dealt with as the master shall choose? You and I know full well the character which the word of God attributes to fallen human nature. We have all been taught how insufferably arrogant and cruel the mind of man becomes, when intrusted with irresponsible power. What, then, must be the condition of a human being left without remedy to the exercise of this power? I know it may be said that there are laws for the protection of slaves. But I ask, is there one of these laws which is not a blot upon a statute-book, if we believe the creatures to whom they refer to be *human beings like ourselves*? But these laws, bad as they are, seem to me merely a mockery. Of what use is a law, when the testimony of the parties liable to injury can never be taken in evidence? Who need fear punishment, when the only witnesses to his wrong are universally forbidden to testify? If it be said that the rights of the slaves are protected by public opinion, I ask, when has public opinion defined these rights? And who is the man that has dared to give utterance to this public opinion? Nay, more, I cannot but consider the laws on this subject a tolerably fair index of the general sentiment of the community. If the public opinion had decided that the slaves had rights, which it was the duty of society to protect, I cannot but believe that a great and radical change would long since have been effected in the statute-books of our Southern States.

It is one of the fundamental principles of society, that no human being shall lay an unkind hand upon another, whatever may be their difference in rank. If wrong have been done, *society* ascertains the facts, and by the trial of our peers, according to equitable law, inflicts the punishment. What, then, must be the condition of those who, men, women, and children, are exposed to the lash without limit and without mercy, at the will of a single individual; and who are liable thus to suffer from weakness, infirmity, nay, for the conscientious obedience to God, as well as for fault? To every innocent woman, her personal honor is instinctively dearer than life. What, then, must be the condition of women who are held to be the property of the owner "to all intents and purposes," and who are, without redress, subjected to his will? What must be their condition, when the use of them for the purposes of profligacy is defended as a social convenience and pecuniary advantage? What must be the domestic condition of those who by law are not permitted to form marriage contracts, and who, if such contracts are formed, are liable to be separated forever at the pecuniary convenience of another?

It seems to me an elementary principle of justice, that when capital and labor combine in the creation of product, the proceeds of such creation should be divided by some equitable law in which the rights of both parties shall be fairly, represented. But what must be the condition of those who have no voice whatever in this distribution of their products, but are obliged to submit to just such a division as the caprice or pecuniary interest of the other party shall appoint?

It seems to me that the soul is the most important part of a human being, and that its capacity for improvement is one of the most precious gifts bestowed upon it by its Creator. It seems to me that the liberty to read, reflect, know, to develop its powers, and look back upon the past, and forward to the future, is an inalienable right; and that the exercise of it is a most precious solace to those who are obliged to devote themselves for a great part of the time to physical labor. What, then, must be the condition of those who are looked upon by law and by public opinion as merely physical beings, for whose intellectual happiness no provision whatever is made; nay, more, who are by the severest penalties prohibited from imbibing even the rudiments of instruction? What must be their condition, when, having been by this prohibition rendered ignorant, stupid, and sensual, this very ignorance, stupidity, and sensuality is pleaded as a reason why they should be held down to this degradation forever?

Again, God has made to us a revelation of his will, and the knowledge of that revelation is essential to our eternal salvation. *Every human being has a right to that knowledge*; for the message which it contains was *addressed directly to him*. What must be the condition of those who are wholly, by the will of another, deprived of that knowledge—who are shut out by law from obtaining it, and who are never permitted to open their eyes upon those oracles which are able to make us wise unto salvation, through the faith that is in Christ Jesus? I know it may be said that they are permitted to attend church with their masters. I know they may be so permitted. They are allowed to hear us tell what, as we affirm, God says to them; but they are not permitted to hear what *God says to them himself. I* confess myself utterly at a loss to conceive how a human being can assume the responsibility of thus interfering between an immortal soul and its Maker.

But suppose that, by means of this glimmering light, a human being should obtain some view of his relations to God, and become a real disciple of Christ. He is then introduced to a new class of duties—duties which he owes to his family, to his fellow-creatures, and to God. He must pray—he must teach others the way of salvation—he must obey God rather than man—he must give all diligence to make his calling and election sure. He needs time, opportunity, social privileges, and the communion of saints, to accomplish all this. But what must be the condition of him who is subject in every respect to the will of another, a will at all times liable to be moved by passion, caprice, or the insane love of gold? What is his condition whose private devotion may at any time be interrupted by the sound of the lash, and whose social meeting for prayer may be made an occasion for the infliction of a punishment which a humane man cannot think of without shuddering?

If, then, it would be our duty at once to free ourselves from the guilt of slavery, and labor with our whole power to free our country from it, were slavery merely involuntary servitude guarded by all the power of merciful and vigilant legislation, how much more is it our duty when it is accompanied by such intense aggravations as I have here suggested! If nearly three millions of our fellow-men are thus degraded from their position as moral, and social, and intellectual creatures, and made the mere instruments of pecuniary gain, can any man, aware of his responsibilities as a moral creature of God, look upon it with indifference? But yet more. A considerable portion of these sufferers are our Christian brethren, partakers of the same inheritance, members of the body of Christ, whom he so loved that he gave up himself for their redemption. Jesus Christ is the comforter of those that are cast down; and can we, who are his disciples, trample the cast down yet deeper in the dust? He has said, "Come unto me, all ye who are weary and heavy laden, and I will give you rest [Matthew 11:28];" and can we lay yet heavier burdens on the weary and heavy laden, whom he thus receives into his bosom? Jesus Christ has said, "It is impossible but that offences should come, but wo to the man by whom they come. It were better for him that a millstone were hanged about his neck and he cast into the sea, than that he should offend one of these little ones [Matthew 18:6]." How, then, can we stand before him, after having inflicted on these little ones these aggravated wrongs? Jesus Christ has taught us that the hungry, the thirsty, the naked, the sick, the prisoner, the stranger, are his representatives on earth, and that our love to him is to be measured by the Universal sympathy which we extend to every form of human distress; and he adds, "Inasmuch as ye did it not to one of the *least of these* my brethren, ye do it not unto me [Matthew 25:40]." The special representative of Christ in this country seems to me to be the oppressed, and I fear I must add the frequently lacerated, Christian slave. How shall we stand before the Saviour, if we make no effort to comfort and deliver this slave—much less if we count ourselves among the number of his oppressors?

To place this subject in what seems to me a correct point of view, let us imagine a very possible case. We have sent the gospel to the Karens,[29] and thousands of them are, we hope, partakers of the faith in Christ Jesus. Suppose that they, hearing that there are in the United

---

[29 The Karens were an ethnic group located in Burma. Adoniram Judson, the earliest American Baptist missionary, was the first person to introduce Christianity to the Karens. Wayland wrote a biography of Judson. See Francis Wayland, *A Memoir of the Life and Labors of the Rev. Adoniram Judson D.D.* (Boston: Phillips, Sampson, and Co., 1853).]

States millions of persons in great moral destitution, should send a missionary and his wife from their own number, to labor among the slaves in the Southern States. They are not of the Circassian[30] race. They are of darker skin than many of our slaves. The race is as weak in intellect, and as rude in knowledge as the native Africans. Precisely, so far as I can see, the same reasons exist for making slaves of the one race as of the other. Let these missionaries land on our shores. They can show no certificate of freedom, written either on paper or parchment, as the law directs. On the first day of their arrival they might, for aught I can see, be arrested, lodged in jail, and after the legal time had elapsed, be legally sold for payment of jail fees to different owners, separated from each other for life, and their children, if they had any, consigned to endless bondage. But suppose them to escape this peril. They go among the destitute and open schools, such as we have established among them, for the purpose of teaching these immortal Africans to read the Word of God. They are immediately arrested and, fined for each offence, it may be, five hundred dollars. In default of payment they are again sold to endless bondage, and separated from each other for life. But suppose them to escape this danger. They attempt to preach Christ crucified. There are more than five slaves present, and there are not present five slaveholders. They are fined again, and the same sale and endless separation takes place. They are made slaves for life. They attempt in despite of the fear of men to preach Christ crucified. They are whipped, They do it again, they are whipped again. And if they persevere, they would, as it seems to me, soon perish under the overseer's lash. They ask, with their Master, "Why, what evil have we done?" They are told that all this is done because it is for the pecuniary advantage of the masters. It is done on a calm calculation of dollars and cents. They learn also that all this system is established either by, or with the consent of, their own brethren in Christ; the very men through whose contributions they had been taught the way of life, convinced of their duty to love all men as themselves, and to preach the gospel to every creature. Would

---

[30]The Circassians were an ethnic group located in the Caucasus Mountains of southestern Europe.]

they believe that their persecutors were the disciples of that Jesus of whom they had read in the Evangelists and the Epistles? Would Christians at the South seem to them to be acting under the eye of that God who cannot bear the appearance of evil, and who has said, ye cannot serve God and mammon? Could the blessed Saviour look with indifference upon such wrongs inflicted, upon these his little ones? And is not this, in all essential particulars, an illustration of the case of all the colored Christians in the Southern States?

It is with great unwillingness that I have alluded to facts which I know must give pain to many brethren whom I love and esteem. I love and esteem them as brethren. But is not the slave, ignorant, degraded, whom no man cares for, my brother as truly as his intelligent and accomplished master? Is not the one as much as the other a member of the body of Christ? Does not the gospel teach me especially to *"remember those that are in bonds as bound with them* [Hebrews 13:3a]?" Can I do otherwise than set before my brethren what I consider to be truth, truth so important that the happiness of millions, for time and eternity, both free and enslaved, seems to me to be most vitally involved in it? I have already made every distinction that can be demanded between the different classes of those who hold their fellow-men in bondage. This, however, does not affect the *system*, and *the system* is the result of the action of the *whole community*. The whole community therefore is responsible for it; and for this reason, how painful soever it may be, it must be spoken of as it is.

But it will be said, the abolition of slavery will ruin the Southern States. Should it be so, as you have well remarked, if it be wrong, it ought to be abandoned. But I cannot see how this is to happen. The soil will neither become diminished in quantity, nor inferior in fertility. The number of laborers will be the same. The only difference that I can perceive would be, that the laborer would then work in conformity with the conditions which God has appointed, whereas he now works at variance with them; in the one case we should be attempting to accumulate property under the blessing of God, whereas now we are attempting to do it under his special and peculiar malediction. How can we expect to prosper, when there is not, as Mr. Jefferson remarks, "an attribute of the Almighty that can be appealed to in our favor?" I would gladly discuss this subject as a question in Political Economy; but this is not the place for it, and I must with these few remarks pass it by.

But it may be said, what can we do? Men of all classes are so excitable on this subject, that they will not allow us to utter a word in opposition to slavery. To do this would be to destroy our influence, endanger our property, ruin our reputation, and it may be, to peril our lives. You, my dear brother, would not make this objection, but you know it would be made. I fear that the objection is well-founded. It is in accordance with the general law, that those who enslave the bodies of others, become in turn the slaves of their own passions. But what if it be so? Are we in such a case to listen to the teachings of a craven and wicked expediency? If this be a sin against God, ought we to hesitate to testify against it, because our fellow-men will persecute us? Ought we not rather to adopt the language of the Hebrews, "Our God whom we serve is able to deliver us, and he will deliver us out of thy hand, O king; but if not, be it known unto thee we will not serve thy gods, nor worship the golden image which thou hast set up [Daniel 3:17]." I do believe that even now it is the duty of every Christian in the slaveholding States to bear his testimony against this enormous wrong, and at once to free himself from the guilt of participation in it. I fear that those who first set this glorious example would suffer persecution. Their names would be cast out as evil. They would be branded with every epithet of reproach. But they would be suffering to rescue millions of men from aggravated oppression, and to deliver their country from a sin that must bring upon it the selectest judgments of a God that loveth justice. They would not, however, long suffer alone. Thousands of slaveholders who now groan under the weight of this infliction, and are praying for deliverance from it, would soon enlist under their standard. The church universal would without ceasing supplicate the throne of grace in their behalf. Every attribute of the Most High would be put forth to ensure their success. He that ever liveth to intercede for us would offer up their prayers with much incense, and would strengthen their hearts by infusing into them a double portion of his spirit. God himself will undertake for them, and they will assuredly triumph, and the glory of a more resplendent moral victory than has been achieved since the day when He ascended up on high and led captivity captive, will encircle the diadem of the Redeemer.

In the remarks which I have made, you will perceive that I have offered no suggestion as to the manner in which emancipation, whenever it occurs, shall be conducted. This is altogether a practical question, and requires for its solution not only genuine and disinterested philanthropy, but also great practical wisdom, large observation of the effects of social changes, and an intimate acquaintance with the habits, manners, and states of feeling of the South. To these I make no pretension, as I have no skill in managing affairs, and have never visited the Southern States. There is, however, knowledge of this kind in abundance with you. To your statesmen, and philanthropists, and Christians, I willingly leave it, in the full confidence that it can be done, done safely, and done to the inconceivable advantage of all the parties concerned.

In the commencement of these letters I think I mentioned that I wrote in behalf of no one but myself, and that no other individual whatever was in any manner implicated in any of the sentiments which I might utter. Such has been the case to the close. I believe it has not chanced that a single idea in these letters has been suggested to me by any other person. Yet I have reason to suppose, from several circumstances, that they express the opinions, perhaps I might say the almost universal opinions, of Christians of every denomination in the Northern States. They look upon slavery as a grievous wrong, and a wrong specially at variance with the spirit and teachings of the gospel of Christ, a cruel injustice towards their fellow-men, and specially towards their brethren in the common faith. It is not therefore remarkable that they feel strongly on such a subject. It is not to be wondered at that any real or even apparent connection with it, should give rise to conscientious scruples in the minds of fair, upright, and candid men. They may well be acquitted of the charge of unkindness or incendiarism, if they shrink from any act which might seem to imply that they consider slavery in any other light than as irreconcilably at variance with the teachings of the gospel of Christ. Thus in our labor to propagate the religion of the Redeemer, we may surely without offence pause before we do any thing that could be construed into indifference to slavery, in the establishment of churches among the heathen. It may here be proper for me, specially in connection with the office to which I was unwillingly chosen at the late Triennial Convention, to state my own views on this subject. I do it without unkindness and without reserve. I am perfectly willing to have it understood, that whatever may be my view as expressed in my third letter of the connection between the holding of slaves, and profession of religion, in a state of society where the institution has become long established, I never could, without doing violence to my conscience, do any thing towards the establishment in a heathen land of a church into which slavery could by any means find admittance. I believe that I should sin willfully against God, if I ever promulgated a slaveholding Christianity. I use the word without opprobrium, and merely to designate a fact. I know that this avowal is not necessary. But I prefer to make it, lest I should, under any circumstances, be accused of acting with duplicity. You, at least, will appreciate my motives, and will at once perceive that no other course of conduct could legitimately flow from the sentiments which I profess. And I do not see how Christians at the South can look upon the subject in any other light. I never found one who would be willing to introduce slavery into this country, were it not established; nay, who would not consider such an act both wicked and unwise. And can a brother expect me to do in another country what he would not do in his own; or can he expect me to take any step, which by the remotest legitimate consequence might lead to this result? I am sure that every reflecting Christian must see that I could never do it, either in honor or with a good conscience.

My task is ended. I have written in haste, and amid the pressure of other and imperative engagements. I have, however, long felt that I owed a debt of humanity and charity to my Christian brethren at the South, both free and enslaved. I have desired to bear my testimony in favor of those whom I believed to be suffering the greatest injustice, and to bear it in the presence of those, many of whom I believe, through erroneous views of the teachings of the Scriptures, to be responsible to God for that injustice. I rejoice that I have had the opportunity of addressing them through one who, whatever he might think of my argument, will do justice to my motives. If, my dear brother, in aught that I have written, I have betrayed a spirit at variance with the kindness of the gospel; if a word that I have uttered has been designed to give the slightest pain to a Christian brother, you will believe me when I say it is not merely unintentional, but directly in opposition to my most thoughtful and vigilant intention. I have desired to address the understanding and conscience of my brethren, and to avoid every allusion that would even remotely tend to deter them from examining this subject in the light of what seems to me to be the teaching of the Holy Scriptures. To them I commit what I have written, with the humble prayer that God may use it to advance the cause of righteousness and mercy.

Now the God of peace that brought again from the dead our Lord Jesus, that great Shepherd of the sheep, through the blood of the everlasting covenant, make us perfect in every good work to do his will, working in us that which is well pleasing in his sight, through Jesus Christ, to whom be glory forever and ever. Amen.

I am, my dear brother, yours, with every sentiment of Christian affection,

The Author of the Moral Science.

# DR. FULLER'S LETTERS

*Letter I*[31]

## To the Rev. Francis Wayland, D.D.

My Dear Brother,

I have been compelled for several weeks to abandon my charge, and am now in the country, seeking to recruit my health. Your very able letters have reached me here slowly and with long intervals, and I need not say that the importance of the matter, and my great love and esteem for the writer, have commanded all the attention I can now bestow on any subject. The chaste style and luminous thought of these communications, their earnestness and truthfulness, and admirable Christian spirit, make them just like every thing I have known of the "Author of the Moral Science;" and I am far more anxious that they should be circulated at the South than any remarks from my pen. To establish great moral principles is your province; mine be the humbler office of an inquirer. Peace and truth are all I seek, and if in this discussion my arguments be refuted, I shall be well content, provided peace and truth are secured; I shall at least fall by no weak hand, and enjoy whatever of consolation Abimelech coveted, when he "called hastily unto his armor-bearer, and said, Draw thy sword, and slay me, that men may not say of me, A woman slew him [Judges 9:54]."

Indeed I am not quite sure how far I am required to encounter you at all. My letter was sent at the suggestion of the *Reflector*, a paper which seems to me to be conducted not only with ability, but remarkable frankness and independence—and its single object was to employ my feeble effort against the fundamental dogma of the modern abolitionists, that slaveholding is necessarily "a heinous crime in the sight of God." Such is the position assumed in the constitution of the American Anti-slavery Society; and the inference is manifest—all slaveholders should be

---

[31*Christian Reflector* 13/4 (23 January 1845): 14.]

excommunicated from Christian fellowship, no matter how pious; indeed, to apply the term pious to such persons, is as if one should speak of devout hypocrites, or holy pirates. Now this doctrine is really as monstrous as it is uncharitable; it finds its prompt refutation, not only in a thousand examples among those whom it insults, but in the verdict of the whole Christian and civilized world, and I do believe in the consciences of the abolitionists themselves. It is a doctrine peculiar to the restless and turbulent fanaticism of this country; for in England no such ground was taken by the churches, even in periods of the intensest excitement. There, slavery was regarded as a national evil, and the energies of those wishing its removal were exerted, not in denouncing their fellow-citizens, on whom the national policy had entailed the sad inheritance, but in moving parliament to adopt measures by which the rights both of the master and the slave were regarded. And hence it is worthy of observation that every respectable minister of the gospel from that country—no matter how zealous there against slavery—has, on coming to the United States, kept aloof from the Northern abolitionists; and this, not from any abatement of zeal in crossing the Atlantic, but from a perception of the different state of things here, and an invincible repugnance to the reckless and proscriptive intolerance everywhere characterizing that party—and which, in fact, will characterize any body of men, however pious and otherwise amiable, who allow their minds to be poisoned by the sentiment above mentioned. You have seen Dr. Chalmers'[32] late letter, deprecating this dissociating system, and he expresses, no doubt, the views of all in Great Britain, who contemplate American slavery with calmness and wisdom.

Now as you condemn this distinguishing tenet of abolitionism, and as I referred to your treatise only because it appeared to favor it, I might very well let the matter rest where it is. And to this course, I confess, I am the more inclined, because unwilling to appear in any controversy, which can, even by implication, place me in a false and odious attitude, representing me as the eulogist and abettor of slavery, and not as simply

[32 Thomas Chalmers was a Scottish Presbyterian minister who served as the first moderator of the Free Church of Scotland.]

the apologist of an institution transmitted to us by former generations, the existence of which I lament; for the commencement of which I am not at all responsible; for the extinction of which I am willing to make greater sacrifices than any abolitionist has made or would make, if the cause of true humanity would thus be advanced; but which, for, all that, I do say it is wrong to pronounce a moral evil and a great crime in the sight of God. If, then, I disregard my ill health and my wishes, and venture to join issue with you, it is because I fear that, notwithstanding your caveat, the correspondence you so skilfully manage will be pressed, by bits and shreds, into the service of those with whom you disclaim all sympathy; and become prolific of inferences—forbidden indeed by you, but recognized by them as legitimate and irresistible, and to which your charitable admissions will scarcely serve even as pleas in mitigation. There is, indeed, (and, knowing my affection, you will pardon my speaking plainly), there is a passage of your second letter which, I venture to say, will be cited in every inflammatory address for a twelvemonth; and which I the more regret, since it does not minister, I humbly apprehend, to the elucidation of the truth, and will serve—though nothing was farther from your design—to confirm one of the most unfounded prejudices by which the Northern conscience is misled and exacerbated in reference to slavery. You say, "Suppose that I should set fire to your house, shoot you as your came out of it, and seizing upon your wife and children, oblige them to labor for my benefit without their contract or consent," &c., &c. Now, my dear brother, I submit to you that, in a disquisition like ours, such a picture as this can serve only to excite the imagination by fictitious horrors, and to divert the mind from a calm and unbiased investigation. If slavery be a crime necessarily and essentially, the manner in which it was originated is just nothing at all to the purpose. Slavery is a condition; and if it be one of guilt, then not only is the master bound to clear his skirts of it without regard to its origin or consequences, but (as with a woman detained in adultery) it is the duty of the slave—his duty, not only to himself but to his master—to revolt and escape; and the apostle enjoined a continuance in sin when he said, "Servants, obey your masters [Ephesians 6:5]." After blackening the conduct portrayed with every diabolical ingredient, you add, "The question before us I suppose to be simply this—would I in so doing act at variance with the relations existing between us as creatures of God?" But there is not, never was, and never can be, such a question. The question before us I suppose to be simply this—*is slaveholding always a sin?* and the moment you make such an hypothesis as yours, it is manifest that another and very different question has been substituted, and the only proposition you undertook to maintain is virtually abandoned. The case to be proved was, that slavery is always a crime, a crime amid the most favorable and extenuating circumstances. The case made out is, that slavery created by murder and arson, and perpetuated by oppression and cruelty, is a crime.

While, however, this mode of reasoning does not aid our inquiry, it does, as I said, serve to nourish an undefined opinion, common at the North, as to the introduction of slavery into this country, than which nothing can be more unjust to the South. If the truth were considered as to this matter, I believe many at the North would regard the whole subject in a perfectly new light; and therefore it behooves that I put, not a fanciful case, but the facts as recorded in history. Let it be borne in mind, then, (1) that it was the mother country which devised and prosecuted the system of supplying her colonies with laborers from Africa; (2) that these importations were made, not only without consulting the colonies supplied, but in spite of frequent protests from them; (3) that in this commerce the importations were all, with I believe not a single exception, in English and Northern bottoms, and by English and Northern speculators; and (4) that, on the arrival of a vessel thus freighted, there remained for the negro only one alternative—deliverance from his loathsome dungeon by the planter, or protracted and daily increasing suffering, to terminate in death. These are historical facts, which ought to be pondered before any man forms his opinion. Very old persons are now living here, and perhaps in Rhode Island too, who well remember the tears of joy shed by the unhappy prisoners when their chains were stricken off; and the gratitude manifested by them, in every look and gesture, towards those whom they blessed, and continued to bless during life, as their benefactors; and the horror with which they would cling to the knees of their deliverers, if the ship were only pointed to, and a return there hinted at. Let me also mention another fact; it is that the condition of the African has been vastly improved, physically, intellectually, morally, and religiously, by his transportation to these shores. This, I presume, will be admitted on all hands, and therefore it is unnecessary for me, to insist upon it. The unmeasured cornucopia vituperation sometimes emptied on us, might make one fear that even this concession may be too great a stretch of charity for some bitter spirits among the agitators. But the thing is incontestable; and, indeed, all who mingle much with slaves will bear me witness, that, whether they be preachers or private Christians, one of their most common themes, in or out of the pulpit, is the great goodness of God in transferring them from the thick darkness of their own land to the privileges they enjoy in ours.[33]

You know Whitefield's character; by all in the ministry it ought to be made a study. He was, I think, the greatest preacher who ever lived, in what constitutes preaching. He was, too, one of the purest and most benevolent and holiest men. Writing in March 22d, 1751, he says: "This is my comfort; 'all things work together for good to those that love God.' He is, the Father of mercies and the God of all consolation. He can bring light out of darkness, and cause the barren wilderness to smile. This, I trust, will be verified in Georgia. Thanks be to God, that the time for favoring that Colony seems to be come. I think now is the season for us to exert our utmost for the good of the poor Ethiopians. We are told, that even they are soon to stretch out their hands unto

---

[33]At this day, it is computed by eyewitnesses, that probably nine-tenths of the population of Africa are slaves; the master's power being, in most cases, arbitrary even over life. Mr. Hazlehurst, a missionary just from that country, states that many of the tribes eat their prisoners; and when a prince dies, a thousand slaves are often first mutilated, and then buried with him. A map of the world, showing the geographical extent of slavery, would, in truth, cause the proceedings of the little meeting in London, which grandiloquently styled itself "The World's Convention," to appear, not ludicrous, for such a term would be improper, but certainly most chimerical and Quixotic.

God. And who knows but their being settled in Georgia may be overruled for this great end? As for the lawfulness of keeping slaves, I have no doubt, since I hear of some that were bought with Abraham's money, and some that were born in his house." "It is plain, that the Gibeonites were doomed to perpetual slavery, and though liberty is a sweet thing to such as are born free, yet to those who never knew the sweets of it, slavery perhaps may not be so irksome. However this be, it is plain to a demonstration, that hot countries cannot be cultivated without negroes." "Had Mr. Henry been in America, I believe he would have seen the lawfulness and necessity of having negroes there. And though it is true, that they are brought in a wrong way from their own country, and it is a trade not to be approved of, yet as it will be carried on whether we will or not, I should think myself highly favored if I could purchase a good number of them, in order to make their lives comfortable, and lay a foundation for breeding up their posterity in the nurture and admonition of the Lord." "It rejoiced my soul, to hear that one of my poor negroes in Carolina was made a brother in Christ. How know we but we may have many such instances in Georgia ere it be long? By mixing with your people, I trust many of them will be brought to Jesus, and this consideration, as to us, swallows up all temporal inconveniences whatsoever."[34]

And now, all this being so, it appears to me the only question for a pure and enlarged philanthropy is, what ought to be the policy of the Anglo-Saxon race, influenced by principles of sound wisdom, and true religion, towards this other race, thus thrown among them, constituting a strange and distinct people, from their introduction known by others and knowing themselves only as slaves, and whose retrocession to Africa is, at least at present, both undesirable and impossible? Such I conceive to be the momentous and solemn inquiry for the South; and on this point, it is plain that a diversity of opinions may exist among those who are inspired with the sincerest love for God and man. In these States it is the settled conviction of many who devote their lives to the spiritual

---

[34] If Whitefield were now living, he would be *deposed*.

good of the slave population, that the principles and precepts of the gospel, and the course pursued by Christ and the apostles, are exactly adapted to the consummation most to be wished; and that, slowly but certainly, Christianity, as an alterative, is elevating the negro in the scale of being, and educating his mind and heart for purposes as yet concealed from us by an inscrutable Providence. And whatever may be the design of God, they are confident he needs not the wrath and fury of man; and that "if a good work cannot be carried on by the calm, self-controlled, benevolent spirit of Jesus, then the time for doing it has not come." At the North I have been honored with the friendship of some of the holiest and wisest Christians, and have found them differing from each other as to the practical *and excommunicated,* and regarded as unfit to be employed as a missionary question; confessing that they had no matured views at all; painfully conscious that a wisdom and a power high above man's are required for such a cause; and devoutly lifting their souls to God, in a prayer now breathed night and day by thousands at the South—that he will work both to will and to do, and bring to pass all his good pleasure, and cause his kingdom everywhere to come and his will everywhere to be done.

In the remarks just made I have supposed, of course, that slavery is not proved to be a great crime; for if it be, no such question as that above stated can be entertained. That sin must at once be abandoned, is a proposition which admits of no debate. If slavery, then, be a sin, it should at once be abolished. It is true the experiment with us would be very different from that in the British West Indies. There the masters were conciliated, the slaves were few compared with our millions, and they are awed into subordination by a powerful military force. Yet even there the wisdom and benevolence of the measure are extremely problematical, and becoming every day more so. The parliamentary reports confess that the freed negroes refuse to work for hire, and England is compelled to rescue her colonies from destruction by reviving the slave-trade under a new name, and importing cargoes of Africans into her islands, there to starve or accept any wages offered, or, as will probably be the result, to augment the evil by swelling the crowd of drones around them.[35]

But in these States it is believed by men of the most devoted piety, and exalted philanthropy, and after patient and prayerful survey of the whole ground, that immediate and unconditional abolition would be a revolution involving the entire South in ruin; breaking up all social order and peace and safety; and, in fact, inflicting on the slaves themselves irreparable mischief. It would suddenly give them a liberty for which they are wholly unprepared, and which would be only a license for indolence and crime. It would convert them, inevitably, from a contented and cheerful peasantry, into a horde of outlaws, a multitude of paupers with whom white population could never amalgamate, who must forever feel themselves (witness their condition even at the North) degraded and outcast from the kindred and privileges of the superior caste; who, deprived of the master's protection, and no longer bound to their governors by the kindly and almost filial ties now existing, would endure perpetual humiliation and insult, and drag out a sullen life of envy and hatred and wretchedness; or, if instigated to revenge and insurrection, be certainly crushed, and either annihilated, or subjugated to an iron bondage, a military rule, from the rigors of which they would look back to their former state as one, not only of comparative, but real, substantial, contrasted liberty and happiness.

If, however, slavery be a crime, I repeat it, the consequences of abolition should not be considered at all. It is, then, of first rate importance that we inquire into the moral character of slavery. If it be a sin, all discussion as to the policy which should be adopted towards the Ethiopian race among us is precluded and superseded.

---

[35]See an able article on this subject in a late *Westminster Review*. [*The Westminster Review* was a politically liberal periodical established in 1824 by a group of British progressives known as the Philosophical Radicals. Key leaders of the movement included the noted Utilitarian philosophers Jeremy Bentham and John Stuart Mill. Many of the periodical's articles addressed the issue of slavery, both in the British West Indies and in the American South.]

Let me finish this letter by assuring you that, if my great distance from you did not prevent it, I would submit all I write to your judgment before allowing it to be published; since nothing could mortify and grieve me more than to utter a word which you or anybody can regard as not deferential and affectionate. If, then, a syllable escapes me in this correspondence which you think might have been softened or omitted, I beg you, once for all, to forgive it. Ascribe it to the haste with which I have to write. Ascribe it to the state of my nerves, which keep me constantly restless and in pain. Ascribe it, in short, to any thing but a want of that sincere esteem and love with which I am, my dear brother,

Yours,

R. Fuller.


*Letter II[36]*

*To the Rev. Francis Wayland, D.D.*

My Dear Brother,

The issue now before us regards the essential moral character of slavery; and on such a question I am strongly disposed to pass by all ethical and metaphysical dissertation, and appeal at once to the only standard of right and wrong which can prove decisive. For my own part, I am heartily sick and weary of the controversies and debates waged and waging on every side, in which each party is contending, not for truth, but victory, and which have effected just nothing, for the want of some arbiter recognized by all, and whose decree shall be final and infallible. Now such an umpire we have. Whatever importance others may attach to the deductions of human reasoning, and thus impiously array against the Scriptures those "oppositions of science falsely so called [1 Timothy 6:20]," which the Apostle terms "profane and vain babblings [1 Timothy 6:20]," you and I have long since put on our shields one motto—"Let God be true and every man a liar [Romans 3:4]." There are, indeed,

---

[36*Christian Reflector* 13/5 (30 January 1844): 18.]

some truths which are seen, like the sun, by their own light; but when the character of any human action admits of discussion at all, it admits, almost always, of indefinite discussion. The question itself of innocence and guilt is necessarily complex; and it is vain, too, in this day of knowledge and mental discipline, to expect any such signal results as formerly belonged to the trial by battle. No matter how an advocate seems to establish his opinions, they will not prove invulnerable. "He that is first in his own cause, seemeth just; but his neighbor cometh and searcheth him [Proverbs 18:17];" and the result of this searching invariably is, that, at least in the judgment of the neighbor's party, the first becomes last and the last first.

It is, then, the responses of the sacred oracles to which we must after all appeal. But as we may rest assured that no science, truly so called, will be found opposed to revelation; and as I abhor and abjure the blasphemy which would charge the Bible with countenancing sin; I shall suspend what still appears to me (with deference) to be the unequivocal argument from the Scriptures, until I examine the logic usually employed on this subject—my principal object being to vindicate the inspired volume from having, at anytime or place, permitted and regulated a crime of the darkest malignity.

Now, in order to clear away rubbish, and arrive at once at the point, let me remind you that it is simply the essential character of slavery which we are discussing; and that slavery is a term whose meaning can be easily and accurately defined. Slavery is bondage. It is (to give Paley's idea in other language) the condition of one to whose service another has a right, without the consent or contract of the servant. The addition you make to this definition is really included in it; the original right involving, of course, all rights necessarily and properly implied. But, my dear brother, while I concur fully in the conclusions you draw from the premises assumed, it really seems to me that those premises beg the whole question, and take for granted the only thing I ever denied. I am now referring to your second communication. Nothing can be more carefully and lucidly reasoned, and the abolitionists declare they "have read no argument from any quarter so simple and yet so conclusive against slavery." And yet, after several times perusing this letter, will my brother forgive my saying that it presents to my mind precisely the following problem, and no other:—Slavery being admitted to be an aggregate of crimes, it is required to prove that slavery is criminal. As to which you very justly add, "I do not perceive how the subject, in this view, admits of any argument."

Let me go a little into detail. Your conclusion is, that slavery is not only a moral evil, but as great a sin as "we can conceive of;" and this you derive from two propositions, both of which I humbly apprehend to be fallacious. First, you affirm that the right of the master is irreconcilable with the right of the slave to "the blessings of moral and intellectual cultivation, and the privileges of domestic society;" which I deny. Why, indeed, should it be? When you hire a servant for a year, he is under obligation to "labor for your benefit" that year; but does your right to his service, or your right to "use all means necessary to the original right," conflict with his right to "the blessings of moral and intellectual cultivation, and the privileges of domestic society?" The terms "moral cultivation" signify, I presume, improvement in holiness. Now, suppose a slave to have the word of God, and to enjoy all the means of grace, why should his moral improvement be impossible because he labors for my benefit? In fact, might not his very position shelter him from many of those temptations of pride, and avarice, and ambition, which are most fatal to piety?[37] Then, again, as to intellectual cultivation: the laboring population in all countries have but little taste or time for literature; but if our slaves were taught to read, I know no class of people employed in manual industry who would have more leisure for books. Many Roman slaves were hard students: they were employed as amanuenses, and their value was in proportion to their education. And so, too, as to domestic society; why should it not be enjoyed by those who labor for a master?

---

[37]All the Greek fathers, and many eminent commentators, maintain that the true meaning of 1 Corinthians 7:21, is, "Even if liberty may be thine, remain rather in the state of the slave, as it is propitious to piety." [See John Chrysostom, *Homilies on Ephesians*, trans. John A. Broadus, ed. Philip Schaff, Nicene and Post-Nicene Fathers, 38 vols. (1889; reprint, Peabody MA: Hendrickson, 2004) 12:108.]

The right of the master, I repeat it, does not confer any such rights as you suppose. He may require the just and reasonable service of the slave, but it is a service exactly such as is due from a servant hired for the year or for life. Nor does the absence of "the contract or consent of the slave," nor the right of transfer, at all alter the nature and extent of the master's right. The case is analogous to that of parents and children. A father has a right to the services of his child during minority, without the contract or consent of the child; and he may transfer that right, as in case of apprenticeship. But is he therefore justified in debasing the moral and intellectual character of the child? Nay; does not the very law which gives him the control of his child, place him under the strongest obligations to promote that child's best and eternal interests? And, beyond a doubt, this is the true light in which Christianity would have masters regard themselves—a view which must cause the holiest among us to tremble at our fearful responsibility, and bow down in contrition and penitence at our unfaithfulness. But this is only what I fear to be too true as to most parents; and, in each case, it is not the relation which is sinful, but infidelity to the solemn trust which that relation creates. The proposition adduced by you is only a modification of another which has so often been urged; viz., that man cannot be made a subject of property; as to which who but sees that the whole perplexity arises from a confusion of terms? The affirmants mean, that it is wrong to treat human beings as brutes and inanimate chattels; which is self-evident. Those who support the negative intend only, that one man may have a just right to the services of another, and that this right may be transferable; which is also self-evident. Here the dispute would at once cease, if the term *property* were defined. And just so with us. Your conclusions are quite indisputable, if slavery be essentially and necessarily the compound of palpable infractions of right which you suppose. But this you surely do not maintain. You certainly do not believe that in Abraham's family, and among Christians in the apostles' days, the right was claimed, and exercised, to deprive the slaves of "the blessings of moral and intellectual cultivation and the privileges of domestic society." Indeed, in your third letter, when speaking of a slaveholder, you say, "he may cultivate their" (the slaves') "intellects, and improve their morals." It is conceded, then, that slavery may exist without those evils which you mention. The right, therefore, to commit them is not necessary to ensure the exercise of the original right of the master, and slavery does not confer it as you affirm.

If instead of *right* you had used the word *power*, and had asserted the great danger of confiding such irresponsible power in the hands of any man, I should at once have assented. There is quite abuse enough of this authority to make me regret its general existence. But the possession of power is, in itself, neither good nor evil. Were I invested with despotic power over the whole earth, there could be manifestly no guilt in this. Good and evil, right and wrong, would depend on my use of such power. Mr. Birney,[38] the abolition candidate for the Presidency, says, "He would have retained the power and authority of an emperor; yet his oppressions, his cruelties would have ceased; the very temper that prompted them, would have been suppressed; his power would have been put forth for good and not for evil." Now what is this but an avowal that he could, conscientiously, have held a vast population in the most abject slavery—having power over labor, and property, and liberty, and life; and that, in itself, this would be no crime? The power of the master I therefore admit. I admit, too, its frequent and shameful abuse, and I unite with you in deploring and condemning this as heinous sin. But to include in the idea of slavery "the right" to oppress and degrade, is to confound two things entirely distinct, and which really have no sort of connection.

It is urged, however, that slavery is a sin, because it does violate those primary rights which belong to all human beings, and of which none can deprive them without doing aggravated wrong. This is your second proposition, in enforcing which you consider man, (1) as an immortal being preparing for eternity; (2) as an intelligent being capable of knowledge; (3) as a moral agent bound to serve his Creator; (4) as endowed with personal liberty; (5) as a fallen creature to whom the

---

[38]James Gillespie Birney ran for president of the United states as the Liberty Party candidate in 1840 and 1844.]

gospel is sent; (6) and, lastly, as sustaining marital and parental relations; and I understand you to affirm, that, in all these respects, slavery is necessarily an outrage on the rights of man. "To put the matter in a simple light" you suppose one to "set fire" to his neighbor's house; to shoot him as he comes out of it; to seize his wife and children, and keep them as slaves, and forbid them to read, and consign them and their offspring to mental imbecility, and deny them the knowledge of God: and I understand you to affirm (for otherwise the supposition is wholly irrelevant) that slaveholding necessarily involves all this crime. You then remark, that "the question before us simply is, whether this would be criminal?" and add, "I do not see how any intelligent creature can give more than one answer to this question." And, verily, so say I; and my only surprise is, that the very enormity of your premises did not startle you, and cause you to suspect error somewhere, and admonish you that what you supposed to be "the only question before us," never was, and never could be, a question at all with any intelligent creature.

You admit that the holiest men in the Old and New Testaments were masters of slaves; but do you believe they were the monsters of wickedness depicted in your portrait, or that they violated all the rights which you have specified? Slavery, then, may exist without inflicting these aggravated wrongs. Again, allow me to refer to your third letter, where the heart of my dear brother argues, (for the heart hath its reasonings, and they are often truer than the slow deductions of the head,) and to cite the following language: "I have known Christian slaveholders who have devoted themselves through life to the welfare, temporal and spiritual, of their slaves, with the spirit of the most self denying missionaries; and who, I confidently believe, if they could do it with a reasonable prospect of improving the condition of their slaves; would gladly manumit them, and support themselves by daily labor at the North. Such men and women do honor to human nature. They are the true friends of their race." Now, here is slavery. Here is no painting of fancy; no impracticable, Utopian abstraction; but slavery as you have known it, and as others know it to exist. And, is this one of the greatest crimes which can be conceived? Or is it not here conceded, that cases may occur where there is, not only no guilt in the act, but no moral evil in the thing? You agree with me "that if slavery be a sin, it is the immediate duty of masters to abolish it, whatever be the result;" and I say, too, this is their duty, whatever be the law of the State. Suppose, now, the laws of South Carolina should forbid an adulterer to dissolve his criminal connection; or require one of her citizens living by piracy to continue his desperately wicked career. These enactments are felt by all to be impossible, while no such emotions are excited by laws protecting slavery; a truth of itself showing that, in the instinctive consciousness of mankind, slavery is not necessarily in the category of crimes. Suppose, however, such a code; and suppose the adulterer and pirate should persevere in their courses, and plead these laws; could you—could even your kind disposition bring you to regard them as innocent? How would it sound to hear my brother say, "I have known Christian adulterers who have devoted themselves through life to the welfare, temporal and spiritual, of their paramours, with the spirit of the most self-denying missionaries; and who, I confidently believe, if they could do it with a reasonable prospect of improving the condition of their paramours, would gladly leave them, and discontinue the guilty intercourse. Such adulterers do honor to human nature. They are the true friends of their race!!" In fact, a single glance at the definition of slavery will convince anybody, that the argument advanced is precisely like that which proves murder of the most aggravated sort to be criminal, when the only issue is, whether in any case it be justifiable to take human life. Of all the rights enumerated by you, slaveholding necessarily interferes only with personal freedom; for we have before seen, what is perfectly manifest, that a man may be held in bondage, and yet be treated in every respect as an immortal, intelligent, moral, fallen, ransomed being, yea and a Christian brother, and his conjugal and parental relations be sacredly respected; which I take to be the exact precept of the gospel. The question then is simply this—is it necessarily a crime in the sight of God, to restrict or control that personal liberty which every man is supposed to have in a state of nature?

Most affectionately, dear brother,
Yours,
R. Fuller.


## Letter III[39]

## The Rev. Francis Wayland, D.D.

My Dear Brother,

I trust I have shown that slavery is not essentially the comprehensive wrong you make it; that a right to the services of a man without his contract or consent, does not confer any such rights as you suppose; and that slavery does not interfere necessarily with any of those rights called primary, except personal freedom. The discussion is then pruned to this, —Is it necessarily a crime in the sight of God to control or curtail the natural personal liberty of a human being? A question admitting no debate at all.

It will not be disputed that government is the ordinance of God. But government is restraint; the very idea of government includes an abridgment of that personal freedom which a savage has in the forest, and a modification of it into political freedom, or civil rights and privileges.

Is it, then, necessarily a crime for a government to discriminate between those whom it controls, the distribution of civil privileges and political liberty? It would surely be preposterous to affirm this. Every government has necessarily a right to pass laws indispensable to its existence;[40] and it has, a right, also, to establish those regulations which shall best promote the good of the whole population. Whether any particular enactments be necessary, and whether they do secure the greatest good, are points as to which error may be committed, but as to

---

[39]*Christian Reflector* 13/6 (6 February 1845): 22.]

[40] "Whatever concessions on the part of the individual, and whatever powers on the part of society, are necessary to the existence of society, must, by the very fact of the existence of society be taken for granted." [Wayland, *Moral Science*, 391.]

which each government is the judge; and if it acts uprightly, with all the lights possessed, there is no crime. We boast of our liberties, and are forever quoting the words of the Declaration of Independence; yet in this country it has been deemed most for the good of the whole, that one half of the citizens (and I believe by far the noblest, purest, and best half) should be disfranchised of a great many civil rights. This is true, also, of all citizens until they reach an age wholly conventional,—viz. twenty-one. Is this a sin? Will it be urged that all are born free and equal, and that it is wicked to violate the indefeasible rights of women and minors? The day is coming, I venture to predict, when our regenerators will utter such frantic arguments; for they drive on, unrecking and unheeding alike the plainest dictates of reason and experience, and the stern lessons of the French Revolution, and the warning voice which spoke in such fearful accents amid the havoc and butchery and desolation of St. Domingo. But no good citizen considers the inequalities existing in these States criminal.

When we pass to England and France, we find these social distinctions far more numerous, and marked, and exclusive. Multitudes there are due to the existence of society, must, by the very fact of the existence of society, be prived of all right of suffrage in reference to laws which affect their property and lives;[41] and Parliament and the Chambers think this most conducive to the great end of social organization, the general good. In Russia civil power is vested in one man. The liberty of the noble is restricted; that of the plebeian is still less; and that of the serf scarcely more than is enjoyed by the African in this State. And in Russia this is believed to be best for the good of the empire. Now what political organization is most desirable for a particular people depends on circumstances;[42] but whatever be that

---

[41]In France there are thirty-four millions of people, and only one hundred thousand are electors of Deputies to the Chambers.

[42] "If it be asked, 'which of these is the preferable form of government ?' the answer, I think, must be conditional. The best form of government for any people is the best that its present moral condition renders practicable." [Wayland, *Moral Science*, 397.]

adopted, whether democracy or despotism, the rights of man, as a human being, are trenched upon; and visionary have proved, and will prove, all projects of constructing and fashioning society according to philosophical notions and theories of abstract "inalienable rights." That slavery, or any civil institution, interferes with the liberty of a man or a class of men, does not, then, make it necessarily and amid all circumstances a crime.

To put this in a plain light, let me suppose that one of these Southern republics should be inspired with the truest philanthropy; that her constituency should, for the first time, regard piety as important in a representative; that the benignant spirit of Jesus should penetrate her halls of legislation, and pervade all her councils; and that the present government—finding the African race under its control—satisfied that even if their removal were practicable, it is not desirable for their own good—should address itself with paternal assiduity to their welfare and happiness. All obnoxious laws are abrogated. The slaves are educated, their rights as immortal, intellectual, moral, and social beings are protected, and their religious instruction secured. If you choose, we will say that their labor is regulated, and instead of the compensation resting with the master, it is fixed by statute. Suppose, however, this government, using the lights of wisdom and experience, is convinced that the black population cannot be admitted to the privileges of free citizens, but that the good of the whole community, the safety and existence of the republic, and the negroes' own best interests, require that their personal liberty be restrained. Will it be pretended that such conduct would be criminal? Nor is there any thing impossible in the hypothesis. It might become fact to-morrow; and no doubt among the Christian masters addressed by the apostles, and in the patriarchs' families, such a picture had many originals, as far as it portrays the fostering and parental character of the relation. Onesimus might have been mentally, and morally, and religiously cultivated, and yet have been a slave; and his very piety would have caused him to "be obedient unto his master." Among the Romans it was not unusual for slaves to be men of much learning.

As soon as slavery is mentioned at the North, there is conjured up, in the minds of many persons, I know not what confused, revolting combination, and heart-rending spectacle, of chains, and whips, and cruelty, and crime, and wretchedness. But, I repeat it, even at the peril of tediousness, that necessarily and essentially—(and in a multitude of instances, practically and actually)—slavery is nothing more than the condition of one who is deprived of political power, and does service, —without his contract and consent, it is true, but yet it may be, cheerfully and happily, and for a compensation reasonable and certain, paid in modes of return best for the slave himself. With what is strictly physical liberty, the master interferes no more, in such cases, than you do with a hired servant. The work assigned is confessedly very light—scarcely one half of that performed by a white laborer with you. When that is performed, the slaves (to use an expression common with them) are "their own masters." And if you ever allow us the pleasure of seeing you at the South, you will find slaves tilling land for themselves; working as mechanics for themselves, and selling various articles of merchandise for themselves; and when you inquire of them some explanation, they will speak of their rights, and their property, with as clear a sense of what is due to them, and as much confidence, as they could if free; and tell you (to use another of their phrases) that they do all this "in their own time."

I hope, my dear brother, I have now shown that your ethical argument does not hold good. And I hope so, not only because it is most painful to me if I am compelled to differ from you on any subject, but because, if your view be correct, you will sooner make people infidels, than convince them that the Bible does not look with allowance on "as great a crime as can be conceived"—which is downright blasphemy. Let me recapitulate the views I have tried to express in this and the last letter.

(1.) A right to the service of a man without his contract or consent, conveys no additional rights but those proper and absolutely necessary to this original right. But it is not proper and necessary to this original right, that a human being be deprived of any right which is justly his, as an immortal, intelligent, moral, social, and fallen creature. Therefore, a right to the services of a man without his contract or consent, does not justify any wrong done to his mind, or soul, or domestic relations. Therefore your first assumption fails.

(2.) Slavery may exist without interfering with any of man's natural rights, except personal freedom. But to interfere with personal freedom is not necessarily a sin. Therefore slavery is not necessarily a sin. Therefore your second assumption fails.

These *sorites* appear to me almost self-evident, and to present the subject in its true light—a light too often darkened by a cloud of words about "making man a brute, and a mere piece of property." Such language is in itself absurd, for nothing but a miracle can effect these transformations. It is, also, the most sheer verbiage of shallow declamation. As well might it be said, that a child is a brute, and a mere piece of property, because his parent has a right to his services, and this right is a transferable one. The most nefarious code of laws ever perpetrated, recognized the slave as a sentient, moral, human being, at least, by holding him accountable for his actions. Nor are the views I have advanced at all affected by the fact that the children of the slaves are born to slavery. This is only saying that their position in society is determined by the accident of birth; which is equally true as to the position of the woman in this country, the commoner in England, and the serf in Russia. Slavery may or may not be hereditary; but this depends not on the parent's being a brute, or a mere piece of property, but on the political organization.

By far my greatest embarrassment in these letters has been, and is, about language by which to dispute your allegations, without seeming to overstep the modesty becoming me, or to depart from that affectionate deference I cherish towards you. After all, however, I am more familiar with the subject under discussion than my Northern brethren can be, and my position discloses to me the truth, which I will express in so many words by saying, *that slavery, absolute and unqualified slavery, is despotism.* Indeed, *despoth (despotes) is* the very Greek term used by the apostles for "master." But now it is conceded on all hands, that despotic power is not a sin, and may be "put forth" most beneficently "for good and not for evil." This the most vehement abolitionist admits. I have, however, much higher authority than any abolitionist. I have, in fact, Job's wish; mine adversary hath written a book—a book justly regarded as a classic—and he says, "A people may be so entirely surrendered to the influence of passion, and so feebly influenced by moral restraint, that a government which relied upon moral restraint could not exist for a day. In this case, a subordinate and inferior principle yet remains, the principle of fear; and the only resort is to a government of force, or a military despotism."[43] And what is all this but yielding the whole question? Let us not be imposed on by names, nor dazzled by magnificent titles. A despot is the absolute master of a whole nation of slaves, and has power of life and death. His authority, however, may be conscientiously retained, and instead of a cruel tyrant, he may be a splendid benefactor, whose name shall glitter on the pages of history. And I venture to say that if Mr. Birney had this authority, and "put it forth," (as I dare say that gentleman would) "for good and not for evil," he would not only be welcomed by the abolitionists to the eucharist, but be applauded to the skies. Why, then, must slavery be necessarily "a heinous sin?" Slavery, in its worst form, is only despotism. Even the Roman master was only a despot. At the South the phrase cannot be employed in its proper import, for the authority of the master is greatly restricted by law; and it is a capital offence in him to murder his slave. Yet, no matter how the Southern Christian "puts forth his power"—he may employ it "for good and not for evil," and be most just, and humane, and benevolent—it does not signify; he is a monster of wickedness, and his very power a great crime. On a small scale, slavery is as great an iniquity as can be conceived, and violates all the rights of man as man. But on a large scale it is quite a different thing. A throne, a sceptre, a strip of velvet sprinkled with diamonds, and clasped around the master's brows, exert a super-magical influence, and achieve a miracle

---

[43]Moral Science, page 397.

impossible even to Deity—that of altering the entire moral character of an action.

If the view I now press was taken of the subject, (and it is unquestionably the strongest view allowed by the Bible), I do not see why Christians might not concur in their wishes to improve and meliorate the condition of the slaves, though disagreeing as to the best mode. May not the most zealous abolitionist be satisfied with the concession that slavery, if not restrained by law, is despotism? And does not truth require of him the admission, in return, that at the South this despotism is (if I may so speak) not absolute, but mitigated and limited? And does not that charity which "hopeth all things and believeth all things [1 Corinthians 13:7]," demand of him the hope and belief, that a brother, whom he knows to be a Christian, is "putting forth his authority for good and not for evil," and doing what he conceives best for the Africans themselves? These are questions to which but one reply can be given. But if all this be so, how will men answer to God for that high-handed, arbitrary temper, which denounces, and cuts off from Christian fellowship, the whole South, because differing from some at the North in honest convictions? I would affectionately ask such brethren, whether, while promising liberty to the negro, they are not attempting towards the master the worst sort of tyranny, the most odious despotism—I mean spiritual tyranny, and despotism over the conscience?

There are a few of these brethren who do not hesitate to insinuate that we all see the sin, but cling to it through selfishness. To such we can only return "blessing for cursing." I, of course, cannot consent to argue with them, except to say, they ought not to excommunicate us for being slaveholders, but to pray for us as unconverted persons. There are others who are forever perplexing a great question with quirks and quibbles, regarding it as a matter of mere property, and saying, "If the original title were vicious, nothing can make the present title good." Such arguments are as little suited to your mind as to this topic, and therefore are not offered by you, and need only be glanced at by me. The Africans have been brought here. The manner in which any particular individuals were procured we know not; they, and those who enslaved them, have, almost all, long since stood before the Judge. I have in my first letter referred to this part of the subject. Here the black race are, nor have they any other home. If their importation was without their consent, it was equally without mine. And can there be a more unsophisticated impertinence, than to divert my mind from the great inquiry as to present duty before me, in order to examine into the original title? The right of a parent springs from the dependence of his child; and by dependence, by very necessity under the existing political organization, the slaves are placed in their present relation to me. As a mere legal subtlety, this sophistry, so frequently urged with an air of triumph at abolition meetings, would discredit a young attorney whose astuteness had been called into play by his first retainer. It is as if one should make a title to land in New York depend on the manner in which the land was obtained from the Indians; and by those Indians from their predecessors; and so on until its antediluvian soundness were ascertained. Or rather, as if, to establish the right of a reigning sovereign to the throne, it were required that he ascend to the origin of all government in the country, and prove that the existing organization was introduced without violence or injury to a single forefather of the land.

You must already have perceived that, speaking abstractly of slavery, I do not consider its perpetuation proper, even if it be possible. Nor let any one ask, why not perpetuate it if it be not a sin? The Bible informs us what man is; and, among such beings, irresponsible power is a trust too easily and too frequently abused. All must feel that, in this country, the subject is surrounded and encumbered with peculiar difficulties, inasmuch as the slaves are a distinct race. On this topic, however, I need not speak. My sole business now is with present duty. That duty is not the emancipation, but the instruction, moral and intellectual, of the slave; just as in a despotism, the duty is, not granting a free constitution, but improving the subjects. I do hope, then, that you may acquiesce in the sentiments above expressed, and not insist that slavery is necessarily, and amidst all circumstances, a sin. This you can do without the slightest compromise of truth, and with the best, hope of advancing our common object. We should thus, too, be reconciled, not only with each other, but with the Scriptures, and you be relieved from the laborious, up-hill, Sisyphus-task, of overcoming the word of God.

In all I have been writing, you see that I have kept strictly to the essentials of slavery, and it is inaccuracy here which occasions much of the dispute existing between the North and South. For example, how constantly do we find the abolition prints intolerant of calm reasoning on what they call *abstract slavery*, and exclaiming, 'let us have it as it is.' But how is that? Upon no two plantations is our servitude the same thing. In some instances there may be all the injustice and heartlessness you so well describe; while, in others, the definition of Paley requires no addition, but material retrenchment—for the slaves are not only watched over with guardian kindness and affection, but prefer to remain with their masters, so that it cannot be said they serve him without their contract or consent.[44]

It will be replied, that we must take slavery as it is embodied in the Southern laws; and this, in fact, is the great and fruitful source of misconception. What I am writing about is slavery, but let no one suppose that I am defending all the slave laws. The statutes of a government for the regulation of slaves may be most oppressive and wicked; this, however, does not prove slavery a sin, any more than harsh and cruel enactments towards apprentices, prove apprenticeship a sin; or than a law giving parents the power, or requiring them, to abuse their children, would prove that it is criminal to have children. The distinction here is certainly palpable, and yet, it appears to me, your entire argument—though put abstractly against slavery—was really framed against the slave laws, and applies only to them. What my relation as master, or parent, gives me a right to do, is one thing; what the law may permit, or even enjoin, is another. The Roman law allowed masters to kill their slaves, and throw them into their ponds to feed fish;

---

[44]In an early letter, copied by the *Reflector*, I referred to, the case of the Rt. Rev. Dr. M——, of Virginia, who, after preparing a family of slaves to provide for themselves, sent them to Pennsylvania. But they soon implored him to receive them back. [Fuller may be referring to the Rt. Rev. Dr. James Madison. See *Annals of the American Pulpit*, vol. 5 (New York: Robert Carter & Brothers, 1859) 318–23.]

does it therefore follow that a Christian master had a right to do this? Human laws have permitted kings to murder their subjects at will, and with the most cruel torments; does it follow that a king has a right to do this, or that the exercise of regal authority is necessarily a crime? It surely cannot be requisite for me to dwell on this point. Yet it is because good men among the abolitionists shut their eyes to the difference between a domestic or social relation, and the enactments concerning it, that they persist in denouncing slavery as a sin.

In reference to the laws of South Carolina I am not called to express myself in this discussion. Suffice it to say, that most of them are virtually repealed by universal practice. The law, for example, forbidding slaves to assemble without the presence of so many white persons, is a dead letter, whenever the meeting is for religious purposes. Missionaries are everywhere traversing the land, and preaching the gospel to multitudes of slaves without molestation. The Beaufort church employs six or seven brethren constantly in this good work; and here, in the country, I walk, every Sabbath, and occasionally in the week, about a mile, and violate this statute most industriously.

I might make the same remark of many other statutes. Most of them are only permissive, and the liberty granted should of course be controlled, or overruled, by what is just and equal. And those which prohibit a discharge of the master's duty are often notoriously inoperative. The most important law is that forbidding slaves being taught to read; yet how many are taught! And this act would, long since, have been expunged, but for the infatuated intermeddling of fanaticism. It is but a year or two since, at the request of the President of the State Agricultural Society, I wrote a letter, to be read before that body, on the religious instruction of our negroes; and, in that communication, I urged the abrogation of this law. The President, however, a gentleman of age, experience, and exalted humanity, desired permission to strike out that clause. And when I had considered his reasons, and seen the character of the incendiary publications with which the South had just before been deluged—works evidently appealing to the worst passions of the slave—was not surprised that the best and most benevolent individuals should regard the provision as necessary, and wise, and even kind. I had, of course; to yield; and this is only one of the instances in which those who are the true friends of the slave, and whose position enables them to plead his cause, have found themselves defeated by the lamentable and cruel system of vituperation and agitation recklessly persisted in at the North. Of these defeats upon whom does the heaviest guilt rest?

Nor should good men among the abolitionists complain, if, in rebuking the wicked and mischievous measures of the party, no exceptions are made; for it is these very men who lend influence to the abolition associations. In its proper import, the anti-slavery party comprehends nineteen-twentieths of the people of the United States. The abolitionists, however, are a band by themselves. With them the rudimental, initiating article is, that slaveholders are heinous culprits, and as such to be universally treated. This bitter, persecuting creed is the great bond of union, and faith in it a cosmetic for most serious blemishes. If a man subscribe to this fierce tenet, he is a brother, and admitted to the pulpit and communion table, however destitute of the meek and holy spirit of Christ. But no matter what the character of one who is by birth placed in the painfully responsible situation of a slaveholder, the damnatory clause does not suffer him to be spared. He is to be anathematized, and the church armed with her most awful sentences against him. Nay, he is deemed unfit to be a missionary to his own slaves; or even to take the lowest place among those who wish to advance the Redeemer's cause upon earth. Such is the malignant spirit of the party—a spirit never engendered by truth, and over which charity can only weep—and all who belong to that party are responsible for the mischief it does. They all sow the wind, and the whirlwind is only the harvest they have reaped.

I think, my dear brother, it will appear to yourself, on a review of our letters thus far, that, in order to justify your condemnation of slavery, as always a crime, you have constantly found it necessary to surcharge it with merely imaginary, or at worst, accidental evils; and to blacken it as much as possible. Fire, sword, gunpowder, and the wanton violation of all human rights, are put in requisition; whereas, you were bound to confine yourself to the strict essentials, and prove them sinful. On the contrary, while my proposition required me only to speak of the most benignant form and origin of the institution, I have purposely adopted the definition of Paley, an antagonist, to every part of which I might object. He includes in slavery an "obligation to labor," and this "without the slave's contract or consent." But slavery is only bondage; and this may be voluntary, and by one's own contract;[45] and there may be no obligation whatever to labor, since a man who should sell himself to another on condition that he be allowed to sleep out his life, would be in all respects a slave. I avoid, however, all nice distinctions, that I may meet the subject practically.

Having described the condition of a slave, I ought now to advert to the obligations of the master; but I have not space, nor is it requisite. Let me only say, (and with the most solemn earnestness, for God forbid I should ever utter a word which may perpetuate cruelty and sin,) that the right of the master not only does not give him any such license of wholesale oppression and wrong as you suppose, but really places him under the deepest corresponding obligations to promote the interest, temporal and eternal, of his slaves. And though we have all been "verily guilty concerning our brethren" who are dependent on us, yet I trust the South is becoming every day more alive to its responsibility. Already much has been effected; and, as a class, I believe our slaves to be now better compensated, and, in moral, intellectual, and religious condition, superior to most operatives in Europe. From parliamentary reports, it appears that in Ireland three millions and a half of people live in mud

---

[45]Such was the slavery mentioned in Genesis, when the Egyptians said to Joseph, "Wherefore shall we die of famine? Buy us and our land for bread. And Joseph said unto the people, Behold, I have bought you and your land for Pharaoh. And they said, Thou hast saved our lives [Genesis 47:23, 25]." It is not uncommon in this State for slaves to be conveyed absolutely, and at their own request, to some friend who will allow them to work for themselves. I am thus legatee of several. Here the power is legally given, and the bequest absolute, and the slavery really exists; but it is, of course, overruled by the wish of the testators. And just so in all cases the power is, with "believing masters," controlled by a sense of duty to the servant, and accountability to God, and love to both.

hovels, having one room, and without chimney or window. In England and Wales there are three millions of people without any pastoral provision. In London itself the statistics of misery and vice are appalling. On one occasion, said a speaker in Exeter Hall, four families occupied one small room, each hiring a corner; and in one of these corners there was a corpse lately dead, and four men using it as a table to play cards upon. And if this be so in Great Britain, need I speak of Spain and Russia, or attest what I myself have seen of ignorance and superstition and degradation in Italy? We are far, however, from having acquitted ourselves of our duty; and I do not wish to palliate, much less defend by recrimination, the unfaithfulness of the South to the sacred trust imposed upon us. I therefore dismiss this part of the subject without enlarging, as I easily might.

Let me finish this letter; and I do it by repeating the hope that my brethren at the North will not continue to confound slavery with its concomitants, and denounce it as necessarily a heinous crime in the sight of God. This assertion is not true. It is truth mixed up with error, and, like all half truths, is more pernicious than pure falsehood. At the South such a charge is felt to be unjust, and serves only to exasperate. At the North it foments a bitter and unrelenting spirit of proscription. It does not aid, but injure, the cause of the slave; for it must require, not his improvement, but his immediate emancipation, which you do not advise. It will rend apart those in this country who ought to be united, and on whose union, I am persuaded, the integrity of our national existence depends. It outrages the convictions of the mass of the wise and good in every land. It is contradicted by the venerable testimony of every Christian church for ages. And, what is infinitely worse than all, it arrays those who adopt it in irreconcilable conflict with the Bible—a conflict hopeless indeed, and serving only to vindicate the impregnable stability of the truth, but yet a conflict greatly to be deplored.

Most affectionately, dear brother,

Yours,

R. Fuller.

*Letter IV*[46]

## *To the Rev. Francis Wayland, D.D.*

My Dear Brother,

Up to this point I have considered the subject before us as a pure question of moral and political science, and attempted to show that, like other social organizations, slavery is not necessarily a crime; and that even the power of the Roman master, though perfectly despotic, was not in itself a sin. To establish this was the more important, because good men are justly shocked, when they understand slavery to be a heinous sin, and find people attempting to shelter themselves under the sanction of the Bible. Perish the thought! they exclaim, and I cordially join them. To charge this impiety upon Christians at the South, however, is to do them great injustice. Such an accusation takes for granted the very thing we deny. We believe that all just moral institutes are only an expansion of those golden maxims, "Whatsoever ye would that men should do unto you, do ye also to them [Matthew 7:12];" and, "Thou shalt love thy neighbor as thyself [Matthew 19:19b]." We believe these precepts apply to masters and servants, just as to masters and apprentices, or parents and children, or kings and subjects. We believe that they reach every abuse of slavery; and condemn all intellectual, moral, and domestic injustice. But we do not believe that they make the relation itself sinful, or require, as they must do if it be a crime, its prompt dissolution. Such disruption might, and in some cases would, subvert society itself, and be real charity neither to the masters nor the slaves.

It will not do, then, for you to conduct the cause as if we had been proved guilty, and were put on our defence. This is the ground always taken at the North, and because Southern Christians reply with the Bible in their hands, they are misunderstood. Politically, and ethically, I have proved that despotism itself is not necessarily a sin. In appealing to the word of God, we are not required to prove a negative, and justify ourselves; but you, to make out your case, and prove us guilty. "Sin is a

---

[46*Christian Reflector* 13/7 (13 February 1845): 26.]

transgression of the law [1 John 3:4b]," and you are bound to show the law we transgress. All will acknowledge this to be the fair position of the accuser and accused. Whereas I submit to you, that your Bible argument entirely overlooks our forensic rights, and is an examination of the question whether the Bible justifies slavery. Suppose the Bible does not justify it; still; unless condemned by the Bible, slavery may remain among things indifferent, and be classed with that large number of actions whose moral character depends on the peculiar circumstances of each case. Nor am I surprised that those who undertake your arduous office always pursue this line of reasoning, since the assertion that slavery is itself and always a sin, jars harshly with what appears to plain men as the unequivocal teaching of the Scriptures; and, therefore, it is felt, in the outset, that much explanation and ingenuity are indispensable; otherwise, not only must the charge fail, but the prosecutors themselves incur a serious impeachment.

The assertion just mentioned as to the inherent guilt of slavery, is the distinctive article with modern abolitionists. But after studying the subject in all its bearings, they have clearly perceived, that if the Hebrew and Greek terms rendered servant in our Bibles really signify slave, there is an end either of their dogma or of submission to the Scriptures. Hence, after trying in vain the whole apparatus of exegetical torture, they have—with, I believe, much unanimity—set all philology and history at defiance, and resolutely deny that such is the import of those words. When Paul says, "We are all baptized into one body, whether we be Jews or Gentiles, whether we be bond or free [Galatians 3:28]," the terms "Jew" and "Gentile" mean something; but "bond" and "free" imply no distinction at all! And to get rid of the Old Testament, various interpretations have been contrived, of which the latest is quite curious. While moving earth and heaven about the thraldom of the negro, the abolitionists refuse to the white man even liberty of speech, and wish to erect an inquisition over the mind. A very pious Presbyterian pastor has lately been arraigned by them, not for holding slaves, but for daring even to utter his honest convictions on the subject of slavery. And at that trial it was declared (if the newspapers did no injustice to the orators) that

slavery was not known in Abraham's day except among the heathen; that
the patriarch was a prince, and the persons bought with his money were
subjects, whom he purchased to improve their condition. So that, after
all, the objection is entirely to the *name*, and will at once be withdrawn if
Southern masters only call themselves princes, and their slaves
subjects—for assuredly, if we ourselves had purchased the African
captives from their native masters, we might plead that their condition
has been immeasurably improved.

You do but give vent to the pious indignation of a candid heart,
when, speaking of such escapes from the dilemma, you say, "I wonder
that any one should have the hardihood to deny so plain a matter of
record. I should almost as soon deny the delivery of the ten
commandments to Moses." Yet these are good men, nor is their perfect
sincerity to be questioned. The truth is, that when an opinion has been
expressed, and pride of intellect and consistency thus enlisted for its
support, no one can say to what lengths he may be carried by its blinding
influence; and our opinions are not unfrequently defended with an
obstinacy exactly proportioned to the precipitation with which they were
adopted.

How it seems to others I know not, but my mind one of the most
lamentable effects of modern ultraism is the collision it is producing
between Christians, and that volume to which all Christians profess to
bow in reverence. God has revealed his whole will. The Scriptures are
"able to make us wise unto salvation [2 Timothy 3:15b]," and these
Scriptures have been purposely written by plain men, so that plain men
may understand them. If we "wrest these Scriptures," it is "to our own
destruction;" and most righteously, for what guilt half so aggravated and
heaven-daring? Nevertheless it is becoming quite common in these days,
for the authorized expounders of eternal truth to treat that truth as a
thing which must pliantly adjust itself to any extravagance their
enthusiasm may take up. I every day more and more admire and adore
the fulness of the Bible; and I know that there is no form of human
suffering to which it is not an antidote. But the Bible operates too slowly
for our reformers. With them, as that brilliant ornament of American

literature, Dr. Channing, remarked, "whatever be the evil opposed, it is exaggerated as if no other evil existed, and no guilt could be compared with that of countenancing it."[47] Every disease they undertake, is to their fiery zeal and disordered imaginations a violent one, and demands a violent remedy. The gospel, however, works always as a corrective, and its precepts forbid violence; those precepts must therefore be frittered away, or distorted; or if this cannot be done, there is still one course,—it is boldly to deny that the original Hebrew and Greek warrant the sense which the translation conveys. And as their audiences are generally, according to the testimony of Dr. Channing himself, "old and young, pupils from schools, females hardly arrived at years of discretion, the ignorant, the excitable, and the impetuous," this assertion is received with a credulity only surpassed by the "hardihood" with which it was advanced. By this unhappy intemperance, how much has not the temperance cause suffered! Nothing could satisfy the unbridled vehemence of the reformers, but such distortions of the word of God as would make all use of wine, even at the Lord's supper, a crime; and the consequence has been unavoidable; the enemies of that great cause have been furnished with formidable weapons against it. The true interests of the slave have been retarded in the same way, and by the same reactions. And so it will be in every cause, whenever excessive zeal runs counter to the manifest instructions of the holy oracles.

Discarding and rebuking the violent misconstruction to which I have alluded, you still deny that slavery can be vindicated out of the Bible. I have already remarked on the utter irregularity of requiring me to take up this issue, when you ought from the Bible to make out your charge that slavery is a crime. But I pass this, and, waiving my clear logical rights, undertake to prove the negative, and to show that the Bible does, most explicitly, both by precept and example, bear me out in my assertion (the only assertion I ever made) that slavery is not necessarily, and always, and amidst all circumstances, a sin. This is the position to be established, and the entire reasoning (reasoning, which, if

---

[47] William Ellery Channing, "Slavery," in *The Works of William Ellery Channing* (Boston: American Unitarian Association, 1892) 732.]

the premises be true, really seems to me to commend itself at once to every man's conscience) is this, WHAT GOD SANCTIONED IN THE OLD TESTAMENT, AND PERMITTED IN THE NEW, CANNOT BE SIN.

In this proposition I assume that both Testaments constitute one entire canon, and that they furnish a complete rule of faith and practice. "All Scripture is given by inspiration of God, and is profitable for doctrine, for reproof, for correction, for instruction in righteousness, that the man of God maybe perfect, thoroughly furnished unto all good works [2 Timothy 3:16]." If, then, a work be good, we are thoroughly instructed in the Bible as to it; and have there reproof and correction, at once convincing us of any work which is evil. So complete and plain, too, are the sacred institutes, that God makes it the duty of each man, "though Paul or an angel preach," to compare his doctrine with the record, and to say, "let him be accursed if he preach any other gospel [Galatians 1:8]." Now there was a time when Roman Catholics alone refused to receive the Bible as the perfect rule of faith; when Protestants read it on their knees with Bunyan; and, as soon as its revealments were discovered, exclaimed, with Whitefield, in the letter before quoted, "we can have no doubt;" and trembled at that declaration, "If any man shall add unto these things, God shall add unto him the plagues that are written in this book: and if any man shall take away from the words of the book of this prophecy, God shall take away his part out of the book of life [Revelation 22:18]." Such a time, however, is fast getting to be no more. In Germany, even men like Neander,[48] while they admit the futility of pleading apostolic authority for some time honored, hereditary sanctities, yet adhere to them, on the ground (to use the ingenious phraseology of the present Bishop of Norwich, in his plan for so subscribing the articles of the Church of England, as to permit every body to take the oath) that the Scriptures have "an *expansion of sense and meaning.*" In this country it is with profound grief that I see the same spirit at work, although in a more insidious shape. The present Bishop of

---

[48August Neander (1789–1850) was a noted nineteenth-century German theologian and church historian.]

London is shocked at the iniquity of his brother of Norwich, and angrily exclaims, "What is this expansion?" "expansion with a vengeance!" and contends only for *a "prudent and accommodating elasticity!"* And it is so in this country with regard to interpreting the Word of God. The Bible must have (not the German "expansion"—O no!—that is too bad, and "with a vengeance"—but) a "prudent and accommodating elasticity," so as to suit itself to the mature philosophy which has outgrown the childish ignorance and simplicity of the apostles. The truth, as the primitive churches had it, was only inchoate. It was the germinal principle, which, in subsequent ages, and under the genial influence of reformers, should expand and ripen. Already do we find it the motto of all abolition harangues, and prospectuses, and papers, that "the times of this ignorance" (all previous times) "God winked at; but now commandeth" (by them of course) "all men, everywhere to repent." And I shall be forgiven for expressing my undissembled apprehensions lest your deservedly great reputation should even seem to countenance this dangerous tendency of fanaticism. You say—"Suppose, then, that slavery were permitted in the New Testament, and at the same time these truths at variance with it are inculcated, it would be evident that the permission must yield to the principle." Now, I submit to you, that this supposition not only makes the Bible contradict itself, but opens the door to a flood of error. The "permission" is truth teaching by apostolic example. It is the contemporaneous, infallible exposition of the doctrines promulgated, and it is plain. The "principle" is to be known only by deduction and argument, in which men will differ. And what would be the inevitable consequence, if your system prevailed? Why, every innovator would contend that he had just discovered "the true principle." *C'est moi*, would be the *cry*; and enthusiasts, flaming and furious—hierophants, chafing and rampant, would rave, recite, and madden round the land, all armed with their "principles," to which the clear permission of God must yield; and each imitating one of the early fathers, who, whenever hard-pressed by an antagonist, was accustomed to cut the debate short by declaring that God had lately vouchsafed him a fresh revelation.

Nor is your theory defended by referring to polygamy in the Old Testament. We shall presently see if that case does not make conclusively against you. It applies not, however, here, since your rule of interpretation is for the whole Bible. That I may not do you injustice, I will quote your illustration: "You may give your child, if he were approaching to years of discretion, permission to do an act, while you teach him principles which forbid it, for the sake of teaching, him to be governed by principles rather than by any direct enactment." Now, in all kindness, would this be parental fidelity? and is it not a shrewd presumption against a cause that it requires such an illustration? A father sees around him children who depend wholly on his instructions for the knowledge of what is right. He sees them growing up in the commission of a sin; living in this sin; and dying in this sin. Yet he not only does not "restrain them," (*which* was the guilt of Eli,) but (unlike Eli) he does not even remonstrate—nay, breathes not a word of direct disapprobation, but (as if God does not require children to obey their parents) satisfies himself with "teaching them principles which forbid" the sin;—thus leaving them to practise the sin constantly under his own eye, and with express permission. "In such a case you would expect him to obey the principle, and not avail himself of the permission." Not I. I should expect the children to reason thus: "Whatever our father's general principles and reasonings mean, they do not mean that this conduct is wrong, otherwise he would tell us so"—and if I continued in this faithlessness until death, I should expect my family to be confirmed in the sin by my wanton delinquency. And, now, to think that the parent of this illustration is, in the argument, the Holy God; and that this kindest and tenderest of fathers, *knowing sin to be in itself present and eternal misery*, is supposed to see his poor creatures utterly blind and corrupt, and to hear their earnest supplications, "What we know not, teach thou us;" "Lead us, O God, by thy truth, and make thy paths plain before our feet;" and yet to give a revelation, not only not forbidding, but permitting as great a sin as can be conceived—my dear brother, I dare not proceed. I repeat it, the cause may in advance be pronounced wrong which requires such an illustration.

There is another expression (over and over I beg your forgiveness) which I must notice, —it is this. "If the religion of Christ allows us to take such a license from such precepts as these, the New Testament would be the greatest curse that ever was inflicted on our race." This is not the place to show that your reasoning here proceeds on a confusion of slavery with the Roman slavelaws; what I am saying is, that such sentences I always read with sorrow. Not but that in a dispute with an infidel the purity of the Bible is an overwhelming argument. The sermon on the mount, if all the circumstances be considered, will be regarded, by any profound thinker, as a greater miracle than the raising of Lazarus. But when the Scriptures have been received as a revelation, and the inquiry is about their meaning, how does it sound to affirm authoritatively as to what they ought to teach; and to designate them a great curse if they teach otherwise? A word, however, is enough as to this. I am sure you abhor as sincerely as any man the idea that "dust and ashes," folly, and ignorance, and guilt, should erect a tribunal, and summon the High and Holy One to the bar of our puny reason, and sit in judgment upon his wisdom, and justice, and goodness. I now take up the proposition advanced, and the first thing I am to prove is, that God did sanction slavery in the Old Testament; and here can any prolonged examination be required? First, you admit that the patriarchs, whose piety is held up in the Bible for our admiration, were masters of slaves. Of all these holy men, Abraham was the most eminent. He was "the friend of God," and walked with God in the closest and most endearing intercourse; nor can any thing be more exquisitely touching than those words, "Shall I hide from Abraham that thing which I do [Genesis 18:17]?" It is the language of a friend, who feels that concealment would wrong the confidential intimacy existing. The love of this venerable servant of God in his promptness to immolate his son, has been the theme of apostles and preachers for ages; and such was his faith, that all who believe are called "the children of faithful Abraham [Galatians 3:7, 9]." This Abraham, you admit, held slaves. Who is surprised that Whitefield, with this single fact before him, could not believe slavery to be a sin? Yet if your definition of slavery be correct, holy Abraham lived all his life in the commission of one of the most aggravated crimes against God and man which, can be conceived. His life was spent in outraging the rights of hundreds of human beings, as moral, intellectual, immortal, fallen creatures; and in violating their relations as parents and children and husbands and wives. And God not only connived at this appalling iniquity, but, in the covenant of circumcision made with Abraham, expressly mentions it, and confirms the patriarch in it; speaking of those "bought with his money," and requiring him to circumcise them. Why, at the very first blush, every Christian will cry out against this statement. To this, however, you must come, or yield your position; and this is only the first utterly incredible and monstrous corollary involved in the assertion that slavery is essentially and always "a sin of appalling magnitude."

The natural descendants of Abraham were holders of slaves, and God took them into special relation to himself. "He made known his ways unto Moses, his acts unto the children of Israel [Psalm 103:7];" and he instituted regulations for their government, into which he expressly incorporated a permission to buy and hold slaves. These institutes not only recognise slavery as lawful, but contain very minute directions. It is not necessary for me to argue this point, as it is conceded by you. Slaves were held by the priests. "A sojourner of a priest, or an hired servant, shall not eat of the holy thing. But if the priest buy any soul with his money, he shall eat of it, and he that is born in his house, they shall eat of it [Leviticus 22:10–11]." They might be bought of the Canaanites around, or of strangers living among the Hebrews. "Both thy bondmen, and thy bondmaids, which thou shalt have, shall be of the heathen that are round about you; of them shall ye buy bondmen and bondmaids. Moreover, of the children of the strangers that do sojourn among you, of them shall ye buy, and of their families that are with you, which they begat in your land; and they shall be your possession [Leviticus 25:45]." They were regarded as property, and were called "money," "possession:" "If a man smite his servant or his maid, with a rod, and he die under his hand; he shall be surely punished. Notwithstanding, if he continue a day or two, he shall not be punished: for he is his money [Exodus

21:20–21]." They might be sold. This is implied in the term "money;" but it is plainly taken, for granted: "Thou shalt not make merchandise of her, because thou hast humbled her [Deuteronomy 21:14]." See also Exodus 21:7–8. "And if a man sell his daughter to be, a maid-servant, she shall not go out as the menservants do. If she please not her master, who hath betrothed her to himself, then shall he let her be redeemed: to sell her to a strange nation he shall have no power, seeing he hath dealt deceitfully with her." The slavery thus expressly sanctioned was hereditary and perpetual: "Ye shall take them as an inheritance for your children after you, to inherit them for a possession. They shall be your bondmen forever [Levitivus 25:45]." Lastly, Hebrews, if bought, were to be treated, not as slaves, but as hired servants, and to go free at the year of jubilee. "If thy brother that dwelleth by thee be waxen poor, and be sold unto thee, thou shalt not compel him to serve as a bondservant; but as an hired servant and as a sojourner shall he be with thee, and shall serve thee unto the year of jubilee: and then shall he depart from thee, both he and his children with him, and shall return unto his own family, and unto the possession of his father shall he return [Leviticus 25:29]." If during the Hebrew's time of service he married a slave, and had children, the wife and children were not set at liberty with him. If he consented, he might become a slave for life: "If thou buy a Hebrew servant, six years shall he serve: and in the seventh he shall go out free for nothing. If he came in by himself, he shall go out by himself: if he were married, then his wife shall go out with him. If his master have given him a wife, and she have borne him sons or daughters, the wife and her children shall be her master's, and he shall go out by himself. And if the servant shall plainly say, I love my master, my wife, and my children; I will not go out free: Then his master shall bring him unto the judges: he shall also bring him to the door, or unto the door-post; and his master shall bore his ear through with an awl; and he shall serve him forever [Exodus 21:2–6]."

Such are some parts of the Mosaic institution. Let me add, also, that the decalogue twice recognises slavery, and forbids one Israelite to covet the man-servant or maid-servant of another. And, now, how does all this appear if your assumption be for a moment tenable, that slavery is as great a crime as can be committed? Suppose these regulations had thus sanctioned piracy, or idolatry, would they ever have commanded the faith of the world as divine? How conclusive this that slavery is not among crimes in the estimation of mankind, and according to the immutable and eternal principles of morality!

In struggling with such difficulties as these, I expected from you all that man could do, and I have not been disappointed. The apostles, however, declared they "could do nothing against the truth," and with the portions of the record already before us, I do conceive, that either proper reverence for the Bible, or your proposition, must be abandoned. Nor do I perceive that your explanations bring your doctrine at all more within the range of probability. I believe your reasonings may be summed up thus:

*Plea first.*—"God did not see fit to reveal his will on this subject, nor indeed on many others, to the ancient Hebrews. He made known to them just as much of his moral law as he chose. He has seen fit to enlighten our race progressively, and he withheld from them his will as to slavery."

*Answer.*—It is true God has unfolded gradually his plans and purposes; but there is a great difference between this, and his making a revelation expressly authorizing any thing. He did not withhold from the Jews his will concerning slavery, but both by precept and example sanctioned it. The Jews had the ten commandments, which are an abridgment of the whole moral law; and even in this slavery is recognised; God may and does conceal much; but he cannot deny himself; he is of purer eyes than to behold evil, and "cannot look on iniquity [Habakkuk 1:13]," much less expressly sanction it.

*Plea second*—The permission granted to the Jews was peculiar. God had authorized them to destroy the Canaanites; their slaves were to be only of these Canaanites thus devoted to destruction; and the authority to hold slaves was a part of this grant; but it is not true that what God sanctioned among the Hebrews, he sanctions for all men and at all times.

*Answer*—It has never been pretended that any man can claim under a grant but those to whom the grant was made; nor was any one ever so silly as to affirm that because Jehovah authorized the Jews to hold the Canaanites as slaves, therefore we might enslave the Canaanites. But it is affirmed that the moral character of actions is immutable; that sin is always "the abominable thing which God hates;" that if slavery be essentially and necessarily a sin, it was a sin among the Hebrews; and that it is impiety to say that God, at any time, or in any place, gave his express sanction to sin. If the character and will of God, and what he approves, and permits, and condemns, are not illustrated by his dealings with individuals and nations, then, almost the whole of both Testaments is useless now. The ten commandments were delivered to the Hebrews; the addresses of Christ were to his audiences; and the instructions of the epistles were to particular churches. This is the answer.

Besides, there is inaccuracy in your premises. You say, "This grant was made to one people only, the Hebrews. It had respect to one people, and to one people only, the Canaanites." Not so. "Strangers sojourning among the Hebrews," might be held in bondage as well, as the heathen around; and Hebrews might, in your own words, "be held in slavery for six years;" and they might, by their consent, become slaves for life. Be it remembered, too, that long before this, the patriarchs held slaves, and not under any grant. "Abimelech took sheep, and oxen, and men-servants, and maid-servants, and gave them unto Abraham [Genesis 20:14]." Pharaoh, too, enriched him with "sheep, and oxen, and he-asses, and men-servants, and maid-servants [Genesis 12:16]." Permit me also to say, that M. Henry not only does not agree with you as to the right of enslaving being a part of the right to destroy the Canaanites, but thinks that slaves were not to be bought from the seven nations doomed to destruction. "They might purchase bondmen of the heathen nations round about them, or of those strangers that sojourned among them, *(except of the seven nations to be destroyed,)* and might claim a dominion over them, and entail them on their families, as an inheritance, for the year of jubilee should give no discharge to them."[49] I pass this, however.

---

[49] Matthew Henry, *The Third Book of Moses, Called Leviticus,* in *Matthew Henry's Commentary on the Whole Bible*, vol. 1 (1721; reprint, Peabody MA: Hendrickson, 1991) 432.]

My answer, as above, may be thus given in the syllogistic form which your letter invites:

(1.) Whatever the holy God has expressly sanctioned among any people cannot be in itself a sin.

(2.) God did expressly sanction slavery among the Hebrews.

(3.) Therefore slavery cannot be in itself a sin.

*Plea third.*—The Mosaic regulations were very different from the laws of the Southern States respecting slavery. "Every one must perceive the unreasonableness of pleading the Jewish laws as authority for an institution so entirely dissimilar, and so forgetful of the limitations by which the practice was originally guarded."

*Answer*—This whole plea is founded on that confusion of slavery with the Southern slave–laws which I have so often mentioned, and which is so glaring. A very good argument it would be with our legislatures to amend our laws, and I wish you would urge it there. On the present issue it is wholly out of place.

*Plea fourth.*—If God sanctioned slavery among the Jews, he also commanded them to "destroy the Canaanites;" and he commanded Saul to destroy the Amalekites. Were these commands to all men and at all times?

*Answer*—Nobody is capable of drawing such an absurd inference. But these commands do prove that it is not always, and amid all circumstances, a sin to take human life. And just so the sanction of slavery proves that it is not always and amidst all circumstances a sin to hold slaves.

*Plea fifth.*—But God did in the Old Testament permit and regulate sin. He did permit and regulate polygamy and divorce, which are sinful, and so pronounced by the Saviour, in Matthew 19:3, 9.

*Answer*—(1) Slavery is declared by you to be in itself, and essentially, a sin, a violation of the eternal and unchangeable principles of right and wrong, or what is called, "*malum in se.*" Neither polygamy nor divorce is in this class of actions. Each is only what is termed "*malum prohibitum.*" They do not conflict with the immutable principles of right and wrong, but only with the relations designed at first by God between the sexes.[50] God might, then, without any impeachment of his character, permit them; and such subsequent permission would overrule the original prohibition, which cannot be done in case of an act which is *"malum in se."*

(2) But, in truth, the whole force of this plea recoils fatally against the proposition asserted by you in this argument, since polygamy and divorce were condemned and abolished by the New Testament. Jesus and his apostles saw these and slavery existing together, and permitted by the Mosaic law. It will be conceded that, if your affirmation be correct, there was no comparison between the heinousness of the practices. Polygamy and divorce are at once and forever condemned and forbidden; but not a syllable is breathed against slavery. I confess this single view of the matter brings with it a conviction, which to me is overwhelming, that slavery is not, in itself, a sin, So great a hardship was it esteemed by the Jews not to be allowed the right of divorce, that, when Jesus restricted it to cases of adultery, the disciples said, "It were good then not to marry [Matthew 19:10]." Yet this privilege, so valued, and granted by Moses, is not spared for a moment; while slavery is not only not forbidden, but, as we shall see in the next letter, permitted still both by precept and example. Can any ingenuity evade, or any power of argument rebut, or any candid mind deny, the consequence which follows irresistibly from this fact in the history of Christ and his apostles?

Very affectionately, my dear brother,
Yours in the Lord,
R. Fuller

---

[50]"From the beginning it was not so" [Matthew 19:8).]

*Letter V[51]*

## To the Rev. Francis Wayland, D.D.

My Dear Brother,

"If slavery be a sin at all," you say, "it is a sin of appalling magnitude." I have attempted to analyze slavery, and to show that your entire definition of it is incorrect, and involves doctrines revolting to all our Christian feelings, and injurious to God, if the Old Testament be received as a revelation. I have also considered your plea, which is, that God did not see fit to reveal the true character of slavery under the patriarchal and Mosaic dispensations. We come now to the new dispensation, where, of course, if slavery be "a sin of appalling magnitude," we shall find it explicitly condemned; and the more explicitly, because the Holy One of Israel having, (according to your supposition,) both by his conduct to the patriarchs and his express precept to the Hebrews, permitted this great wickedness, every attribute of his character required now a most distinct and unequivocal reprobation. This, at least, you will concede. And you will also admit that, in deciding on the import of apostolic precept and practice, are to construe the actions and language of the apostles as they would naturally be construed by the persons who witnessed those actions, and to whom that language was addressed. Nothing can be more utterly sophistical than the idea that we have any light, as to matters of pure revelation, which the first Christians had not. That the world has made prodigious progress in all the arts and sciences, during the last three or four centuries, we know; and we know, too, that libraries on libraries have been written to elucidate the Scriptures. But what advantage do we derive from all this, in our inquiries respecting the teachings of the Bible? Here the book is just as the primitive disciples had it, and not an invention nor discovery has added to it a single letter. And then, as to the volumes of commentaries and expositions, why, they have served really to perplex the truth. The first believers found every precept plain and

[51*Christian Reflector* 13/8 (20 February 1845): 30.]

determined, while with us, the accumulation of learned rubbish has made it difficult to discover the simplest matters. Each year the press groans, and the pulpit resounds, with fresh controversies and disquisitions, all darkening God's counsel, casting doubt on the plainest things, causing that word whose "entrance giveth understanding" to be received through discoloring and distorting mediums, and enveloping in hopeless obscurity that gospel which to the meek-minded Christian is so full of light—such an unerring guide to his feet, and prompt casuist as to every duty. I recollect here the words of a Persian traveller writing from France to his friend at home:—"Father" said I to the librarian, "what are these huge volumes which fill the whole side of the library?" "These," said he, "are the interpreters of the Scriptures." "There is a prodigious number of them," replied I; "the Scriptures must have been very dark formerly, and must be very clear at present. Do there remain still any doubts? Are there now any points contested?" "Are there?" answered he with surprise, "are there? There are almost as many as there are lines." "You astonish me," said I "what, then, have all these authors been doing?" "These authors," returned he, "never searched the Scriptures for what ought to be believed, but for what they did believe themselves." But I have been carried away from the question before us: I return to it, and inquire whether under the new dispensation slavery was permitted.

Now in support of the affirmative of this question we have, I think, argument, inference, proof, and demonstration; all which I shall content myself with just indicating, as I can aim in these papers only at making myself fully comprehended.

(1) I say, then, we have argument. And by this I mean that, even if the New Testament had not alluded to slavery at all, I should be sustained in denying your proposition. In the days of the Saviour and the apostles, this institution existed everywhere. And among one people, and that the very people to whom the gospel was first addressed, it had been sanctioned by Jehovah himself. All the proudest and most hallowed associations of a Hebrew—all his devout meditations upon the simple beauty of patriarchal piety—and all the soul-stirring memories of the august era, when Israel's God had been Israel's immediate lawgiver, and

had marshalled her hosts for the battle, spreading over them that terrible banner of fire and cloud—all recognised this institution as most ancient, and resting upon authority most venerable and sacred. And what I say is this—that a clear and conclusive declaration of Jehovah's will would have been given, if slavery be an awful sin. Every conception of the character of God which nature and revelation inspire, at once proclaims this. Otherwise there is *a suppressio veri*, a suppression of the truth; and this, too, in a case where the very thought of such conduct must shock us. It was not by any impalpable "spirit" and concealed "principles" of revelation, that slavery had been countenanced, but by express precepts. And that God should allow slavery still to exist, and never breathe a hint as to the former permission having ratified what was criminal, this is what I dare not believe, and scarcely dare utter. It is to assert that Jehovah first, by his conduct and express enactment, confirmed his chosen people in a sin of appalling magnitude, because he saw fit to keep back the truth as to some things, and then completed the only revelation he will ever give, and assured the world it was complete, and still suppressed the truth as to this sin, and left Gentile and Jew to live in it, and die in it, unless they had the strange penetration to discover (what Jew and Gentile cannot now discover) that the Author of the Bible said one thing and meant another—and the singular sanctity to detect, behind the plain language and law of God, a subtle spirit and lurking principle which contradict that language, and condemn that law as a license to commit crime! If any man can believe this, and thus charge God with mocking his poor creatures, and sporting with their guilt and consequent wretchedness, and trying on their blindness and weakness and corruption an experiment which he knew would prove fatal even to those most sincerely desirous to do his will—then that man can surmount the first New Testament objection to your broad statement that slavery is in itself and always a heinous sin.

(2.) We have on the question before us not only argument but inference. And here I have my eye upon the precepts given to slaves. The New Testament is not silent as to slavery; it recognises the relation, and commands slaves to obey their masters; and what I now affirm is this, that, when we consider the previous permission by the Old Testament, such commands to slaves are not only *a suppressio veri*, but a *suggestio falsi*—not only a suppression of the truth, but *a* suggestion of what, is false—if slavery be a sin of appalling magnitude. Let it be borne in mind that the previous sanction had been both by God's conduct and express precept, and demanded, therefore, a countervailing revelation of no equivocal sort. Yet, not only is no condemnation uttered, but slaves are addressed as such, and required to obey. You have quoted some of these precepts. There is one you have omitted, and which I only cite because it teaches us what is faith's true estimate of things that are now embroiling the churches, and embittering hearts once united in love, and filling the sacred ministry with violent spirits, who are no longer the humble preachers of Christ and him crucified, but the fiery apostles of headlong reform—haranguing their hearers on the exaggerated horrors of some evil to be corrected, and surpassing the martial anchorite of Amiens in the ardors of a crusading ambition.

The passage I allude to, you at once recollect. It is very fine indeed, and when we remember the condition of a slave then, under a heathen master, there is in it a simple grandeur of thought, compared with which all the vaunted sublimity of Homer is unutterably mean.

"Is any man called," says the apostle, "being circumcised? let him not become uncircumcised. Is he called in uncircumcision? let him not be circumcised. Circumcision is nothing, and uncircumcision is nothing, but the keeping of the commandments of God. Let every man abide in the same calling wherein he was called. *Art thou called being a servant? care not for it;* but if thou mayest be made free, use it rather. For he that is called in the Lord, being a servant, is the Lord's freeman: likewise, also, he that is called, being free, is Christ's servant [1 Corinthians 7:18–22]."

His ardent soul on fire with the great salvation, and the anticipations of the glory to be revealed, Paul declares that the true spirit of the gospel, instead of interfering with social relations, should cause the believer to soar above them; and that the advantages and disadvantages of all earthly conditions ought to be forgotten and swallowed up in the thought of those transports and raptures to which he is hastening. In the verse just copied, while he says liberty is to be preferred to slavery, yet he adds that, in the light of faith, the soul alone has true value, and even the hardest bondage is nothing at all, the most cruel treatment nothing at all, not worth a thought, if the slave has been called to the glorious liberty of the gospel. And he classes the distinction between master and servant in the same list with circumcision and uncircumcision, which made no sort of difference. "Hast thou been called," says Chrysostom, "being a slave? Care not for it. Continue to be a slave. Hast thou been called, being in uncircumcision? Remain uncircumcised. Being circumcised, didst thou become a believer? Continue circumcised. For these are no hinderances to piety. Thou art called, being a slave; another, with an unbelieving wife; another, being circumcised. Astonishing! Where has he put slavery? As circumcision profits not; and uncircumcision does no harm, so neither doth slavery, nor yet liberty."[52] What gives peculiar importance to this passage is, that it was written in answer to a letter from the Corinthian church touching certain matters, and among them, the duty of Christians sustaining to each other the relation of master and slave. Now here, if slavery be heinous crime, would not these inquirers have been told so? But we see the answer which the apostle, or rather which the Holy Spirit returns.

Reverting to the precepts you cite, I remark that the relation of master and slave is five times recognised, and is mentioned in immediate connection with the other domestic and civil relations, and the duty of obedience enjoined upon slaves, just as upon children, and wives, and subjects; and if this be not an implied permission of the relation, I am at a loss how ever to draw an inference. When the legislature of South Carolina enacts laws requiring slaves to obey their masters, does it not permit slavery? Nor do I perceive the force of your pleas here. (1) You

---

[52Chrysostom, *Homilies on the Epistles of Paul to the Corinthians*, 108.]

say the apostles always add as a reason for these precepts, the relation in which the slave stands to Christ. I answer, the Bible does this as to every duty. It never degrades the Christian to any rule or motive lower than the will and glory of God. Its language always is, "Whether ye eat or drink, or whatsoever ye do, do all to the glory of God [1 Corinthians 10:31]." "None of us liveth to himself, and no man dieth to himself. But whether we live we live unto the Lord, and whether we die we die unto the Lord [Romans 14:8]." "That God in all things may be glorified through Jesus Christ [1 Peter 4:11]." "For of him, and through him, and to him are all things [Romans 11:36]." Besides, the same reason is assigned for the subjection of the child, and wife, and citizen. "Wives, submit yourselves unto your own husbands, as it *is fit in the Lord* [Colossians 3:18]." "Children, obey your parents in all things, for this *is well pleasing unto the Lord* [Colssians 3:20]." "Wives, submit yourselves unto your own husbands, as Unto *the Lord* [Ephesians 5:22]." "Submit yourselves to every ordinance of man *for the Lord's sake*; whether it be to the king, as supreme, or to governors, as unto them that are sent by him for the punishment of evil-doers, and for the praise of them that do well. For so *is the will of God*, that with well-doing you may put to silence the ignorance of *foolish* men [1 Peter 2:13–15]." And just so as to the obedience of the slave: "Servants, be obedient to them that are your masters according to the flesh, with fear and trembling, *as unto Christ.* Not with eye-service, as men-pleasers; but as the servants of Christ, doing *the will of God* from the heart [Ephesians 6:5–6];" in which, and the other passages, the will of God is expressly declared, that slaves obey their masters, and the duty placed on the same principle with the other relative duties. (2) But, you say, the apostle only requires "patience, meekness, fidelity, and charity, duties obligatory on Christians towards all men, and of course towards masters;" and ask, "Do our obligations to practise fidelity, honesty, charity, to avoid purloining, lying, eye-service, depend on the justice of the authority which the master claims over the slave?" "The fact," you add, "seems to be simply this—there are certain vices to which ignorant people laboring for others are specially liable, and the apostle only forbids these, as dishonoring to Christianity." Such

---

is your second plea, but I submit to you if it be not wide of the whole case. You omit "*obedience*," which is the very duty enjoined. The apostle does not simply require the duties to which the master, in common with all men, had a claim. He commands "*obedience*," and obedience "to their own masters," not to all men, nor to the masters of other slaves; and the duty of obedience does depend on "the justice of the authority which the master claims." It is precisely the same inference as that by which the right of the husband, and parent, and governor is deduced from the command to the wife, and child, and citizen. In neither case is any injurious conduct of the superior justified; in one command to servants it is condemned—but the relation is in each case acknowledged and ratified. The fact, dear brother, seems to me to be simply this: it never entered the apostles' minds that the authority of Christian masters was sinful, and by the strongest implication they confirmed it. And not only so, but they declared that if the master was a "believing master," and discharged his duty to his slaves, and put forth his power for good—he was "faithful and beloved." "And they that have believing masters, let them not despise them, because they are brethren; but rather do them service, because they are *faithful and beloved par takers of the benefit.*" Such is the language of God. God says of such Christian masters, they are "FAITHFUL and BELOVED." My dear brother declares them guilty of a sin of appalling magnitude; and the abolitionists only carry out his doctrines, when they excommunicate and consign to perdition the whole South. Well might David exclaim, "Let me fall into the hand of the Lord, for very great are his mercies; but let me not fall into the hand of man [2 Samuel 24:14]" —even the kindest and best man.[53]

---

[53]While writing this, a number of my servants have come into my study, to tell me what God has done for their souls. "It rejoiced my soul," said Whitefield, "to hear that one of my poor negroes in Carolina was made a brother in Christ." How would his heart have overflowed, if, like many masters in these days, he had seen almost all his slaves brothers, and happy in the Lord! I do not know whether this note should be printed. However, I rejoice, yea, and will rejoice, and what I have written is written, and I will let it remain.

(3) Wishful to avoid every appearance of attributing to my reasoning more force than it possesses, I have called my first view only an argument, and my last only an inference,—leaving it to every candid reader to say, if I might not have designated each, and especially the latter, proof, and convincing proof. I come now to what I have announced as proof on the question before us. It is the precepts to masters. And here let it be still remembered, that the Old Testament is constantly referred to by the apostles as of divine origin, and that there slavery had by express precept been sanctioned; and I put it to any one whether the precepts to masters, enjoining of course their whole duty, and not requiring, not exhorting them to emancipate their slaves, are not conclusive proof that the apostles did not consider (and, as a New Testament precept is for all ages, that no one is now justified in denouncing) slaveholding as a sin. These precepts are so regardful of the slave that they even require the master to "forbear threatening," yet not an intimation as to emancipation. These precepts were to men anxious to know the whole will of God, and ready to die (as multitudes did die) rather than commit sin, and who were not prevented by law, as we are, from giving liberty to their bondmen. Yet the apostles do not even insinuate that slaveholding is a sin. The apostles solemnly took heaven to witness that they had "kept back nothing;" and in addressing, not only the people, but the pastors who were to teach the people, and bequeath their ministry to their successors, they asserted their purity from the blood of all men, because they "had not shunned to declare the whole counsel of God [Acts 20:27]." Yet they had shunned even to hint to masters that they were living in a "sin of appalling magnitude;" and had kept back truth, which, if you are right, was of tremendous importance. Lastly, a whole epistle (to which you do not allude) was addressed to a pious master whom Paul styles a "brother dearly beloved" and its entire contents were about his slave. This letter was written, too, when the apostle styles himself "Paul the aged," sixty or seventy years after the first promulgation of the gospel, and when surely the spirit and principles you speak of ought to have begun to operate. And, now, what does this epistle teach us? I will let McKnight answer this question. He

says, "Onesimus, a slave, on some disgust, having run away from his master, Philemon, came to Rome, and falling into want, as is supposed, he applied to the apostle," &c.[54] "After his conversion, Onesimus abode with the apostle, and served him with the greatest assiduity and affection. But being sensible of his fault in running away from his master, he wished to repair that injury by returning to him. At the same time being afraid that on his return his master would inflict on him the punishment which, by the law or custom of Phrygia, was due to a fugitive slave, and which, as Grotius says, he could inflict without applying to any magistrate, he besought the apostle to write to Philemon requesting him to forgive and receive him again into his family," &c. "To account for the solicitude which the apostle showed in this affair, we must not, with some, suppose that Philemon was keen and obstinate in his resentments, but rather, that having a number of slaves, on whom the pardoning of Onesimus too easily might have had a bad effect, he might judge some punishment necessary, for a warning to the rest, &c. The apostle would by no means detain Onesimus without Philemon's leave; because it belonged to him to dispose of his own slave in the way he thought proper. Such was the apostle's regard to justice and to the rights of mankind!"

(4) The demonstration furnished on this question, I need only mention; it is the baptism by the apostles of slaveholders, and the admission of them into the churches. Before baptism they required men to repent, that is, to abandon all their sins; yet they baptized masters holding slaves. They fenced the Lord's table with the most solemn warnings that men should examine themselves, and that to eat and drink unworthily was to eat and drink condemnation; yet they admitted to the supper masters holding slaves. They declared that "without holiness no

---

[54]James MacKnight, *A New Literal Translation, from the Original Greek of All the Apostolical Epistles, with a Commentary, and Notes, Philological, Critical, Explanatory, and Practical, to Which Is Added, a History of the Life of the Apostle Paul* (1809; reprint, Grand Rapids: Baker, 1984) 495. James MacKnight (1721–1800) was a leading clergyman and Bible scholar in the Church of Scotland. Like many of his contemporaries, Fuller refers to MacKnight as "McKnight."]

man could see the Lord [Hebrews 12:14]," and at once condemned all the darling sins of the day. Idolatry was interwoven with the very elements of society, yet they spared it not, but at the sight of "a city given to idolatry [Acts 17:16]" their "spirits were stirred [Acts 17:13]," and they told the people plainly that they worshipped devils. They abhorred the thought that "the temple of God, could have any agreement with idols [2 Corinthians 6:16];" and stigmatized idolatry as one of the "works of the flesh," "as to which," said they, "we tell you before, as we have told you in times past, that they which do such things shall not inherit the kingdom of God [Galatians 5:19–21]." Voluptuousness reigned in city and country, and even philosophers considered it innocent; but the heralds of Christ assailed it everywhere. In a word, going in the strength of the Lord God, they, with lion-hearted dauntlessness, struck at and warred with the superstitions of the Gentiles and the prejudices of the Jews. They attacked the passions of the vulgar and the pride of the noble. They defied the priests, and confronted the Sanhedrim, and thundered before unjust and licentious princes "of righteousness, and temperance, and judgment to come [Acts 24:25]." Yet as to slavery, they not only never forbade it, but received believing masters into the churches, and declared them "faithful and beloved" brethren in Christ Jesus. After this shall I be told that they considered slaveholding as a sin of appalling character, and meant it to be condemned by some covert and slow spirit or principle of their teaching? Is this supposable? Is it possible? Does it even verge towards possibility? Did they thus treat any infraction of God's law? And what would we say, I ask again, if our missionaries should thus act towards idolaters and fornicators in heathen lands? To put a case not half so strong as that here made out, let me suppose it could be proved that the apostles baptized children, would not that litigated question be at once settled? Yet then it might be urged that the very New Testament idea of a Christian church requires its members to be believers, and that the only commission to baptize excludes infants; whereas, in the instance before us we have clear, universal, apostolic practice, and not only no command with which it clashes, but the previous precepts and dealings of God all in conformity with it. If any one with all this—this argument, and inference, and proof, and demonstration—before him, still doubts, why then no good can come to that man from farther discussion. But it is impossible. So incurable a skeptic does not live, and my proposition is established, that slavery was sanctioned in the Old Testament, and permitted in the New Testament. If, however, slavery was sanctioned in the Old, and permitted in the New Testament, it is not a sin; and he who says it is, will answer to God whom he affronts, and not to me. You and I cannot, I know, differ as to the impiety of such a charge.

My letters are becoming, I fear, quite too long for your patience or the attention of our readers. I will conclude this by adverting as briefly as possible to the consequences which you think must follow if the New Testament permitted slavery. Now, to all objections of this kind, my dear brother will recollect that inspiration supplies one proper and compendious answer: "Nay, but who art thou, O man, that repliest against God [Romans 9:20]?" The Christian, however, need not fear that the teaching of the Holy Spirit can ever be found to inculcate doctrines at variance with truth or piety, and, therefore, he may be confident that all attempts to fasten upon the Scriptures any error in science, moral or physical, must fail. Nor is my humble assurance shaken by your objections. Those objections may be condensed thus.

*Objection first.*—If the New Testament permitted slavery among Christians in the apostles' days, then it permitted all the atrocities and enormities of Roman slavery, if the master only forbore threatening, and gave his slave suitable physical comforts as the reward of his toil; for this is all that the precepts to masters required.

*Answer.*—Here is a manifest confusion of slavery with the Roman slave-laws. What you affirm is, that slavery is always a sin. But slavery may exist, and did exist, among "faithful and beloved" Christian masters in apostolic times, and does exist now, without any of the horrors legalized by the Roman code. The gospel condemns cruelty, oppression, and injustice. It, therefore, denounced the system of servitude allowed among the Romans; and, moreover, by expressly enforcing justice, and reciprocal rights, and reminding the master of his subjection and accountability to God, it altered entirely the relations of the parties. The case is analogous to that of the Roman despotism. Indeed, Dr. Channing uses the very example, when he says, that if the Bible precepts to slaves sanctioned slavery, then the precepts to subects sanctioned all the tyranny of the reigning emperor, the tiger Nero.[55] Let us now suppose that the apostles had not only enjoined subjection to rulers, but that one of the Caesars having been converted and received into the church as a brother "faithful and beloved," an epistle had been addressed to him, exhorting him "to give unto his subjects things which are just and equal, and to remember that he also had a King in heaven"—what would this prove? It would establish conclusively the proposition that despotic power is not in itself a sin; but would it justify the profligate and sanguinary reigns of Tiberius, and Caligula, and Nero, or the crimes which the royal penitent himself might have formerly committed by the abuse of his power? And this supposed case is exactly the fact as to slavery. The precepts and example of the apostles settle the point that slaveholding is not in itself a sin; but they did not, and do not, sanction any abuse of the master's power; and had a master been guilty of cruelty or injustice to his slaves, the apostles would never have suffered him to continue in the communion of the church, much less would they have pronounced him "faithful and beloved."

*Objection second.*—A gospel permission is a general permission; and if the New Testament permitted slavery formerly it permits it now; nay, it sanctions the slave-trade, and "I should be as much justified in sending a vessel to Africa, murdering a part of the inhabitants of a village, and making slaves of the rest, as I should be in hunting a herd of wild animals, and either slaying them or subjecting them to the yoke."

*Answer.*—Jesus and his apostles found slavery existing as a part of the social organization. Should they appear now, they would find the same institution here. They did not declare it to be a sin, but by precept and example permitted it to continue; making it, however, a relation not of oppression and crime, but of justice and love. And they would act now

---

[55Channing, "Slavery," 732.]

just as they acted then; or rather, they are here in the gospel, and are now doing what they then did. If you can show that they permitted Christians to murder and hunt down men, and rend them from their homes and families, and stupify and imbrute their intellects, and destroy their souls, then you may plead that a gospel permission is a general permission, and that the permission of slavery is a license for every abominable barbarity. It will be time enough then for me to reply to this objection. You admit that the New Testament authorizes government. Suppose, now, one should thus reason. "The government in the apostles' days was a military despotism. If then the Bible justifies government, it justifies a citizen of the United States in becoming, if he can, a military despot; nay more, it sanctions the whole system of Roman conquest and tyranny; and I should be justified in planting my armed heel upon the necks of all the sovereigns of Europe, and trampling upon all the nations of the earth, and wading to a throne through seas of blood, and then wielding the sceptre for purposes of lust, and rapine, and ferocity." What would you say to such an argument? Yet it is exactly your objection to the New Testament permission of slavery. The very condition of a devout man, placed by birth under the responsibilities of a master, causes him to admire that wisdom of God which in the Bible shines with such lustre for all times and places. To him, as to you, the atrocities you mention are most revolting. But he feels, dear brother, what you do not, I mean the difficulties of his very solemn position; and after seeking most earnestly to know his duty, he perceives that the gospel prescribes for him in this situation, (as for all men in every emergency), that course which, faithfully pursued, would insure at once the peace of society, and the best temporal and spiritual interests of the individual.

*Last objection.*—If the Bible permits slavery, cannot be said to correct its abuses, for "where shall we find the precept?" "Where have we ever known the New Testament to be called upon to decide the question, what constitutes the proper use, and what the abuse of the institution of slavery?"

*Answer.*—No master, with the Bible before him, will ever be able to plead at the bar of God any obscurity on this point. The express precepts are full, nor do I think your paraphrase gives by any means their import. The New Testament solemnly calls upon a master whose power was irresponsible, to "remember," in all his conduct to his servant, "that he had a Master in heaven [Ephesians 6:9]," who would judge him. For slaves, who in the eye of the law had no rights, the New Testament claimed, "that which was just and equal,"—not merely "suitable, physical comforts,"—but whatever was equitable, and due to one intelligent, social, immortal being, standing in such a relation to another. In a word, the command to masters is a special application of the rule, "Whatsoever ye would that others do unto you, do ye also to them [Matthew 7:12]." And the very application of it by the apostles, proves that they did not regard it as requiring the emancipation of the slave; but (to use the words of Neander) as "imparting to masters such a knowledge of their duties to their slaves, and such dispositions towards them, and as teaching them so to recognise as brethren those who were among their slaves, as to make the relation quite a different thing."[56]

Very affectionately, my dear brother,

Yours, &c.,

R. Fuller

## Letter VI[57]

### To the Rev. Francis Wayland, D.D.

My Dear Brother,

So far from being offended at your plainness of speech, I see in it only that smiting of the righteous which is a kindness, and receive it as a proof of the esteem with which you have always honored me. And you, in return, will suffer my boldness, when I ask you whether truth ever

---

[56]It seems likely that Fuller is not quoting Neander, but rather paraphasing his thoughts on slavery. For Neander's interpretation of slavery during the New Testament era, see August Neander, *General History of the Christian Religion and Church*, vol. 1, 2nd ed., trans. Joseph Torrey (Boston: Crocker & Brewster, 1849).]

[57*Christian Reflector* 13/9 (27 February 1845): 33–34.]

requires, or is advanced by, exaggeration, and whether the sweeping charge I am combating be not a manifest exaggeration, that must be abandoned, and which in effect you do abandon? I am not unmindful of the distinctions of charity you make in your third letter, and I know that charity covereth the multitude of sins. But no charity can devise a distinction by which a man may live knowingly in the commission of a sin of appalling magnitude, and be free from its guilt; no affection—not even self-love—can invent a refinement by which one may inflict on others as great a wrong as can be conceived, and do it for their benefit; all which I understand you several times to suppose. I will not, however, dwell on this matter. If you still adhere to your assertion, that slavery, in itself, and always, and everywhere, was, and is, a sin of appalling magnitude, then there is nothing left for us but to pray for each other, and to love each other, and to recollect always the diffidence and forbearance becoming those who now "know but in part [1 Corinthians 13:12]." I write, and have written, with my health, as well as the patience of our readers, admonishing me to stop. But the subject is too important; and, moreover, a committee is soon to meet in your city, upon whose decision will depend the co-operation of Northern and Southern Baptists in any Christian enterprise. Of course Southern ministers are the proper missionaries to the colored population. If, then, the monstrous proposition be sustained, that they are all unfit to be employed in the Home Mission Society, and the proscriptive spirit of a few Northern enthusiasts thus annul a constitution under which our fathers have acted so long and happily, you readily foresee the consequences. Never again shall we assemble in any society. The spirit of fanaticism will exult in the accomplishment of its baleful plans. And one of the largest and noblest bodies of Christians ever constituted for the glory of God, will at once be broken into fragments—not hostile, I hope, but forever irreconcilable. That the great enemy of Christ will exhaust all his devices to secure such a result, no one can doubt. He has suffered too much from our assaults, not to long for such ample revenge. But who can love the Redeemer, or the heathen, without deprecating this disaster, and wishing to avert it? Nor do I see how disruption can be avoided, and peace and harmony permanently established, unless upon the basis that our associations are agents strictly limited in their trusts and operations, and never to be perverted by any of the principals into engines of inquisition and annoyance.

In this correspondence it only now remains that I notice one or two arguments advanced by you; gladly assenting when I can, and when I venture to dissent, doing so with reluctance.

(1) And first, as to expediency, it is unnecessary to examine how far anybody might have a single grain of a scruple about all you advocate. But how can your theories shelter the apostles, if they were guilty of the conduct you attribute to them? Whether the word "expediency" be good English in the evil sense now generally attached to it, I need not inquire. It is very good American; and as such we will use it, meaning thereby a truckling and trimming so as to make the principles of right and wrong comply with circumstances. And now, thus defined, was there ever expediency more abominable than that practised by the apostles, if your supposition be correct? If they knew slavery to be a sin of appalling magnitude, it was their duty to condemn it. They were bound to dismiss all unworthy comparison between two evils, and, rejecting all evil, to do the will of God, and leave consequences to him. The abolitionists feel themselves under sacred obligation to denounce slavery, and rather tear society to pieces than rest while the horrid sin is committed on the earth. My brother has "long felt that he owed a debt of humanity and charity to his Christian brethren at the South, both free and enslaved. He has desired to bear his testimony in favor of those whom he believed to be suffering the greatest injustice, and to bear it in the presence of those, many of whom he believes, through erroneous views of the teaching of the Scriptures, to be responsible to God for that injustice." And he feels this, I know, most sincerely and affectionately, although he has published against the idea that responsibility rests upon the North. What then? Were Jesus Christ and the apostles less compassionate and faithful? Consider, too, the office intrusted to the apostles. Their precepts and example were to furnish to all ages a pattern. Or rather, let me forget them, and say, that what they spake the Holy Ghost uttered, and what

they did the Holy Spirit prompted; and we have seen what they spake and what they did as to slaveholders. And now, I ask, how could these apostles indignantly repel the thought of "doing evil that good might come"—nay, how can they escape the charge of having done evil by which evil has come—if you are right? If you are right they did evil, and evil such as no other men ever did: evil to the slaves, they were faithless to them—evil to the Christian masters, they were faithless to them—evil to the churches, they were faithless to the churches—evil to the world around, they were faithless to the world—evil to the gospel, they were faithless to the gospel—in fine, evil to posterity, they were faithless to posterity, down to January, 1845, as this very discussion testifies.

(2) You affirm, however, that although the apostles did not condemn slavery by express precept, they did so by the inculcation of truths that must abolish slavery. As to which allegation, occupying the ground I now do, it would be quite enough for me to reply, that no matter what truths the apostles taught, if they received slaveholders into the churches, and pronounced them *"faithful and beloved,"* they put to silence the charge that slaveholding is always and everywhere a sin.

If you had said that the gospel, wherever received, at once eradicated the Roman system of slavery, and made the relation "a very different thing;" and if you had added, that everywhere the gospel requires of a master the moral and intellectual improvement of his slaves; I at least should have had no controversy with you. Then, too, while Christians at the South are enjoined to perform their solemn duty, the good and the wise through the Union might consult in the spirit of a prospective and far-seeing philanthropy, as to the designs of God for the African race. But the proposition defended by you has no connection with all this. Slavery is averred by you to be always, and every moment, a sin of appalling magnitude. And if this be so, I do not see how you can either respect the apostles, or censure the most vehement abolitionists.

The discrepancy between pious men, as to the teachings of so plain a book as the Bible, on the subject of slavery, is owing, I humbly apprehend, to our overlooking the obvious distinction to be made between the gospel, viewed as a civil code, and the gospel, viewed as a rule of Christian duty. In the former sense Christianity operates indirectly, through the spirit of its precepts, and the character of its professors. And its beneficial effects thus produced—the blessings it scatters in its path to immortality—how noble! The spirit of peace and justice infused into society, and by this the appeal to arms fast becoming, among nations as well as individuals, a barbarous and obsolete wickedness and absurdity. The spirit of love blending with every relation, civil and domestic; and by this, tyranny and cruelty mitigated, and governments converted into engines for human happiness, and women exalted to their true station, and purity and sanctity diffused through all the walks of private life; in a word, the spirit of religion everywhere expelling idolatry, and its obscenities and horrors. These are a few of the fruits of Christianity, regarded as a civil code for all nations. And in acting thus upon the world, and reaching and reforming political abuses, or public institutions, the gospel operates gradually and indirectly, by the announcement of a few grand truths, and chiefly through the influence of Christian character in individuals. In no other way could it operate for all times and places; and in no other way would we expect it to operate. The object of the gospel is to turn the heart from sin to holiness. Its direct business is never with masses, but individuals; and its aim is the conversion, and sanctification, and salvation of the soul. The revolutions it achieves in social manners and establishments, are only secondary effects: and therefore the operation of the gospel as to these is indirect and secondary.

But as a perfect rule of duty for each Christian, making the man of God thoroughly furnished to every good work, the gospel does not act indirectly, but by express command and prohibition, and these given dogmatically. Conversion to God is the submission of the heart and life to all his holy will. The language of the renewed soul is, "Lord, what wilt thou have me to do [Acts 9:6]?" And, dealing with Christians, the apostles at once condemned all sin, and never, in any instance, permitted them to live and die in iniquity, keeping back from them the knowledge of its true character. Indeed, as the gospel acts upon any established and public evil chiefly through the influence and character of individuals, it is self-evident that upon individuals it must exert a direct, and thorough, and compromising, and immediate energy. Otherwise its entire object will be defeated. Its primary purpose is the holiness and salvation of the individual; but if the individual be allowed to live and die in sin, this purpose is defeated. The secondary design of the gospel is, the removal of social and political evil by the purifying influence of individual character; but if the individual character of the Christian be blackened by sin, and his participation in the evil confirm the world in it, then this design is defeated.

I will illustrate my meaning, and for this purpose let me suppose myself convinced that slavery is a heinous sin. Now, what would be my duty as to the members of the Beaufort church? In your seventh letter, while assigning reasons why the apostles did not directly condemn slavery by precept, you say, "Is not this the almost universal method of the New Testament teaching? Do you not, my brother, so interpret it? When you attempt to teach men that they are sinners against God, do you enumerate the precepts which they have broken, or do you set before them the character of God and their universal relations to him?" Suppose, then, I should imitate your apostles, and adopt your New Testament method of teaching, and never breathe a hint as to slavery being a sin, and receive slaveholders into the church, and call them "faithful and beloved," would I be the servant of Christ? And would it not be most absurd for me to expect, that, by moral essays on the Sabbath, I could counteract the force of my perfidious conduct to the church; or that, through the church, I could ever act upon the system established by law? In fact, in the very letter after your seventh you say, "I do believe that even now it is the duty of every Christian in the slaveholding states, to bear his testimony against this enormous wrong." But how is this? Are not the New Testament method of teaching, and the, apostolic example, the best guides I can follow?

(3) "But," it is said, "the times are changed our circumstances are not those in which the apostles lived." And it is in this argument. I detect what, I confess, fills me with grief and alarm. "The times are changed." What then? Who but sees the inference? It is that the gospel must have

an expansion or elasticity, so as to adjust itself to the times. But what if the gospel can by no torture be framed and bent to what anybody and everybody chooses to call "the times?" Why, then, the gospel is effete, and obsolete, and must be discarded, as it has been by many of the abolitionists.

I need not say, my dear brother, that I know you detest and abjure such conclusions. But they are, and must be, the results of any doctrine which regards the instructions and examples of the Bible as of private or local interpretation. Moreover, while I enter my most solemn protest against this doctrine, I also deny the premises on which it rests. I deny that there is any such difference between our condition here, and that of Christians in the days of Paul, as is affirmed. It is not pretended that there is any want of correspondence between our circumstances and theirs, except in two particulars mentioned by you. The first of which is, that we make our own laws; and the second, that we possess superior moral light.

Now it is evident, that, in the present discussion, the first distinction is of no consequence, since it is not of the slave-laws, but of slavery, I am speaking; and the character of this, according to the eternal principles of morality, is not affected by any human enactments.

Is it true, then, that a Christian at the South possesses greater advantages than a Christian in apostolic times, for ascertaining his duty? If he does, whence does he derive them? Not from natural religion; for I venture to affirm that neither Paley, nor any writer on natural theology, has advanced a single idea which had not been advanced long before the Christian era. And as to revealed religion, I repeat, what I said before, that a converted master in Corinth, or Galatia, or Rome, had the very same scriptures. And he had, too, the living, inspired apostles—enjoying, in their personal presence and instruction, an advantage, which no succeeding age has known, and which, we feel, would at this moment terminate not only this dispute, but a great many others. I protest, then, against any permission given to men, to tamper with the word of God on the plea that the times are changed. And I deny, too, that my means of deciding on the moral character of slavery are superior to those which

Timothy and Philemon enjoyed—the latter of whom was a slaveholder, and confirmed in slaveholding by Paul and the former was enjoined, as an evangelist, to inculcate precepts, and pursue a line of conduct, utterly at variance with the doctrine that slave-holding is itself, and always, a heinous crime.

(4) "But omniscient wisdom," you say, "has chosen, in imparting moral truth, to teach, not by express prohibition and precept, but by principle; and if slavery had been singled out from all other sins, and had alone been treated preceptively, the whole system would have been vitiated. We should have been authorized to inquire, why were similar precepts in other cases delivered, and if they were not delivered, we should have been at liberty to conclude that they were intentionally omitted, and that the acts which they would have forbidden, were innocent." I ask, however, when and where has omniscient wisdom chosen this method of condemning sin? I do not stop to inquire why if *omniscient wisdom* selects this mode of condemning slavery, my brother and others at the North are dissatisfied with it, and feel themselves bound to be more direct and explicit? But I appeal to the prophets, and ask, whether they ever saw sin of appalling magnitude practised in the world and among God's people, and connived at it in their entire conduct, and satisfied themselves with indirect and inferential condemnation? And I appeal to the Saviour's ministry, and to the ministry of the apostles, and repel at once the imputation of such unfaithfulness. You say, God does not teach by precept. But what does God say? "*Precept must be upon precept, precept upon precept* [Isaiah 28:13]."

Let me take for instance, idolatry. Now we all know that this is not merely an erroneous creed, but a system of practical falsehood, penetrating and pervading society, and so incorporated into its very fabric, and interwoven with all established usages, natural, and social, and domestic, that, to rend a people away from idolatry, is declared by God to be a work of surpassing difficulty. "*Pass over the isles of Chittim, and see, and send unto Kedar, and consider diligently, and see if there be such a thing. Hath a nation changed their gods* [Jeremiah 2:10–11]?" Yet we find how the gospel dealt with idolatry. It assailed every form and ramification of it; separating converts at once and forever from the practice; and, through them, reaching the institution, and attacking it vigorously and unremittingly. Your remark, then, about "singling out," turns against you. For, if slavery be a heinous sin, the truth is, that God has directly and expressly denounced all other prominent forms of sin, but, "singled this out," and acted towards it "anomalously," you say, in the Old Testament, and still more anomalously, I add, in the New. You have eloquently described the gross darkness which covered the earth, and the effulgence poured upon this darkness by the gospel. The truths thus revealed, however, affected every modification of wrong, and served the apostles as weapons mighty through God, with which to attack sin in every shape. With these weapons they did extirpate at once from among Christians the Roman system of slavery, (and let me say, too, that with these arms they are now contending against the Southern abuses of slavery), but slavery itself—softened, and so entirely changed by Christianity, that the relation between the parties was one of justice and love—they not only did not attack, but permitted, both by their precepts and conduct.

(5) "But," you urge, "the most effectual way of forbidding sin, is not by express precept and prohibition, but by inculcating moral principles at variance with it." To which opinion I can only reply, that neither human nor divine wisdom appears to me to concur with you. Not human wisdom; since all nations find it necessary to enact laws, and I dare say, even in Brown University a code has been established for the students. A government which should simply adopt a constitution, proclaiming a few general principles, and expect the people to be regulated by their spirit, would soon be wofully convinced of its delusion. "*A simple precept or prohibition is of all things the easiest to be evaded.*" If this be so, then legislation is folly, and the acts annually passed by our⁻ representatives are only so many provisions for the easier evasion of justice. "*Lord Eldon used to say, that no man in England could construct an act of parliament through which he could not drive a coach and four.*" Suffer me, however, as a lawyer, to assure you, that both in England and America statutes have been constructed, through which all the subtlety of Lord Eldon could

not have driven a single culprit; and if that nobleman had committed forgery, or treason, he would inevitably have found himself, not driving through an act of parliament, but driven by it into the tower, and thence to the scaffold. *"We find this to have been illustrated by the case of the Jews in the time of our Saviour. The Pharisees, who prided themselves on their strict obedience to the letter, violated the spirit of every precept of the Mosaic code."* What does this illustrate? Certainly not your proposition, since it shows that the spirit is readily violated, when the express letter cannot be. Or, if you mean by this example to elucidate the superior binding efficacy of general principles, then, to my apprehension, your argument stands thus: *"The Pharisees, who prided themselves on their strict obedience to the letter, violated the spirit of every precept of the Mosaic code;"* it would, therefore, have been wiser, and a more effectual restraint on the Pharisees, if the precepts of the Mosaic code had never been given at all. To settle this point at once, suppose there had been in the Bible an express command against slaveholding, could the present controversy exist between us for a moment? Good men may not require precepts in many cases. But laws are made for the lawless and disobedient; and if there be no laws, why, the most carefully framed general principles will, in the administration of justice, prove to be only "barren generalities," and possess scarcely more practical tenacity and cogency for the conviction of a criminal, than one of Euclid's problems.

> "And be these juggling fiends no more believed,
> That palter with us in a double sense,
> That keep the word of promise to our ear,
> And break it to our hope."[58]

This jugglery—how constantly do we find artful men succeeding in it, when rights are protected merely by abstractions. And though the passions will still attempt evasion, however explicit the precept, yet it is plain, that by special precept and prohibition alone, can all paltering in a

---

[58 William Shakespeare, *McBeth*, act 5, scene 8.]

double sense be prevented, and duties and obligations be at once unambiguously defined, and unequivocally enforced.

Human wisdom and experience do not sustain your position. Nor does the divine wisdom act upon it. For in both dispensations we find God giving specific laws, and these often very minute, extending to every relation of life—and discriminating most nicely between actions. It is true, as Whately remarks, the gospel could not go into every detail. But it does, in all cases, erect a complete standard, and never abstains from such an express denunciation of any sin as to leave room for doubt. Much less does it, by precept and example, ever afford countenance to any thing which is an appalling crime in the sight of God.

(6) "But the duty of emancipating slaves depended on the general truths promulgated; it was reasonable, then, to postpone the inculcation of the duty, until the truths were promulgated on which this duty was founded." Be it so. I acquiesce. The duty of emancipation, however, is not inculcated at all. The course of the gospel always is, to announce God's will, and to prescribe dogmatically and peremptorily, as becomes the Majesty of heaven, whatever duties are exacted by such annunciations. This it did as to all existing iniquities, and as to the abuses of Roman slavery. But it promulgated no truths, and uttered no hint, requiring emancipation.

(7) "But slavery was established by law, and could only be abolished by a change in the public mind." *Answer.* The precepts and conduct of the apostles were to Christians, and not the public. Moreover, how could the public mind be convinced that slavery was an appalling sin, when the churches everywhere practised it, and were confirmed in it by the apostles?

(8) "But if slavery had been declared to be a sin, it would have led to a servile war." *Answer.* This argument forgets God altogether, and his power, and makes him abstain from denouncing, sin through fear of consequences. It conflicts, also, with your own declaration, that "if slavery be a sin it should be abolished, although the whole South would be ruined." Besides, where is the ground for this plea? The masters would be either converted or unconverted. If converted, they would

obey the command. If unconverted, things would remain just as before, and the slaves continue in their power.

(9) "It is unreasonable for masters at the South to object to the gospel method of treating slavery, since they oppose immediate emancipation so strongly." *Answer*. Not only Southern masters, but every man of wisdom, (and, I know, my brother among them,) deprecates immediate abolition. Paley and Robert Hall were peculiarly anxious that no one should suppose they thought slavery could cease wisely, and beneficially, except by provisions of law, and gradually, under the protection of civil government. As soon, however, as it is conceded that slavery is to be gradually abolished, it is also conceded that slaveholding is not always and in all circumstances a heinous sin.

(10) "The early church interpreted the teaching of the gospel as requiring slavery to be abolished." *Answer*. Do you mean they understood the gospel as teaching that slavery is a sin? If so, what early church? Not the Galatian, nor Corinthian, nor any apostolic church, nor, indeed, any church, until these radiant days of abolition illumination. The cases you cite from a contemporary journal have really nothing to do with the question at issue. Suppose a band of marauders should seize and carry off yourself and family, and the church in Providence, and that you could all be redeemed from shocking indignity and outrage only by a ransom. Does my brother believe there is in Carolina a Christian who would hesitate about contributing to the sum required? Exactly such are the cases mentioned by you. As for slavery, though the preachers of the earlier ages are very bold in denouncing all cruelty in masters, yet never is slaveholding regarded by them as a sin.[59] The excitement of our own days may convince us what would have been the treatment of emancipationists in the Roman Empire. But in no single

---

[59]In the third century, Origen says, "We wish all slaves and children to be trained in the word of God." And at the end of the fourth century, Chrysostom thus preaches, "Hast thou bought thy slave? Before all things, enjoin him what God would have him [to] do." [See Origen, *Contra Celsum*, trans. Henry Chadwick (Cambridge: Cambridge University Press, 1953) and Chrysostom, *Homilies on Ephesians*, 13:159.]

persecution were Christians accused of abolition principles, although every sort of crime was falsely charged upon them. Masters, in fact, allowed them to preach to their slaves so freely as to occasion the sarcasm of Celsus in the second century, "that the Christians addressed only flocks of women, and idiots, and slaves." The truth is, that during the apostolic periods, and for centuries after, the most holy men and martyrs held slaves; and Eusebius, speaking of the death of his patron, Pamphilius, one of the most illustrious of the proto-martyrs, A.D. 309, draws a picture which is very affecting, and which, in like circumstances, would no doubt find many originals at this day among us. Pamphilius had a slave named Porphyrius, a young man eighteen years of age, whom he educated with parental affection, and for whose religious, moral, and spiritual edification he provided in every way, and to whom he had communicated an ardent love for the Redeemer. When Porphyrius heard the sentence of death pronounced against his beloved master, he prayed that it might be conceded to him to show the last proof of love to him, by burying his corpse after the execution of the sentence had taken place. This request at once excited the wrath of the fanatical governor; and, as he now steadfastly avowed that he was a Christian, and was anxious to sacrifice himself, he was most cruelly tortured, and at last, with his flesh entirely torn from his bones, he was led to the stake. He bore every thing with firmness, after he had only once, when the fire touched him for the first time, called to Jesus the Son of God for help.—*Eus. de Mar. Palest. 338.*[60]

(11.) "Slavery was at last abolished throughout the whole Roman Empire; and, by the admission of all, this was purely the result of the gospel." *Answer.* Even if this statement were correct, it would not affect our discussion. But I submit to you that it is inaccurate. At first, myriads of slaves were procured by war; and then the law of self-preservation occasioned the greatest severities. When all nations had become consolidated into one empire, this source of supply almost ceased, and, masters depending on the natural increase, slaves became more valuable,

[60]See August Neander, *General History of the Christian Religion and Church*, vol. 2, 2nd ed., trans. Joseph Torrey (Boston: Crocker & Brewster, 1849) 415.]

and their treatment more kind. Through this cause the laws were mitigated, and in the reign of the Antonines, edicts were published protecting slaves. This was in the second century, nor can this change be at all ascribed to the gospel. In process of time Christianity seconded the humane working of this system, and infused its mild and benevolent spirit into the institution, making it quite a different thing. But slavery never was abolished throughout the Roman Empire.[61] In its latest days there were millions of slaves in the empire, and a living writer thinks, that their number was one of the causes which conspired in producing that most astonishing catastrophe, the subjugation of Rome by the Northern barbarians. Nor did Goth, and Frank, and Vandal abolish slavery; but, by perpetual wars among themselves, they revived the method of obtaining bondmen by captivity, "which," says Gibbon, "had almost ceased under the peaceful reigns of the emperors." And thus Romans were, in multitudes, made to cultivate the lands of the barbarians, who exercised power of life and death over them, and often sent, as a nuptial present to their daughters, trains of slaves chained on wagons to prevent their escape. The practice of enslaving prisoners of war continued, in truth, until the thirteenth century over Europe, and prelates were often masters of hundreds.[62]

I have much more to say, my dear brother, but must close this controversy. In your last letter there is a great deal of truth, and solemn exhortation, which I hope may do good. It applies, however, entirely to the slave-laws, and to abuses not to be defended. In some matters you are grossly misinformed. At least I never heard of the atrocities you mention; such, for example, as the prohibition of marriage, and the

---

[61] Slavery persisted to the end of the Roman Empire, though there were more opportunities to leave slavery for the higher classes. See Allen M. Ward et al., *A History of the Roman People*, 3rd ed. (Upper Saddle River NJ: Pretice Hall, 1999) 402, 456.]

[62] See Gibbon; and Moreri, "Esclavage." See too, Blackwood for Dec., Art. Guizot. [See Edward Gibbon, *History of the Decline and Fall of the Roman Empire* (Basil: J. J. Tourneisen, 1788–1789). See also Louis Moreri, *Le Grand Dictionaire Historique, Nouvelle et Derniere Edition* (Paris: Denis Mariette, 1718) s.v. "Esclavage," and "Guizot"; *Blackwood's Edinburgh Magazine* 56 (December 1844): 786–804.]

defence of profligacy in the abuse of female slaves for purposes of convenience and pecuniary advantage. I regret the intrusion of such statements into your letters, and yet I am not surprised at it. I have several times had under my roof individuals, once abolitionists, and who, on examining for themselves, have been amazed at the calumnies by which their minds had been poisoned from childhood. And if the Author of the *Moral Science* credits these libels, what are we to expect from the ignorant, and young, and impetuous, women, and girls, and children, whom the agitators at the North gather nightly at their feet?

After admitting and deploring much abuse of slavery at the South, I still humbly hope that God sees here the sincerest friends of the African race; nor would we stint our benevolence towards them. In a familiar correspondence like this, I may be pardoned for saying, that, during twelve years, I have devoted the salary given me, whenever at my disposal, to the spiritual instruction of the slaves; and am now doing so. With reference to my own servants, their condition is as good as I can make it. They are placed under a contract, which no instrument of writing could make more sacred. By this contract they, on their part, perform not one half the work done by free laborers; and I, on my part, am bound to employ a missionary to teach and catechize them and their children; to provide them a home, and clothes, and provisions, and fuel, and land to plant for themselves; to pay all medical bills; to guaranty to them all the profits of their skill and labor, in their own time; to protect them as a guardian; and to administer to the wants of the children, and of those that are sick, and infirm, and aged. Such is their state, nor have I any idea that they would consent to be removed. But will my brother, or any man at the North, undertake to remove them, and give me bond and security that their condition shall be improved? If so, let him speak; and I will then make a proposition which shall, at once, and by a test more sure than all the writing in the world, determine who is the friend of the slave, and who is willing to make sacrifices for his good, and how many abolition Acaciuses[63] and Paulinuses[64] are ready to be forthcoming with

---

[63]Acacius may be a reference to either Patriarch Acacius of Constantinople or Bishop Acacius of Caesarea, both of whom were notable heretics during their time.]

church plate for the crucible, and even a moiety of their estates "for the redemption of captives."

In conclusion, let me again submit to you, whether the broad assertion that slaveholding is a sin, must not be modified. Slavery may be a sin; and may be rendered so by the manner in which the present master obtained his power, or by the abuse of that power, or by the means employed to perpetuate that power. But supposing there is no sin (as there is manifestly none) in being the heir or legatee of this power, then the use of it may be most virtuous; as in the bequests mentioned in my third letter; and in all cases where slaves are unprepared for liberty, and the master's authority is exercised for their truest benefit, temporal and eternal.

I have done; and mine has been an irksome and cheerless task. You have had the popular side of the question, and the Reflector has accompanied your letters with accounts of the enthusiasm produced by them at the North. May you ever be animated in your pious labors by multitudes who love and admire you, —among whom I shall always be found, when conscience permits it. For me, I have long been schooled to say, "*My soul, wait thou only upon God; for my expectation is from Him* [Psalm 62:5]." I expect no enthusiasm from the North, and little even from the South. I ask only the calm and honest reflection of wise and good men for truth, which may not be welcome, but is truth for all that. Easily could I have composed papers which would have been copied and applauded here, but truth forbade it. Nor can I approve of the fanaticism of the South, any more than that of the North, on the subject which has been before us. I only wish, in fact, that, —instead of employing my humble efforts in refuting an untenable, and mischievous, and monstrous dogma,—I had been occupied in the more congenial work of attempting to excite masters to a sense of their fearful responsibility, and to the discharge of their solemn duties.

Farewell! Grace and peace be multiplied unto you through the knowledge of God and our Saviour Jesus Christ. That knowledge, we are

---

[64Paulinus may be a reference to either Paulinus I or Paulinus II, the former was archbishop of York, the latter served as an advisor to Charlamagne.]

assured, shall fill this guilty and polluted earth, as the waters cover the face of the deep. And it is with that knowledge, too, as with those waters, when the sea is rolling in. Wave after wave breaks, and is driven back; but the ocean is advancing; and before its majesty and strength, impotent must every barrier prove; —vainly shall nations rage, and rulers take counsel together, and all the kings of the earth set themselves, saying, Hitherto shalt thou come, but no further, and here shall thy proud billows be stayed.

Now unto Him that is able to do exceeding abundantly above all that we ask or think, according to the power that worketh in us—unto Him be glory in the church, by Christ Jesus, throughout all ages, world without end. Amen.

Dear brother, most affectionately yours,

R. Fuller.

P.S. As it does not belong to this argument, I have said nothing of your remark, that you "never could, without doing violence to your conscience, do any thing towards the establishment in a heathen land, of a church into which slavery could by any means find admittance." When it is considered, however, that you speak this as President of the Convention, and that in India there are millions of slaves, your observation is of vast importance; and the public ought to be informed by the Board at once, whether, in reference to slavery in the East, our missionaries are required to pursue a course different from that which, you admit, was pursued in the Roman Empire, by Christ and the apostles. Upon this point I do respectfully, but earnestly, request, that the highly and universally esteemed gentlemen constituting the Board will not allow ignorance or doubt to perplex the Southern mind for a moment.

R. F.

# Dr. Wayland's Letter[65]

## To the Rev. Richard Fuller, D.D.

My Dear Brother,

It is needless to assure you that I have read your letters in reply to mine on Domestic Slavery, with profound attention and unfeigned admiration. To the acuteness of one profession and the learning of another, in both of which you have attained to the highest distinction, you have here added a fervor of eloquence and a richness of illustration peculiarly your own. Never before, I presume, has the defence of slavery on Christian principles been so ably conducted. Never before, I think, has any thing been written so admirably calculated to make a favorable impression on those who hold the opposite opinions. Nor is the singular ability displayed in this discussion by any means its highest recommendation. The warm spirit of philanthropy which pervades every part of your argument, must melt away every prejudice by which it could be resisted; while the love to God and the reverence for his word which are everywhere so apparent, must, I am sure, give you a place in the affections of every true disciple of our common Lord. If slavery cannot be defended by such an Advocate, I shall believe that the defense of it must be hopeless.

Si Pergama dextra
Defendi possent, etiam hac defensa faissent[66]

---

[65 This letter did not appear in the *Christian Reflector*, but was added to the print version of *Domestic Slavery*.]

[66 This Latin phrase comes from the second book of the Aeneid and is a quote from the shade of Hector. It is translated, "If by any right hand Troy could have been defended, it would have been done by this one [of mine]." That is, if the greatest warrior was not able to accomplish something, there is little point for a lesser one to waste his efforts.]

While, however, I say this, and I say it from my heart, I do not perceive that you have overthrown a single position which I have attempted to establish. It was not, therefore, until quite lately that I resolved to offer any thing by way of rejoinder. As, however, with your usual courtesy, you have intimated a desire that I should close, as you had commenced the correspondence, I shall avail myself of your liberal suggestion. It will not be my intention to present any new argument, or introduce any new matter into the discussion, but rather to state the points of difference and coincidence between us, so that the conclusions at which we have both arrived may be the more clearly presented to the view of those who may perchance take an interest in the correspondence.

Before I proceed, I ask the privilege of offering a few remarks explanatory of two or three passages at which you have properly taken exception.

1. In my second letter I supposed, for the sake of illustration, that I had murdered you and reduced your wife and children to slavery. You think that this passage will lead to the belief that I intend to institute a comparison between the moral condition of those who hold slaves in the Southern States, and those engaged in the slave-trade on the coast of Africa. Should such an opinion be formed, I should sincerely regret it; for, in all truth, I declare that it never entered my mind to institute any such comparison. I do most earnestly protest against such a use being made of any thing I have ever either thought, or said, or written. I merely intended by this illustration to show, that neither from the manner in which this power *originated*, nor from the manner in which it is *perpetuated*, is any right *created*. It went to this extent and no farther.

Here, however, that I may avoid the necessity of referring to this topic again, permit me to say that the analogy which you suggest between this case and that in which our present title to land may be good, although the original title may have been vicious, is not to my mind conclusive. The rule of law and equity on this subject, I suppose to be the following. The possession of property is a bar to molestation until some one *who can show a better title* presents himself, and *no longer*. The rightful owner may always oust me, how long soever I may have held possession. Now, in the case of slavery, the rightful owner is always present, and has never relinquished his claim. *He* has a better *right to himself* than *any one else* can possibly have, and this right he has never either forfeited or alienated. My possession bars my neighbor from stealing him from me, but it is no bar to the claim of the man to himself. I submit it to you as a lawyer, whether this be not the principle which rules in the case.

2. In my seventh letter there is another illustration which I also desire to correct, although you have not alluded to it. In order to exhibit my view of the manner in which I suppose the duty of emancipation might be performed, I introduced the case of a person who had *dishonestly* obtained possession of the property of another. I desire to alter it, so as to suppose the owner to have become possessed of property *not knowing that he held it wrongfully*, and then to be convinced of the invalidity of his title. This is all that is necessary for my purpose, and in this form I do not see that it is liable to give offence.

3. In the postscript to your last letter, you allude to the remark which I made touching the principles by which I must be guided in the propagation of the gospel among the heathen, in so far as it was connected with this subject. Previously to the reception of your letter, I had prepared a note explanatory of my views, which, from several sources, I learned were liable to be misunderstood. What I meant to say was simply this. I could never, with a good conscience towards God, do an act which, directly or by legitimate inference, should render me a party to the introduction of slavery into a heathen country. My mind was at the time directed to the Karens, our principle missionary field, among whom slavery does not exist, and it was really in reference to them that the remark was made. The subsequent sentences, in which I allude to the opinions of slaveholders on this subject, sufficiently indicate my meaning. If, however, I were preaching the gospel to the heathen in a country where slavery formed a part of the social organization, I should not make abolition a condition of native church membership, but should leave the principles of the gospel faithfully inculcated to work out the extinction of slavery. Such I believe to be the mode inculcated by

apostolical example. Suffer me, also, to add, that I did not by any means intend to write as President of the Convention. To have done so would have been a gross impertinence. My reason for alluding to the office was simply this. I had perceived, from published correspondence, that opinions on this subject were considered by many of our brethren to affect eligibility to any office in the convention. I felt, therefore, called upon, in honor, immediately to avow what my opinions were.

Having thus disposed of this preliminary matter, I address myself at once to the consideration of the argument before us.

In the first place, my dear brother, permit me to remark, that the more frequently I have read your letters, the more deeply have I been impressed with the coincidence of opinion that exists between us. The reasonings which we employ are dissimilar. We arrive at our conclusions by different trains of argument, but the conclusion seems to me almost precisely the same. From your reasons I often dissent, and sometimes dissent totally; but in the results to which you are led I perceive but little to which I can object. The proposition which you prove, and to which, as you repeatedly assert, you strictly confine yourself, is this, to be the holder of slaves is not always and everywhere a sin; and hence you infer that the simple holding men in bondage ought not to be a ground of ecclesiastical excommunication. Now, if you refer to my third letter, you will find all this repeatedly and explicitly asserted. This you say is the whole matter that you intend to discuss. As, therefore, I had affirmed the same truth, and you disclaim the affirmation of any thing else, it is not remarkable that our conclusions should be really identical.

There is, however, as I have intimated, a difference in the grounds on which our opinions rest. And here you will, I know, permit me to observe, that your argument would have been clearer to my understanding, if you had kept in mind the distinction between right and wrong, and innocence and guilt. This distinction seems to me essential to any complete conception of the matter in dispute. I do not remember an allusion to it in the whole course of your argument. Being from this cause frequently unable to discover which of their two meanings you attach to the words crime, sin, moral evil, I have sometimes been much embarrassed in attempting to define the position which you intended to defend. Supposing, however, that we agree as to the truth of your assertion that slavery does not always involve *sin*, understanding *sin* to mean guilt, I shall dismiss at once this branch of the discussion. The only question between us, then, is this: is slavery a violation of the relations which God has established among men; that is, is it a moral wrong. I think that even here we are not so much at variance as at first sight it might appear.

The question that first presents itself is the following: What is slavery? In the answer to this question we seem to differ widely, but the difference is mainly a matter of terminology. You define slavery to be the right to oblige another to labor for us without his contract or consent. I consent to this definition, with the liberty to add, that it also includes the right to all the means necessary to establish and perpetuate the original right, and that it thus includes the right to control the intellectual, social, and moral nature of man, in so far as it is necessary to render the original right available.

Suffer me to explain my view of the subject in a very few words. "Slavery," says Dr. Paley, "is the right to oblige another to labor for us without his contract or consent." But what, according to the same author, is the meaning of *oblige?* "A man is *obliged* when he is urged by a violent motive, resulting from the command of another."[67] The right of slavery is therefore the right to *urge* another man *by a violent* motive resulting *from, my own command, to labor for me without his contract or consent.* Now I must say that to the best of my understanding, the conferring of such a right does really confer all that I have asserted. You grant that it confers the power, but that it does not confer the right to use it. I am almost ashamed to say that I do not clearly understand this distinction in such a case. The right, as above explained, is the right *to urge* another *by violent motives*, resulting not from the *law of God*, or the *social laws of man*, but resulting from *my own command*. My command dictates both the kind and the degree of violence; and I do not see, that

[67William Paley, *Moral and Political Philosophy* (London: Printed for R. Faulder, 1785) 49.]

in the conferring of this right, any limitations are imposed upon the exercise of my own will. I do not perceive how we can exclude from this definition the grant of all the rights necessary to secure and establish it, including absolute control over the intellectual, moral, and social nature of the slave. That this has always been claimed as a portion of the rights of the master, is, I suppose, evident, from the whole history of domestic slavery. When, therefore, I have spoken of slavery, I have spoken of the whole system, originating in the claim to hold our fellowmen in bondage, and terminating in those various abuses inflicted on slaves, wherever this system exists. Of course I do not pretend that every slaveholder carries out his principles to their practical results. I am speaking of what the assumption necessarily involves, and of the effects which, as a system, legitimately flow from it.

From this view of slavery, however, you wholly dissent, and declare that it involves nothing, absolutely nothing but mere personal bondage, with the right to oblige the enslaved person to labor. You say, "Slavery is only bondage." "Slavery is *nothing more* than the condition of one who is deprived of political power, and does service without his contract and consent, but yet *cheerfully and happily*, and for a *compensation* reasonable and *certain*, paid in modes of return best for the slave himself. With what is strictly *physical liberty* the master interferes no more, in such cases, than you do with a hired servant." Letter 3d.

Again, "A right to the service of a man without his contract conveys *no additional right* but those proper and necessary to the original right. But it is *not proper and necessary to this original right* that a *human being* be deprived of *any right* which is *justly his* as an *immortal, intelligent, moral, social*, and *fallen* creature. Therefore, a right to the service of a man without his contract or consent, *does not justify any wrong* done to his *mind, soul* or *domestic relations*."

This, I confess, is to me a new view of the institution of domestic slavery, and I must add that it pleases me incomparably better than any that I have ever seen. Slavery, according to this definition, confers on the master no right whatever, beyond merely that of obliging the slave to labor. It gives him no right over the slave as an *immortal, intellectual, moral, social,* and *fallen* creature, and *justifies no wrong done* to his *mind, soul,* or *domestic relations.* In all these respects, then, slavery makes no difference between the slave and any other man. His condition, bating the obligation to labor for his master, is precisely that of a freeman. He has just a same right as any other man to his wife and children, to all the means of education, to the opportunity for intellectual cultivation, to the privilege of worshipping God when and as he chooses, to the trial by jury, to be received as a witness in a court of justice, or in an ecclesiastical tribunal; in a word, to the full benefit of equal law in all cases whatsoever, save only that he is under obligation to render reasonable and cheerful service to his master. The separation of children from their parents, of husbands from their wives, by the domestic slave-trade, and, in fact, the whole system of legislation and practice by which a distinction is made between slaves and freemen, finds no apology in this view of slavery; and it is, like any other case of causeless oppression, wholly indefensible, a wrong, and a sin against God. Here then we entirely agree. I believe all this. We will not contend about words. I care not what you call this wrong. I may call it slavery. You call it by another name. If, however, we agree in what we affirm of its character in the sight of God, I am perfectly content. Here then is a very large part of what I call the system of slavery, concerning which we do not differ in the least. This is certainly a very important point of agreement.

We then have arrived together to this conclusion: every respect in which the intellectual, moral, social, or domestic condition of a slave is made to differ from that of any other man, is indefensible, unauthorized, and wrong. We have next to proceed and consider slavery in the restricted sense in which you understand it; since it is only here that there can be any difference of opinion between us.

Here I am reminded of a remark which you have frequently made, that this is purely an abstract question, a question of simple right, and is by no means affected by the *manner* in which a master may use his slave. He may use him cruelly, but this does not prove that he has not a right to hold him as a slave. In this I fully concur. I also add, that the question of right is not affected by the *humanity* of the master. He might use his slave *cruelly*, but this would not disprove, and he might use him *humanely*, and this would not establish his *right*. It is a question of ownership, just like that of the ownership of any other property. If the question should be brought before a court and jury, whether I was the owner of a particular horse, it would affect the issue in no manner whatever to prove that I had used him either kindly or cruelly. Nor, again, is this a question respecting the treatment of men in any particular *condition*, it is a question respecting the lawfulness of the *condition itself*. Thus, suppose I had kept a child blindfolded from infancy, so that he had never seen the light. I might treat him very well as a *blind child*. I might say that he gave me much more trouble, and was of far less service to me than a child that had the use of his eyes. All this might be, but the question would still return, why do you not strip off the bandage? I am bound to show, not that I treat him well in this condition, but the reason why I keep him in this condition at all. This abstract view of the case is, I think, specially to be borne in mind at the present point of the discussion.

"The right of slavery is then, as we have seen, the right to urge another, by a violent motive resulting from my own command, to labor for me without his contract or consent." This right you suppose to be conferred upon us by the precepts of the New Testament. These precepts were given when men of all nations and colors and grades of civilization were in the universal habit of enslaving each other, and the New Testament confirmed them in the right of so doing. And yet more, the New Testament was given as our moral statute book to the end of time. We can neither add to nor take from it. Whatever permission it gives is a universal permission. It is addressed to men as men, and hence the right which it thus confers it confers on human nature. The right, therefore; for which you contend may be, I think, expressed truly in these words. Every man has the right to urge every other man, by a violent motive proceeding from his own will, to labor for him without his contract or consent.

That this is the meaning of the assertion is evident. The only other form in which it could be expressed would be the following, "*Masters* have the right to urge *slaves,*" &c. But the question would return, who are masters and who are slaves? To this we must reply, a *master* is one who *has* this right, and a *slave* one who *is under this obligation.* The assertion would then be a mere truism. It would affirm that he who had this right had it, and he who is under this obligation is under it; leaving the matter in dispute just where it found it. We must therefore, I think, take the assertion in its abstract and unlimited sense, in the form in which I have stated it. And here, I am constrained to say, I can by no means agree with you. I will not, however, go into extended discussion of the subject. The substance of what I have to urge may be found in the chapter on Reciprocity, in the Elements of Moral Science, to which you have done me the honor to refer. Suffer me, however, briefly to offer the following considerations.

1. This doctrine is really more alarming than any that I have ever known to be inculcated on this subject. If this right to oblige another man to labor for us is thus given to human nature, it is as really and truly given to black men as to white men. It authorizes them to enslave us, just as much as it authorizes us to enslave them. This goes very far beyond any thing that I ever before heard claimed for the slaves. I have heard it said, but I never agreed to it, that the slaves had a right to rise and emancipate themselves by force; but this goes much farther, and claims for them the additional right to enslave their masters. Thus, if the slaves of any state or plantation should rise and enslave their masters, this precept would justify them; and yet more, the other precepts, according to your interpretation, would oblige the masters as Christians to obey them, "doing service from the heart; not only to the good and gentle, but also to the forward." And still more, if this be the precept of the New Testament, and we are allowed to keep back nothing that would be profitable to man, this would be the doctrine that ministers of the gospel would be specially obliged to inculcate upon slaves.

But this is not all. This is, as I understand it, a precept for human nature. It is revealed by God as one of the social laws of man. It is a permission given, not to a few men in a portion of a single country, but to the whole human race. By virtue of it, I have the right to oblige every other man to labor for me without his contract or consent. I may assert this right to-day. I might be well pleased with this permission; but then every *other man* is, by the same rule, equally authorized to oblige me to labor for him. The question which shall be the master, and which the slave, must be decided by physical strength. And after I have subdued him, he has the same right as before to enslave me in return. Here then is war, war interminable, and war to the knife. Nor is this all. While I am *obeying* the gospel in enslaving him, I am at the same moment *disobeying* it, in not also allowing him to enslave me. Here then is a permission given of which every man may avail himself but of which he cannot avail himself without directly violating it. I can by no means believe that Jesus Christ, or his apostles, ever taught such a doctrine as this. And here suffer me to remind you, that, if this be an argument at all, it is a universal argument. It is on the question of abstract right, and is not affected by the cruelty or kindness by which this right may be enforced. It applies to every case in which any deviation from the law of perfect reciprocity of right is pleaded as a matter of revelation in the New Testament.

And here, before I leave this part of the subject, permit me to remark, that the analogy which you have supposed to exist between the innocence of despotism and the innocence of slavery, is, to my mind, by no means convincing. As you have quoted what I have elsewhere said concerning the adaptation of different forms of government to different conditions of humanity, permit me in very few words to explain my views on this subject. I believe society, and its necessary agent, government, to be an ordinance of God, and necessary to the existence of the race; that the object, the all controlling object of society, is to secure to every individual the enjoyment of all his natural rights, or the rights conferred upon him as a human being by his Creator; that in every state of society, that mode of government is to be preferred which will best accomplish this object; that a government is *right* in just so far as it accomplishes this object; it is *innocent* in just so far as it honestly *intends* to accomplish it; and that, for the accomplishment of it, society possesses powers over the individual which the individuals of that society do not possess over each other.

Now between institutions so radically unlike, in every essential particular, I do not perceive what analogy can possibly exist. The one is an ordinance of God; this, as it seems to me, cannot, without absurdity, be affirmed of the other. The one is necessary to the existence of the race, the other certainly is unnecessary. The paramount object of the one is to secure to every man all the rights conferred on him by the Creator; the direct object of the other is to abridge these rights: the one acts by protecting the individual against the aggression of his brother, the other acts by withdrawing this protection; the one acts by providing means for the universal redress of grievances, the other acts by removing the means of redress. How any argument from analogy can be drawn from institutions so radically dissimilar I am really unable to discover.

But let us return again to our definition of slavery. The right of slavery is the right to urge another by a violent motive, resulting from my own command, to labor for me without his contract or consent.

I am not certain, my dear brother, that I clearly understand the nature of that domestic slavery which you defend. If, however, I correctly comprehend your views, the institution which you are *proposing for our consideration*, differs very widely from that which you *describe in this definition* If what you defend be innocent, it will by no means follow that slavery above defined is innocent also.

The slavery which you hold up to our view, and which you contend is innocent, is described in the following passages:

"He (the master) may require the just and reasonable service of the slave; but it is a service *exactly* such as is due from a servant hired for the year or for life." Letter 2d.

Again. "In some instances there may be all the injustice and heartlessness which you describe, while in others the definition of Paley requires no addition, but *material retrenchment;* for the slaves are not only watched over with guardian kindness and affection, but *prefer* to *remain with their masters*; so that it *cannot be said* that they serve him *without their contract or consent.*" Letter 3d.

Again. "Slavery is only bondage, and this may be *voluntary*, and by one's own contract, and there may be no *obligation whatever to labor*." Ib.

Again, in your last letter, you present us with a practical illustration of the form of slavery which you defend. "During the past twelve years, I have devoted the salary given me, whenever at my disposal, to the spiritual instruction of the slaves, and am now doing so. With reference to my own servants, their condition is as good as I can make it. They are placed under a contract, which no instrument of writing could make more sacred. By this *contract*, they, on their part, perform not one half of the labor performed by free laborers; and I, on my part, am bound to employ a missionary to teach and catechise them and their children, to provide for them a home, and clothes, and provisions, and fuels and land to plant for themselves, to pay all medical bills, to guaranty to them all the profits of their labor in their own time, to protect them as a guardian, and to administer to the wants of the children, and of those that are sick, and infirm, and aged. Such is their state, and *I have no idea that they would consent to be removed.*"

Now I might here remark, that all this is really aside from the merits of the question at issue. You have frequently reminded me that this was an abstract question, and had nothing to do with the *manner* in which the right was exercised. If a master uses his slaves kindly, this is surely commendable; but this does not at all bear upon the question of his right to hold them as slaves at all.

I will not, however, pause to insist upon this point. My object is to direct your attention to the fact that the slavery which you defend, is a very different institution from that which your definition describes. As you truly observe, the definition requires "material retrenchment." The condition described by the definition, is that of a man urged by a *violent motive resulting from the command of another*; the condition described by these quotations, is that of a man whose *service may be voluntary*, and is *performed by his own consent.* The one excludes the idea of contract; of the other, "*it cannot be said* that they serve him *without their contract and consent.*" To the one it is essential that the man be obliged to labor; of the other it is true that "there may be no obligation whatever to labor."

Now, these two conditions seem to me so essentially dissimilar, that the defence of the one by no means constitutes a defense of the other. The one describes the condition of *involuntary servitude*, the other describes a condition to which involuntary servitude is by no means essential; and in which, in fact, it frequently does not exist. If a man, whether black or white, serve another *voluntarily*, and would *not consent* to leave that service, here is no *invasion of the right of personal liberty*. It must, however, be a *bona fide* consent, and not merely a consent to do one thing lest he should be obliged to do something worse. A man may choose that I should blindfold him, and take care of him as though he were a blind man. This would be a very unwise agreement for both of us, but this would be no invasion of his rights. But because this is no invasion of his rights, it by no means proves that I have the right "to *urge men by a violent motive, resulting from my own command*," to become blindfolded.

But even this form of what you consider slavery you do not justify, or at least you speak of it as an institution leading to dangerous consequences. Thus you say: "There is, as you remark, quite enough *abuse of this authority* to make me *regret its general existence*." Letter 2d.

Again: "You must already have perceived that speaking abstractly of slavery I do not consider its perpetuation *proper*, even if it were *possible*." Letter 3d.

Here again I am pleased to observe that our sentiments almost exactly coincide. Even this modification of slavery, if indeed that be the *modification* of a thing from which its essential elements are excluded, you consider *dangerous*, *impossible to be perpetuated*, and *improper*. To this I fully subscribe, and I rejoice that these truths have found an advocate so much better able to expound them than myself.

If now we look back over the course of these remarks, I think we may easily discover the manner in which, commencing so widely asunder, we have come at last so nearly to coincide. In the first place, excluding from your definition of slavery all right to interfere with the *intellectual*, *moral*, *social*, and *domestic* condition of man, and admitting that for such interference slavery furnishes neither excuse nor palliation, you limit the institution which you defend to the mere right to oblige another to labor for us without his contract or consent. In the second place, as it seems to me, falling within your own definition, and "materially retrenching" from it, you defend a condition which may be *voluntary, limited by contract,* and one *which the laborer would not consent to relinquish.* In the third place, you affirm that this condition, even thus modified, could not properly be perpetrated. In how much soever then we may differ in our course of reasoning, the practical conclusions to which we arrive are singularly coincident.

Where there is so substantial practical agreement, it might seem that farther examination of the argument was unnecessary. I find, moreover, that I am in danger of extending this letter to an unreasonable length. I will not, therefore, pretend to examine your argument from the Scriptures in detail, but shall merely remark very briefly upon some of the points on which, as I suppose, the controversy mainly hinges.

Your argument drawn from the Old Testament in favor of slavery, is, I think, two-fold. In the first place, you infer that slavery cannot be wrong, that is, cannot be a violation of the relations which God has established, because the holiest men, both in ancient and modern times, have both held slaves and also spoken in favor of slavery. This argument, I fear, will not bear generalization. I have already alluded to the case of Dr. Stiles. You also remember that John Newton, for some years after his conversion, was the captain of a slave-ship, and was thus doing acts which now would condemn him to the gallows, without being aware that he was doing wrong. This surely by no means proves that the *slave-trade is* innocent.

Secondly, you infer that slavery cannot be a wrong because God gave the various precepts concerning it, which you quote from the laws of Moses.

To this I have replied, that he gave various precepts in the same laws respecting other practices manifestly wrong, and that, therefore, your inference is not legitimate.

Polygamy and divorce come under precisely the same class of moral wrongs as slavery. You describe them as acts "conflicting with the relations designed at first by God between the sexes." I consider slavery to be wrong precisely because "it conflicts with relations designed at first by God between" man and man. The generic character of the two act is, that they "*conflict with the relations designed at first by God;*" their *specific difference* is, that in the one case the conflict is with the relations designed by God between *the sexes*; in the other it is with the relations between *man and man*.

Yet God did not prohibit polygamy and divorce among the ancient Hebrews, but enacted laws to regulate them. These practices were nevertheless clearly wrong, and Christ condemned and forbade them. I thence infer that an act may be wrong, a violation of the relations which God has established, and yet, at a particular time, he may not prohibit it, and may even enact laws concerning it. You say Christ forbade these wrongs, but did not forbid slavery. Very true. But this, I think, does not affect the general fact above stated; nay, it rather confirms it. Christ's condemnation of these institutions clearly shows them to have been wrong, and wrong from the beginning; but this only demonstrates the truth, that it is not inconsistent with the dealings of God with men, to give precepts regulating a practice in itself wrong, but concerning which he has not seen fit, at present, explicitly to reveal his will.

It would be improper, it this closing letter to examine at length your argument from the New Testament. I could not do so without introducing new matter into the discussion. I am as confident as I usually am in any of the conclusions of my understanding, that I have interpreted the teachings of our Saviour and his apostles correctly. I must content myself with referring you in general to what I have already stated. I shall here very briefly allude to the different principles on which our argument rests.

Your argument, I think, intends to establish the following points:

1. God could not consistently with his attributes, in making a revelation, be silent as to any course of action and also give precepts concerning it, and yet inculcate principles in the same revelation, intended to subvert and abolish it.

2. God has been thus silent and has thus given precepts respecting the institution of slavery, and

3. Therefore, God has inculcated no such principles. Hence, you consider that by the apostolic directions on this subject the character of God is committed to the innocence of this institution; and to suppose it wrong is to suppose him to deny himself. This argument you have enforced with great copiousness of learning, and with all the advantages of an eloquence which I admire; but which I have no power to imitate. It moves me strongly every time I read it, but I must say it does not convince me. Suffer me briefly to hint at the reasons of my dissent.

1. I do not believe that we are competent thus to decide upon the manner in which God can or may teach us. I am confident, first of all, that God is consistent with himself, and that the Bible is his own revelation, and that therefore I can best justify his ways by receiving in humility all that he has there made known to me. You very well ask, "When the Scriptures have been received as a revelation, and the inquiry is about their meaning, how does it sound to affirm authoritatively as to what they ought to teach;" and I may add, to affirm authoritatively in what *manner* they shall teach it? The adoption of this principle has always led to error. Reasoning thus, you know that Luther is said to have rejected the Epistle of James from the canon, because he supposed that the views of faith taught by this apostle, could not have been dictated by the same spirit which indicted the Epistle to the Galatians.

I take a different view of this subject. I suppose the Most High to deal with us, as with beings endowed with an intelligent and moral nature; and, therefore, that he frequently makes known to us his will by teaching us the relations in which we stand, and the obligations thence resulting, without specifying to us the particular acts which he intends thereby to forbid. Whatever our reason clearly perceives to be contradictory to a relation which he has established, is thus forbidden. In this manner I suppose God to have made known his will concerning slavery. Again, on the other hand, I find in the Bible the precepts concerning masters and slaves which we have both quoted. I receive both of these as a revelation from God; and I hence conclude that it is consistent with the attributes of God to teach us in this manner.

I ask myself, did he ever before teach in this manner? I find that he frequently did so under, the old dispensation. I ask again, is it in analogy with his teaching in the New Testament that he should teach rather by principle than by precept? I find upon inquiry that this is there his ordinary mode of teaching. I ask again, is there any special reason why this mode of teaching should be adapted in this particular case? I find that this mode is specially adapted to the removal of a social evil, and that no other could, on the principles of human nature, be reasonably employed. Hence, I conclude that slavery is by the word of God forbidden, but that the word of God intends to remove it, not by immediate proclamation, as must be the case if it were treated preceptively, but by applying the principles of the gospel to the consciences of men, and thus, by changing the sentiments of the society, gradually and kindly work its entire extermination.

In the use which you have made of the saying of Lord Eldon, I think you have not taken notice of the point which I intended to illustrate. The question is not whether, if Lord Eldon had violated plainly a plain law, he would have been punished. This would have depended on the firmness of the judge, and the honesty of the jury. The question is, whether, the law being as it is, he could not have taught another man how to violate the whole intention of the law, and yet escape conviction, and thus make it necessary that the law should be amended. Nor is this really the question at issue. It is, in fact, this. Suppose a law forbidding forgery had been made by a Roman emperor in the time of Christ, and the law, from the constitution of things, could neither be altered nor amended; would Lord Eldon, or any other man, find the slightest difficulty in doing with impunity the very acts which the law intended to *forbid?* You think that my views of interpretation lead to laxity of morals. To me, their tendency seems exactly the reverse. In my view, a principle is like the flaming sword, which, turning every way, guards on every side the tree of life; while a precept, made only for one age, and looking only in one direction, leaves the approach in every other direction unguarded and defenceless. While, however, there seems to be this wide theoretical difference between us, I again perceive that, practically, we very nearly agree. While you hold that slavery is permitted, nay, sanctioned by God; and that, hence, to have taught any thing at variance with this permission would have been to deny himself; you still express your views of this institution in such language as the following: "If you had asserted the great danger of confiding such irresponsible power in the hands of *any man*, I should at once have assented. There is quite enough abuse of this authority to make me regret its *general existence*." Again, "you must already have perceived that, speaking abstractly of slavery, I do not consider its perpetuation *proper*, *even if it were possible*. Nor let any one ask, why not perpetuate it if it be not a sin? The *Bible informs us what man is*, and among *such beings*, *irresponsible power is a trust too easily and too frequently abused*." It may not be proper for me to ask how these assertions are to be reconciled with the views to which I have above referred. I cannot, however, but observe, that you *regret* the general existence of an institution, of which the general existence is, as you affirm, both *sanctioned* and *permitted* by God himself; and you declare that its perpetuation would be both *impossible* and *improper*. These opinions you must have derived, certainly, from *principles*, for there is, as we both grant, no direct *prohibition* on the subject. Nay more, you inform us that these principles are *derived from the Bible*, and that they result from what the Bible *teaches us of the character of man*. Now this looks to me marvelously like *controlling a permission by a principle*. In fact, I do not perceive that the ground which it covers is not precisely that which is covered by my illustration of the case of a young man and his parent, which you have considered so strangely unfortunate.

Before leaving this subject, suffer me, my dear brother, to ask you whether there be not reason to apprehend that your views on this whole subject will be misunderstood? I very much fear that when slavery is spoken of at the South, it is spoken of, not as you define and defend it, but as it actually exists; and I perceive that it is boldly upheld as a thing desirable, and right—an institution both to be *perpetuated*, and even at all hazards to be *extended*. I ask, is there not reason to fear that, on your authority, the attributes of God will be appealed to, to sanction, *not the*

*abstract idea of it*, which you believe to be in harmony with the word of
God, *but the whole system, just as it exists?* Is it not important that you
should express your views explicitly on this subject, so that the word of
God may not, on your authority, be used to support what you believe it
explicitly to condemn?

And now, to sum up the whole, let us briefly enumerate the points
of agreement between us. In the first place, we both affirm that to hold
slaves is not of necessity a guilt, and under peculiar circumstances it may
not be a wrong; it is, therefore, *in itself*, no scripture ground for
ecclesiastical excommunication. In the second place, you affirm that a
slave is entitled to the same privileges, intellectual, moral, and domestic,
as any other man; and, of course, that all that part of the system which
interferes with those privileges, is wrong, and ought to be abolished. In
the effort to effect this abolition, we can both co-operate. In the third
place, you give us, in your own case, an example of what you believe to
be the duty of masters. You teach your servants to read, you instruct
them in the gospel of Christ, and by every means in your power are
laboring to improve their intellectual, moral, social, and domestic
condition. I do not here allude to your care of their physical comforts,
for you could never be a selfish or unkind man. We can both unite in the
effort to render all slaveholders in this country just such masters as you.
Thirdly, you believe it neither *possible* nor *proper* to perpetuate this
institution. It must, then, in your view, cease. In my judgment, it would
be a great calamity were it to terminate by violence, or without previous
moral and social preparation. In the effort to prepare both the masters
and slaves for this event, we can cordially co-operate. I neither ask you,
nor any other man, to do any more. In the effort to accomplish these
results, I pledge you my services to any extent that you are willing to
accept of them.

In the doing of all this, I am well aware that great difficulties are to
be encountered. I believe that the first labor must be the labor of
preparation; but I think it must be a labor *directed specifically to this end*. I
fear, with you, that the emancipation of the slaves in the West Indies is
not accomplishing what was expected. I say *I fear* for the reports are so

absolutely contradictory, that I am unable to come to a decided opinion. But, aside from this case, all history informs us that absolute liberty is too violent a stimulant to be safely administered to a race who have long been bred in slavery. They must be taught and become accustomed to the responsibilities which it involves, before they can use it aright. All this requires caution, boldness, philanthropy, and humble but earnest trust in God. "Prayers and pains," said Elliot, "with the blessing of God can do any thing."[68] I do not pretend to dictate as to the *manner* in which this is to be done. This I leave to you, who are so much better able to judge. All I ask is, that the views which you entertain, so far as I understand them, be carried out into practice; and, in doing this, I here promise to give you my poor aid to any extent that I am able to render it.

Here I close this long and, I fear, wearisome letter. This is the first time in my life—I hope it may be the last—in which it has fallen to my lot to enrage in controversy. Be assured, my dear brother, that it has given me pain whenever I have been obliged to differ from one for whom I cherish so affectionate a regard. For that Christian urbanity with which you treated whatever I have written, from my heart I thank you. If I have in any manner been able to avoid the errors into which many have fallen who have treated on this subject, I ascribe it mainly to the influence of your example, and to the unfeigned esteem which I entertain for your character, as a gentleman and a scholar, a clergyman and a Christian. Or rather, if we have been enabled without bitterness to express our views to each other on a subject which is so liable to arouse the worst passions of our fallen nature, let us ascribe it all to that love of God shed abroad in our hearts, which teaches us to treat as a brother every disciple of our common Lord, though he may embrace opinions in

---

[68]This quote is from John Eliot (1604–1690), Puritan missionary to the American Indians in New England. Eliot established a settlement for "praying Indians," the popular name for Indian converts to Christianity. He is also credited with translating the entire Bible and numerous other religious works into the Algonquin language. See Eliot, *The Indian Grammar Begun: or, an Essay to Bring the Indian Language into Rules, for the Help of Such as Desire to Learn the Same, for the Furtherance of the Gospel among Them* (Cambridge: Marmaduke Johnson, 1666) 66.]

many respects differing from our own. God grant that we may both meet in that world where neither of us shall any more see through a glass darkly, but where we shall see as we are seen, and know as we are known.

I am, my dear brother, yours with every sentiment of affection,

The Author of the Moral Science

# Appendix I

## Original Wayland Article on "Domestic Slavery"[69]

Domestic slavery proceeds upon the principle that the master has a right to control the actions, physical and intellectual, of the slave, for his own, that is, the master's individual benefit; and, or course, that the happiness of the master, when it comes in competition with the happiness of the slave, extinguishes in the latter the right to pursue it. It supposes, at best, that the relation between master and slave is not that which exists between man and man, but is a modification at least, of that which exists between man and the brutes.

Now this manifestly supposes that the two classes of beings are created with dissimilar rights: that the master possesses rights which have never been conceded by the slave; and that the slave has no rights at all over the means of happiness which God has given him, whenever these means of happiness can be rendered available to the service of the master. It supposes that the Creator intended one human being to govern the physical, intellectual and moral actions of as many other human beings as by purchase he can bring within his physical power; and that one human being may thus acquire a right to sacrifice the happiness of any number of other human beings, for the purpose of promoting his own.

Slavery thus violates the personal liberty of man as a physical, intellectual and moral being.

1. It purports to give to the master a right to control the physical labor of the slave, nor for the sake of the happiness of the slave, nor upon terms mutually satisfactory to the parties, but for the sake of the

---

[69]Francis Wayland, "Domestic Slavery," *Christian Reflector* 12/18–19 (2 and 9 May 1844): 69–70 and 73 respectively.]

happiness of the master. It subjects the amount of labor, and the kind of labor, and the remuneration for labor, entirely to the will of the one party, to the entire exclusion of the will of the other party.

2. But if this right in the master over the slave be conceded, there are of course conceded with it all other rights necessary to [unreadable] inasmuch as the slave can be held in this condition only while he remains in a state of comparative mental imbecility, it supposes the master to have the right to control his intellectual development, just as far as may be necessary to secure entire subjection. Thus, it supposes the slave to have no right to use his intellect for the production of his own happiness; but only to use it in such manner as may be consistent with his master's profit.

3. And, moreover, inasmuch as the acquisition of the knowledge of his duty to God could not be freely made without the acquisition of the other knowledge, which might, if universally diffused, endanger the control of the master, slavery supposes the master to have the right to determine how much knowledge of his duty a slave shall obtain, the manner in which he shall obtain it, and the manner in which he shall discharge that duty after he shall have obtained a knowledge of it. It thus subjects the duty of man to God, entirely to the will of man; and this for the sake of pecuniary profit. It renders the eternal happiness of the one party subservient to the temporal happiness of the other. And this principle is commonly recognized by the laws of all slave holding countries.

If argument were necessary to show that such a system as this must be a variance with the ordinance of God, it might be easily drawn from the effects which it produces both upon morals and upon national wealth.

1. Its effects must be disastrous upon the morals of both parties. By presenting objects on whom passion may be satiated without resistance and without redress, it tends to cultivate in the master pride, anger, cruelty, selfishness, and licentiousness. By accustoming the slave to subject his moral principles to the will of another it tends to abolish in him all moral distinctions: and thus fosters in him lying, deceit,

hypocrisy, dishonesty and a willingness to yield himself up to minister to the appetites of his master. That in all slave-holding countries there are exceptions to the remark, and that there are principles in human nature which, in many cases, limit the effects of these tendencies, may be gladly admitted. Yet, that such is the tendency of slavery, as slavery, we think no reflecting person can for a moment hesitate to allow.

2. The effects of slavery on national wealth, may be easily seen from the following considerations:

1. Instead of imposing upon all the necessity of labor, it restricts the number of laborers, that is, of producers, within the smallest possible limit, by rendering labor disgraceful.

2. It takes from the laborers the natural stimulus to labor, namely, the desire in the individual of improving his condition; and substitutes, in the place of it, that motive which is the least operative and the least constant, namely, the fear of punishment without the consciousness of moral delinquency.

3. It removes, as far as possible, from both parties, the disposition and the motives to frugality. Neither the master learns frugality from the necessity of labor, nor the slave from the benefits which it confers. And hence, while the only party wastes from ignorance of the laws of acquisition, and the other because he can have no motive to economy, capital must accumulate but slowly, if indeed it accumulates at all.

And that such are the tendencies of slavery, is manifest from observation. No country, not of great fertility, can long sustain a large slave population. Soils of more than ordinary fertility cannot sustain it long, after the first richness of the soil has been exhausted. Hence, slavery in this country is acknowledged to have impoverished many of our most valuable districts; and, hence, it is continually migrating from the older settlements to those new and untilled regions where the accumulated manure of centuries of vegetation has formed a soil, whose productiveness may, for a while, sustain a system at variance with the laws of nature. Many of our free and of our slave-holding States were peopled at about the same time. The slave-holding States had every advantage, both in soil and climate, over their neighbors. And yet the accumulation of capital has been greatly in favor of the latter. If any one doubt whether this difference be owing to the use of slave labor, let him ask himself what would have been the condition of the slave-holding States at this moment, if they had been inhabited, from the beginning, by an industrious yeomanry; each one holding his own land, and each one tilling it with the labor of his own hands.

But let us inquire what is the doctrine of revelation on this subject.

The moral precepts of the Bible are diametrically opposed to slavery. They are, 'Thou shalt love thy neighbor as thyself, and all things whatsoever ye would that men should do unto you, do ye even so unto them.'

1. The application of these precepts is universal. Our neighbor is everyone whom we may benefit. The obligation respects all things whatsoever, certainly to a thing so important as the right to personal liberty.

2. Again. By this precept, it is made our duty to cherish as tender and delicate a respect for the right which the meanest individual possesses over the means of happiness bestowed upon him by God, as we cherish for our own right over our own means of happiness, or as we desire any other individual to cherish for it. Now were this precept obeyed, it is manifest that slavery could not in fact exist for a single instant. The principle of the precept is absolutely subversive of the principle of slavery. That of the one is the entire equality of right; that of the other, the entire absorption of the rights of one in the rights of the other.

If any one doubt respecting the bearing of the Scripture precept upon this case, a few plain questions may throw additional light upon the subject. For instance,—

1. Do the precepts and the spirit of the gospel allow [unreadable] my support from a system which extorts labor from my fellow-men, without allowing them any voice in the equivalent which they shall receive; and which can only be sustained by keeping them in a state of mental degradation, and by shutting them out, in a degree, from the means of salvation?

2. Would the master be willing that another person should subject him to slavery, for the same reasons, and on the same grounds, that he holds his slave in bondage?

3. Would the gospel allow us, if it were in our power, to reduce our fellow citizens of our own color to slavery? But the gospel makes no distinction between men on the ground of color or of race. God has made of one blood all the nations that dwell on the earth. I think that these questions will easily ascertain the gospel principles on this subject.

But to this it is objected, that the gospel never forbids slavery; and still more, that by prescribing the duties of a master and servants, it tacitly allows it. This objection is of sufficient importance to deserve attentive consideration.

The following will, I think, be considered by both parties a fair statement of the teaching of the New Testament on this subject. The moral principles of the gospel are directly subversive of the principles of slavery; but, on the other hand, the gospel neither commands masters to manumit their slaves, nor authorizes slaves to free themselves from their masters; and also, it goes further, and prescribes the duties suited to both parties in their present condition.

*First*. Now, if this be admitted, it will, so far as I see, be sufficient for the argument. For if the gospel be diametrically opposed to the principle of slavery, it must be opposed to the practice of slavery; and, therefore, were the principles of the gospel fully adopted, slavery could not exist.

*Secondly*,

1. I suppose that it will not be denied, that God has a right to inform us of his will in any manner that he pleases; and that the intimation of his will, in what manner soever signified, is binding upon the conscience.

2. Hence, God may make known to us his will either directly or indirectly; and if that will be only distinctly signified, it is as binding in the one case as in the other. Thus he may, in express terms, forbid a certain course of conduct, this is forbidding it directly; or else he may command certain duties, or impose certain obligations with which that

course of conduct is manifestly inconsistent; that is forbidding it indirectly. It is insufficient, in either case, in order to constitute the obligation, that the will of God be known.

3. The question, then, resolves itself into this: 'Has God imposed obligations upon men which are inconsistent with the existence of domestic slavery? That he has, may, I think, be easily shown.

*a.* He has made it our duty to proclaim the gospel to all men, without respect to circumstance or condition. If it be our duty to proclaim the gospel to every creature, it must be our duty to give every creature every means for attaining a knowledge of it; and yet, more imperatively, not to place any obstacles in the way of their attaining that knowledge.

*b.* He has taught us that the conjugal relation is established by himself; that husband and wife are joined together by God; and that man may not put them asunder. The marriage contract is a contract for life, and is dissoluble only for one cause, that of conjugal infidelity. Any system that interferes with this contract, and claims to make it any thing else than what God has made it, is in violation of his law.

*c.* God has established the parental and filial relations, and has imposed upon parents and children appropriate and peculiar duties. The child is bound to honor and obey the parent; the parent to support and educate the child, and to bring him up in the nurture and admonition of the Lord. With these relations and obligations, no created being has the right to interfere. A system which claims authority to sever these relations, and to annihilate these obligations, must be at variance with the will of God.

4. That the Christian religion does establish these obligations, will not, I think be disputed. Now they either are, or are not, inconsistent with the existence of domestic slavery. If they are inconsistent with the existence of slavery, then slavery is indirectly forbidden by the Christian religion. If they are not inconsistent with it, then that interference with them which slavery exercises, is as uncalled for as it would be in any other case; and is the infliction of just so much gratuitous, inexcusable and demoralizing misery. And, as we have before said, what is indirectly

forbidden in the Scripture, is as truly forbidden as though it were directly forbidden.

But it may be asked, Why was this manner of forbidding it chosen in preference to any other? I reply, that this question we are not obliged to answer. It is enough for us to show that it is forbidden. It is this which establishes the obligation, and this obligation cannot be in the least affected by the reason which may be given, for the manner in which God has seen fit to reveal it. The reason may be, that slavery is a social evil; and that, in order to eradicate it, a change must be effected in the society in which it exists, and that this change would be better effected by the inculcation of the principles themselves which are opposed to slavery, than by the inculcation of a direct precept. Probably all social evils are thus most successfully remedied.

We answer again, this very course which the gospel takes on this subject, seems to have been the only one that could have been taken, in order to effect the universal abolition of slavery. The gospel was designed, not for one race, or for one time, but for all races, and for all times. It looked not at the abolition of this from of evil for that age alone, but for its universal abolition. Hence the important object of its Author was, to gain it a [unreadable] every part of the known world; [unreadable] by its universal diffusion among the classes of society, it might quietly and peacefully modify and subdue the evil passions of men and [unreadable] without violence work a revolution in the whole mass of mankind. In this manner alone could its object, a universal moral revolution, have been accomplished. For if it had forbidden the evil, instead of subverting the principle; if it had proclaimed the unlawfulness of slavery, and taught slaves to resist the oppression of their masters; it would instantly have arrayed the two parties in deadly hostility, throughout the civilized world: its announcement would have been the signal of servile war; and the very name of the Christian religion would have been forgotten amidst the agitations of universal bloodshed. The fact, under these circumstances, that the gospel does not forbid slavery, affords no reason to suppose that it does not mean to prohibit it; much less does it afford ground for belief, that Jesus Christ intended to authorize it.

3. It is important to remember that two grounds of moral obligation are distinctly recognized in the gospel. The first is our duty to man as men; that is, on the ground of the relation which men sustain to each other: the second is our duty to man as a creature of God; that is, on the ground of the relation which we all sustain to God. On this latter ground, many things become our duty which would not be so on the former. It is on this ground that we are commanded to return good for evil, to pray for them that despitefully use us, and when we are smitten on one check, to turn also the other. To act thus is our duty, not because our fellow-man has a right to claim this course of conduct of us, nor because he has a right to inflict injury upon us, but because such conduct in us will be well pleasing to God. And when God prescribes the course of conduct which will be well pleasing to him, he by no means acknowledges the right of abuse in the injurious person, but expressly declares, 'Vengeance is mine and I will repay it, saith the Lord.' Now, it is to be observed, that it is precisely upon this latter ground, that the slave is commanded to obey his master. It is never urged, like the duty of obedience to parents, because it is right; but because the cultivation of meekness and forbearance under injury, will be well pleasing unto God. Thus, servants are commanded to be obedient to their own masters, 'in singleness of heart, as unto Christ;' 'doing the will of God from the heart, with good will, doing service as to the Lord, and not to men.' Eph. 6:5–7. 'Servants are commanded to count their masters worthy of all honor, that the name of God and his doctrine be not blasphemed.'1 Tim. 6:1. 'Exhort servants to be obedient to their own masters,' etc., 'that they may adorn the doctrine of God our Saviour in all things.' Titus 3:9. The manner in which the duty of servants of slaves is inculcated, therefore, affords no ground for the assertion, that the gospel authorizes one man to hold another in bondage, any more than the command to honor the king, when the king was Nero, authorized the tyranny of the emperor; or than the command to turn the other check

when one is smitten, justifies the infliction of violence by an injurious man.

In a word, if the gospel rule of conduct be directly at variance with the existence of slavery; if the relations which it establishes, and the obligations which it enforces, are inconsistent with its existence; if the manner in which it treats it is the only manner in which it could attempt its utter and universal extermination; and if it inculcates the duty of slaves on principles which have no connection with the question of the right of masters over them; I think it must be conceded that the precepts of the gospel in no manner countenance, but are entirely opposed to the institution of domestic slavery.

Before closing this part of the subject, it may be proper to consider the question, What is the duty of masters and slaves, under a condition of society in which slavery now exists?

I. As to Masters.

If the system be wrong, as we have endeavored to show, if it be at variance with our duty both to God and to man, it must be abandoned. If it be asked, When? I ask again, When shall a man begin to cease doing wrong? Is not the answer always immediately? If a man is injuring us, do we ever doubt as to the time when he ought to cease inflicting injury upon others?

But it may be said, immediate abolition would be the greatest possible injury to the slaves themselves. They are not competent to self-government.

This is a question of fact, which it is not within the province of moral philosophy to decide. It very likely may be so. So far as I know, the facts are not sufficiently known to warrant a full opinion on the subject. We will, therefore, suppose it to be a case, and ask, What is the duty of masters under these circumstances?

1. The situation of the slaves, in which this obstacle to their emancipation consists, is not by their own act, but by the act of their masters; and, therefore, the masters are bound to remove it. The slaves were brought here without their own consent, they have been continued in their present state of degradation without their own consent, and they

are not responsible for the consequences. If a man have done injustice to his neighbor, and have also placed impediments in the way of remedying that injustice, he is as much under obligation to remove the impediments in the way of justice, as he is to do justice. Were it otherwise, a man might, by the accumulation of injury, at last render the most atrocious injury innocent and right.

2. But it may be said, this cannot be done, unless the slave is held in bondage until the object be accomplished. This is also a question of fact, on which I will not pretend to decide. But suppose it to be so, the question returns, What then is the duty of the master? I answer, supposing such to be the fact, it may be the duty of the master to hold the slave; not, however, on the ground of right over him, but of obligation to him, and of obligation to him for the purpose of accomplishing a particular and specified good. And, of course, he who holds him for any other purpose, holds him wrongfully, and is guilty of the sin of slavery. In the mean while, he is innocent in just so far as he, in the fear of God, holds the slave, not for the good of the master, but for the good of the slave, and with the entire and honest intention of accomplishing the object as soon as he can, and of liberating the slave as soon as the object is accomplished. He thus admits the slave to equality of right. He does unto another as he would that another should do unto him; and thus acting, though he may in form hold a fellow creature in bondage, he is in fact innocent of the crime of violation of liberty. This opinion, however, proceeds upon the supposition that the facts are as above stated. As to the question of fact, I do not feel competent to a decision.

II. The duty of slaves is also explicitly made known in the Bible. They are bound to obedience, fidelity, submission and respect to their masters, not only to the good and kind, but also to the unkind and forward; not, however, on the ground of duty to man, but on the ground of duty to God. This obligation extends to every thing but matters of conscience. When a master commands a slave to do wrong, the slave ought not to obey. The Bible does not, as I suppose, authorize resistance to injury; but it commands us to refuse obedience in such a case, and suffer the consequences, looking to God alone, to whom vengeance belongeth. Acting upon these principles, the slave may attain to the highest grade of virtue, and may exhibit a sublimity and purity of moral character, which, in the condition of the master, is absolutely unattainable.

Thus we see that the Christian religion not only forbids slavery, but that it also provides the only method in which, after it has been established, it may be abolished, and that with entire safety and benefit to both parties. By instilling the right to moral dispositions into the bosom of the master and of the slave, it teaches the one the duty of reciprocity, and the other the duty of submission; and thus, without tumult, without disorder, without revenge, but by the real moral improvement of both parties, restore both to the relation towards each other intended by their Creator.

Hence, if any one will reflect on these facts, and remember the moral law of the Creator, and the terrible sanctions by which his laws are sustained, and also the provision which, in the gospel of reconciliation, he has made for removing this evil after it has once been established; he must, I think, be convinced of the imperative obligation which rests upon him to remove it without the delay of a moment. The judge of the whole earth will do justice. He hears the cry of the oppressed, and he will, in the end, terribly vindicate right. And, on the other hand, let those who suffer wrongfully, bear their sufferings with patience, committing their souls unto him as unto a faithful Creator.

# Appendix II

## Union of the Baptist Denomination in Enterprises of Benevolence[70]

A new era now opens in our denominational history. The Baptists of the North and the Baptists of the South are not, we trust, becoming mutual foes, and gathering in hostile array, but they are, without a question, dissolving partnership, by mutual consent. The writings are not yet drawn, but the intention is avowed, and the parties are casting up their accounts. The consummation devoutly wished by some, and solemnly deprecated by others.

For ourselves we contemplate it with neither extreme of feeling. We believe that they who seek it, as an end, have mistaken conceptions of the character of the union, and of the injury of benefit resulting from it to the parties united. We believe that those who regard it as a great calamity, fraught with evil and only evil, have but slightly considered the circumstances attending it, and are sadly deficient in faith, and confidence in the over-ruling providence of God. Undeniably, there are advantages to be derived from the union of brethren North and South. On the supposition that slaveholding is sinful, it is an advantage to have access to those who practice it—to have occasion to meet and mingle with them on terms of friendship; i.e.; if it be understood that by thus meeting we do not express the least approbation of their sin. Under such circumstances, they may be more readily convinced of their error; our influence upon them may be more salutary and direct. Intercourse between Northern and Southern Baptists may contribute likewise to the intelligence and improvement of the latter, in various ways. The South can hardly meet its own literary demands. They want and must have Northern Reviews and Magazines; ay, and Northern ministers too. New

---

[70This editorial appeared in the *Christian Reflector* 13/13 (27 March 1845): 50.]

England and New York supply many of their churches with pastors, and these men draw much of their intellectual life from the fountains of knowledge and thought which open here. This intercourse will be less, when it is understood that Northern and Southern Baptists have ceased to co-operate in enterprises of benevolence. In our opinion, however, there is another view to be taken of this subject. The separation will not be such an evil as many suppose.

It will not diminish the amount of money paid for the support of missions. If it is understood that the South will generally withhold her contributions from the Treasury of the Board in Boston, this very fact will stimulate the friends of missions in the North to increased exertions. They will not suffer our missionaries to want, or the mission schools to be broken up. They will feel that the responsibility is no longer divided with the wealthy and generous planters of the South, but that it rests entirely on them, and cheerfully will they come forward to sustain it. Many, who, from conscientious scruples, have for sometime past withheld their offerings, will now lay them on the altar; and others, who, loving too well their money, were glad of an excuse for keeping it, when this is taken from them, will feel compelled to surrender all that an awakened conscience suggests. Nor will the Southerners, unless they falsely testify, cease to give to the cause of missions. They purpose immediate provisions of their own for the use of funds. They talk of employing missionaries extensively among their own slaves, a large proportion of whom, as they themselves testify, are in a state of heathenish ignorance and darkness. Let it not, then, be said, or suspected, that the cause of missions will greatly suffer from the anticipated separation. It will, in all probability prosper the more. The Board, whose seat of operations is in Boston, has now too wide a field to cultivate. In England much larger sums are raised with the same amount of effort, and one reason is, that all the ministers and churches are so accessible. They concentrate their strength more easily. There is more mutual confidence—a deeper sense of responsibility, and a freer dissemination of intelligence. If only the churches of the Free States are to be visited by the agents of the Board, and relied on for funds, there will be a saving of the expense and an increase of efficiency. The result will show, that in missions as well as in agriculture, a small farm well-tilled, is better than a large one much of which, is entirely neglected, and the rest cultivated but indifferently.

The separation of the Southern Baptists from Northern, in works of benevolence, will not diminish our strength or efficiency as a denomination. The independence of Baptist churches will save us from any ecclesiastical rupture, such as the Methodists have realized. We are already divided into as many parts as we have churches, and our efficiency as a denomination depends, not on these parts being joined, but on the purity and energy of individual churches. We see nothing in present movements that indicates a diminution or loss of these elements of strength. We believe the churches will be more pure and more zealous in good works, rather than the reverse. If any thing has diminished their strength heretofore, it has been their want of unanimity on the subject of slavery—a subject which has for many years agitated the whole country, and embarrassed us beyond almost any other. The attempts of slaveholders and those who abjure the system of slavery, to coalesce—to conduct important religious enterprises together, and harmoniously have brought us, at the North into collision, not only with our Southern brethren, but with each other. Let these attempts cease—let Northern churches act by themselves, and a great source of contention is removed; a stumbling block is taken out of the way; no good or obvious reason will remain why the members of each church should not harmoniously unite to sustain the same Boards and promote the same objects. It inevitably follows, then, that our strength and efficiency as a denomination will be increased rather than lessened by the anticipated event.

The withdrawal of the Southern churches from co-operation with the churches in the Free States, will prevent a far greater evil—the disruption of our Boards themselves, and division and confusion in all our ranks and throughout all our borders. We have alluded above to the past want of harmony in our churches. Were this connection between the North and the South to be much longer maintained, what has been, would be to scenes coming after, as the cool breezes of autumn to the howling tempests of winter. The elements of discord have been controlled with difficulty for the last three years. Opposing sentiments have been cherished and defended, and the utmost efforts on the part of the friends of peace and union have been requisite to keep the churches in a state of comparative quiet, and to prevent the aggrieved and doubtful from rushing into excesses alike injurious to themselves and to the cause of Christian benevolence. There has not been a day nor an hour during the last two years, when it was not in the power of the *Christian Reflector*, (we say it without boasting—it would be true of any paper in the same circumstances) to introduce discord and confusion into a thousand churches. We could have fed the suspicions, aroused the indignation, and influenced the course of a multitude, against existing organizations and against all ministers and brethren who sustained them. We should have done scarcely less, had we only admitted some communications, which we were earnestly desired to publish, and by rejecting which we secured the lasting displeasure of some former supporters and friends. But we were persuaded that such a course would be disastrous. We did not dare to assume the responsibility of contributing to such results. We saw that forbearance, and kindness, and confidence, would be followed, ere long, by a general unanimity of sentiment in the Northern States on the subject of slavery; and that therefore our duty was plain—to cultivate those inestimable virtues, while we continued to reflect light and truth with fidelity and affection. We maintained that any division would be attended with the most serious evils, excepting a division between the churches of the South and the churches of the North; and in consequence we declined to do any thing, or to suffer the *Reflector* to be used in any way, to promote secession and discord among brethren who ought to be united, and, if conciliatory measures were employed, would be; at least sufficiently to save the churches from disruption, and to produce concert of action at the North in promoting the cause of missions.

What we anticipated has, to a great extent, been realized. Such is the position of the Foreign Mission Board at the present moment, that with a willingness to make slight concessions, and a disposition to keep the unity of the spirit in the bonds of peace, the great body of Northern Baptists can be cordially united in enterprises of benevolence. Southern Baptist can also unite, and in their own way, without any suspicions of inequality or 'monopoly of privileges,' can give their thousands for the heathen, and employ such missionaries as they prefer. Whereas, if brethren should resolves that the union between the North and the South must still be maintained, and by concessions on the part of the Northern men touching the subject of slavery the attempt to preserve it should be made, a breaking up of the present organization and a division in the North would be the immediate and inevitable result. From such disunion and its fearful consequences, do we not all devoutly say, Good Lord deliver us!

There is another reason, which has weight with us, and, we presume, with most of our readers, although in the view of all at the South and some at the North it may be of no account. This is found in our conviction of the sinfulness of slavery, and our unwillingness to be bound to it by any ties whatever. But on this point it is not necessary here to enlarge.

In the consideration of this subject, we have endeavored to look at it is a friend of the South as well as the North—as an impartial observer, consulting denominational and missionary interests, rather than the claims of the anti-slavery enterprise. And every view we can take strengthens our conviction, that the separation which some so earnestly deprecate, will be fraught with more of good than of evil. Brethren have looked at the subject superficially. The 'sober second thought' will, we believe, be one of resignation, if not of confidence and hope. It is to be remembered that we cannot co-operate—the North and the South together—without continual jealousies, misunderstandings, and collisions. How often have Northern brethren within the last two years been called upon to make explanations, to remove suspicions and quiet alarms! Do brethren wish to expend their energy and breath in this way for years to come? Is it not better than we should separate, like Abraham and Lot? Our opinions and interests are so widely diverse, we cannot co-operate with advantage. Then why do we regard separation as an evil? We are like two families. They can seldom live together, partakers at the same board, but for a short period, without difficulty. But as neighbors, living under separate roofs, each independent of the other, they can live happily and on friendly terms, through successive generations.

There is another point, however, of great importance to the Baptists of the Free States, which demands the separate and special consideration of us all. It is our union, the union of Northern Baptists, in the cause of missions. We fear no evil, if brethren in New York, Pennsylvania, Ohio, and the other Northern States will adhere to their friends in New England; laying aside minor differences of opinion on questions of expediency, or points which are not of radical importance, and giving to the great object of the world's salvation their earnest thoughts and united efforts. O for a missionary spirit—the spirit of Boardman, or Ann Judson, of Samuel Pearce, of Paul the apostle to the Gentiles—to take possession of our hearts, to pervade and arouse the church! Let us seek it! Let us have it! Nothing else will so enable us to redeem the past, or to provide for the future. With this, our greatest difficulties will disappear—our peace will be confirmed—our treasures will overflow.